Copyright © Scott Harwood 2023

All rights reserved. No part of this book may be r[...]
any electronic or mechanical means, including inf[...]
systems, without written permission from the autl[...]
reviewer, who may quote brief passages embodiec[...]
review. Trademarked names appear throughout tl[...]
trademark symbol with every occurrence of a trac[...]
used in an editorial fashion, with no intention of i[...]
owner's trademark. The information in this book is distributed on an "as is"
basis, without warranty. Although every precaution has been taken in the
preparation of this work, neither the author nor the publisher shall have any
liability to any person or entity with respect to any loss or damage caused or
alleged to be caused directly or indirectly by the information contained in this
book.

CW00508278

First published 29/09/2021. This edition was published on 30/06/2023.

With thanks to Lewis Brennan for helping me with the proofreading of this
book.

https://avantgardetraveller.wordpress.com/
@AvantTraveller

TO ZOË

CÒ-LA BREITH SONA DHUIT!

LE GAOL,

SCOTT Harwood 2023

MISFORTUNE ACCOMPANIES FORTUNE

Travel Tales from the Other Side of the Fence

If you are reading this, it means that the man in the picture, Steve Rudd at *The Kings England Press*, has sadly passed on. As he was initially going to be my publisher, it means that I have had to self-publish the book.

Hence, if you are reading this, what you are reading is the book in its original form. Initially, the plan was to release this book in two parts: the first concerning my adventures in Australia, the second in Nepal. However, as this book is now being published and distributed online, and as such there are fewer costs associated with book-building, I have taken the liberty of combining both parts into what I intended to be the book's original form.

Before you get stuck into my strange tales from around the world, remember Steve Rudd. After all, he was the one who originally suggested to me that I should be documenting my adventures and escapades in the first place.

Of course, I feel like a total bell-end publishing this book. But sadly, time has taken its toll.

So, in memory of that great man in the photo, I give you the full-fat, no-hold-back, version of *Misfortune Accompanies Fortune*.

THE MANDATORY INTRODUCTION

"The course of every intellectual, if he pursues his journey long and unflinchingly enough, ends in the obvious, from which the non-intellectuals have never stirred."
— Aldous Huxley, The Doors of Perception

I am not God. Neither am I Jack Kerouac, nor am I Timothy Leary. I am probably not Henry David Thoreau, although my life turned out like Walden for a notable period of my life. I am definitely not Gina Fenton, the great producer of the milk of human kindness that she is, always will be and, in due course, what she will be remembered for. I am, in all likelihood, not Bibek Maharjan, Thorsten Jones, Aashika Budhathoki, Hamish Finlay (who frequently appears in this book), Cassandra MacLean (who sadly does not), David Peace One Love, Suzette Fialho, Axel Koehler, Lewis Brennan, Ram Kafle, Bòidheach the flat-coated retriever or Jade Blyth, nor am I the old Jewish guy I once met on the Flixbus from Brussels to Rotterdam.

I am merely a stout working-class fellow of mixed Germanic, Celtic, Italian and African (that I know of…) descent, who first saw daylight in the former industrial heartland of northern England in the year of our Lord nineteen-ninety-four, baptised in the Church of England despite coming from a historically-Catholic family (at least on my dad's side), grew up on a large rock in the middle of the Firth of Clyde, and just so happened to be in the right places at the right time through pretty much the entirety of my life, at least up until 2017 anyway. I absolutely hated comprehension at school, failed my Highers (or A-levels or whatever they are called these days), got accepted into college anyway, and ended up dropping out and buggering off to Australia after doing the equivalent of the second year of university in Business Administration with Information Technology. And yet, despite my apparent shortcomings regarding the written artform, I have somehow managed to churn out a book. Thanks be to the influence of the late Steve Rudd of *The King's England Press* for first suggesting the idea, in addition to the subsequent voices of many other people from around the world echoing this thought.

There's something bugging me, though. Just one little thing. I have absolutely no idea what I want to achieve with the publication of this book.

Except maybe I wish to please the large and ever-increasing number of individuals who think that I should have written it a number of years ago, thanks in part to my great number of influential trans-global wacky adventures and mystical experiences that continue to this day. And also, maybe attract a few Captain Beefheart fans and other such weird persons with the subtle subtitle. Or maybe I'm writing this book in a half-baked attempt to encourage people to stop being self-thinking, point-and-snap, 'I'm a tourist, so I'm always right!' morons on the sole basis that they're on holiday, and maybe they should try to see the bigger picture. Or perhaps I merely want to achieve a sense of accomplishment by the publication of this book – as if I need it judging by some of the tales in it. I mean, you're about to read how I've literally saved people's lives and taken steps to secure rural community survival about as much as my ascent to legend.

Either that, or I'm dissatisfied with the day (and night) jobs I've encountered over the years, and I'm constructively channelling my frustration. Seriously, I don't know what I want to achieve, nor do I know what I'm going to achieve. But I'm still going ahead with the publication of it. And if it sells one copy, I'm going to deem that a success.

Now, let's change the subject of this introductory rant. The reader should consider the fact that this book does not exactly describe my adventures exhaustively. I could mention the details of my odd jobs in Sydney, or my numerous trips to the markets at The Channon and Uki, or the extended lives of Gina, Thorsten, Xanda and my various other compatriots. I could, in theory, talk about the fact that a remix of Trans-Europe Express was playing the first time I made out with a girl at the Glasgow School of Art. But I'm not going into that kind of detail. Because I just did. What you are about to read, once you eventually get past all this tripe, were the bits that I felt like need documenting. The rest you can leave to your imagination. If you are not in the possession of one of those, turn on your television. Most channels will do these days.

I should also mention that this book contains elements that I am forced to write about in an attempt to give the reader a fully encompassing experience of what it is like to become the alternative journeyman that I am today. For example, I have included enough foul language to make a docker blush, references to usage of (mostly) non-lethal hallucinogens, and details of occasional tactics which some may interpret as decidedly sneaky, tricky and underhanded, possibly even downright dangerous at times. You know, like siphoning electricity from a streetlight or taking a disinfected bong through several different countries where possession of cannabis carries the death penalty. Omitting these acts would probably result in the reader accusing me of being a cherry-picking bell-end, and would make this book a hell of a lot more boring. So, as you read these tales of derring-do, you should never, ever regard me as a saint, role model or gigolo, but at least think of me as a human who learns from his mistakes.

The book also contains a few graphic sex scenes which may or may not bring about a greater level of horniness in the reader than that erotic trilogy that was released a few years ago. You know the one, the one that women overtly read on trains because posh porn is apparently more socially acceptable than the alternative.

Likewise, any expressions elicited by myself, the author, that may seem offensive to some (including, but not limited to Americans, Australians, the British, drug dealers, law enforcement, and white people in general) should be disregarded as little more than banter that adds effectiveness to my storytelling. In all my years on this planet, I have never meant to deliberately offend anybody on this planet, at least without due cause anyway.

Oh, and I might casually mention the fact that Australia has benefits for some, but not others (read: 'apartheid'), and is populated by a significant number of arrogant bastards – Bogans or otherwise – who glorify the genocide of the indigenous inhabitants in the form of Australia Day (read: 'Invasion Day') and ANZAC Day. I may also allude to the fact that Australia has, at the time of writing, a great crystal meth (or 'ice') crisis. That being said, many of the inhabitants of the Northern Rivers area of New South Wales tend to form an exception to my post-travel interpretation of the Australian norm, as you will soon read about.

So there's more honesty in this book than in the British Parliament in its entire history. You're welcome. Now shut up and read on…

Overthrow the government!

The van I resided in for eight months just outside Nimbin. No national grid, no water main, no toilet.
Eat your heart out, Thoreau.

ACKNOWLEDGEMENT

A deep respect is felt by the author towards the Indigenous Nations, and their elders, of what we now commonly know as the Commonwealth of Australia. Gratitude is particularly felt towards the Bundjalung Nation, whose people are spread across what we now commonly know as north-eastern New South Wales, including the town of Nimbin.
The author acknowledges the fact that the Original Inhabitants were the custodians of the land long before the coming of the white man, that their descendants remain as the custodians of the land in the present day, and that they will remain as the custodians of the land for a great many generations to come.
Furthermore, the author is humbled by the grace, humility and patience shown by the present-day descendants of the Original Inhabitants in the constant face of adversity.

Into the Void

"Why do you go away? So that you can come back. So that you can see the place you came from with new eyes and extra colours. And the people there see you differently, too. Coming back to where you started is not the same as never leaving."

- Terry Pratchett

Prologue

India or Australia?
Those were what my choices had boiled down to.

I was studying at James Watt College at the time, an establishment of mostly-good-natured bunglers and hairdressers in the centre of the Scottish town of Kilwinning. In between studying for my Higher National Certificate in Travel, I was doing one of two things; plotting to travel, and actually travelling. The HNC was a perfect course; I mean, it was taking me three hours to travel from my house on the Isle of Arran to college, and it took me five hours to travel home in the evening – an abnormality brought on by the low frequency of the CalMac ferry from Ardrossan.

What would technically be my third trip to Amsterdam was coming up in July 2012, just after my eighteenth birthday, but already I was yearning for something a little meatier than a twenty-four-hour bus ride each way from Glasgow. Thoughts of the roads on which I would travel were spiralling into outright fantasia. I imagined myself hitchhiking through the mountains of central Mexico with drug dealers and grandmothers at the wheel; riding the ore train through Mauritania, breathing in the desert through a perpetually-dampened scarf; smoking copious amounts of marijuana in the high hills of the Himalayas; even the thoughts of operating various forms of machinery in the Australian bush filled me with ecstatic pleasure.

I have no idea why the Americas and North Africa were way down on my bucket list at the time. Though in hindsight, it was probably because that I was merely a naïve seventeen-year-old who thought that aeroplanes were a pointless endeavour for a genuine traveller. Australia being an exception.

So, I had two options at this point, both of which involved me finishing my studies at James Watt. The first option was to hitchhike to India, or at least catch a bus to Romania and start from there. The hitchhiking would get significantly easier from there, after all. The second option looked more appealing; fly to Australia with a working holiday visa, try and pick up some work on a fruit farm, and possibly buy a banger and drive around that great southern land. Over the months, the plan veered more and more towards the latter, my thoughts being influenced by the possibility of earning some serious money. Australia was a go!

Well, it nearly was. It would take me another two years to finish my studies; only three people had passed the Higher National Certificate, myself being one, and as such the Higher National Diploma (the second year) would not be taking place. So I had to start again on a different course – a Higher National Diploma in Administration with Information Technology. I was naturally good at this sort of thing, but I didn't want to spend all of my freaking life pushing buttons in some godforsaken office with some unethical knobcheese of an employer blackmailing me in a pathetic attempt to have my hair cut. The sole reason I did this course was for the sake of form – it looked good on the curriculum vitae.

About halfway through the course, I applied for my first adult passport to marginal success; Her Majesty's passport fascists initially denied my application on the basis that there was something microscopically wrong with my original photo. But the wee burgundy book, indicating that I was indeed a citizen of the United Kingdom and the European Union, finally arrived in the post. And that was good enough for me.

I had finally obtained my passport as yet another Scottish summer – rain for forty days and nights, maximum temperature nineteen degrees Celsius – drew to a close. And that was the catalyst to do one of the greatest things I had ever accomplished up to that point.

Apply for an Australian Working Holiday Visa.

The visa was specially designed for those aged eighteen to thirty inclusive who wished to travel to Australia and work to support themselves. With a validity of twelve months, the visa would allow me to work in any occupation for any employer during my stay in Australia. Plus, if I worked in certain, mostly rural, areas for three months, I could remain in the country for a second year. Well, in theory anyway.
But I still had to apply for the first year.
CLICK. CLICK. CLICKEDDY-CLICK.
No turning back now...

A week later, the email came through...
"Dear Mr Harwood,
We are pleased to inform you that you have been granted a working holiday visa, subsection..."
An hour later, I had booked a flight from London to Sydney. And the cheapest flight was via Dubai on Emirates! All I had to do was sit it out for the next eleven months; eleven long and tedious months of commuting three hours to college and five hours home again, looking forward to my annual trips to the islands of Eigg and Berneray (it wasn't like I was going to abandon them, not at this stage in my life anyway…), preparing for my first Epic Voyage. And in August 2014, the adventure would begin.

I had no idea what I had let myself in for that day.
No idea at all.

August 10 2014 – Ardrossan

I HAVE LEFT ARRAN AND AM HEADING FOR AUSTRALIA.
Now that I have your attention, I have left Arran and am heading for Australia. Faced with the choice between staying at home and working at the Co-op, or travelling to Australia, where the minimum wage is around £10 per hour and there are more jobs than people, I chose the obvious, despite sickness earlier today. So, I bid you all adieu - see you in ten months!

Interlude #1

On the evening of the 10th of August 2014, you could have found me on the cold concourse of Glasgow's Buchanan Bus Station, thumbing through a copy of Marcus Clarke's *For the Term of His Natural Life* that an Australian backpacker had left in ArCaS – the local charity shop on Arran. I was waiting for a certain bus, fitted out with beds rather than seats, that would take me onwards to the small, quiet mountain village of London. It transpired that the on-board service would be snooty, but at least I would get a little sleep. Until the bloke in the bunk below me accidentally punched me in the gonads during the night, that is.

Upon my arrival in London, I located the nearest outdoor swimming pool (which was just off the Tottenham Court Road) and did lengths for a few hours in the presence of a few Team GB athletes. Leaving them to their own devices, I popped into a local Korean takeaway to devour some kimchi-fried rice before calling in at a local newsagent to purchase an Oyster card. The fancy-schmancy Borismaster-thingies don't accept cash, you see.

Returning to Victoria, I boarded a coach for Gatwick Airport, passing the much-chronicled Empire of Austenasia in the town of Carshalton en route (look it up – I have a knighthood there…).

August 11 2014 – Gatwick Airport

Despite having long hair, sandals and a Toots and the Maytals t-shirt on, I've got through security with no hassle! Shame about that crap NatEx driver chucking me off at Gatwick's South Terminal – "I've got no time to drive you to the North Terminal!" Oh, well. At least there was a free shuttle. Currently enjoying a kofta burger before the flight now. Soon, I will be free...

The Flight

Emirates are the best. End of story. The end. *Fin.*

Although I did get a bit jittery when we were flying over a peaceful little village called Erbil, located in a quaint region known as Iraqi Kurdistan. And when I mean peaceful, it was August 2014, so we were passing over Ambridge-of-the-East at the height of a missile crisis down below.

Then in Dubai, when I was changing planes onto another Emirates Airbus A380 bound for the Antipodes, I had my water bottle confiscated whilst being manually searched and security wanded by a spotty adolescent at the gate.

"What is this?"

"It's my water bottle – I filled it airside at London Gatwick."

"Is not allowed!"

Being deprived of my water in the desert during the middle of summer was, as can be imagined, not a good thing. At least I was still in the air-conditioned airport and about to board another flight. I even ended up seeing the Pakistani national cricket team at the gate… or was that a mirage?

I spent much of the twenty-four hours I spent en route to Sydney discovering the perfumed garden of delights known as the *ICE* in-flight entertainment system, complete with films like *Mr. Peabody & Sherman* and *Mars*

Needs Moms. I squealed with ecstatic delight when I discovered that the virtual jukebox had *Trout Mask Replica* – Captain Beefheart's magnum opus.

The pilots were a barrel of laughs. The pilot on the first leg to Dubai was an Irish guy who amazed everyone by speaking fluent Arabic with an Irish dialect ("Sure, he could be speaking Irish for all I know," I joked with the honeymooning English couple en route for the Maldives sitting next to me). The second pilot was barely competent in English, let alone the national language of the United Arab Emirates; he was an American who, to our collective dismay, had the mentality of 'have microphone, will use':

"Well, good mornin' y'all and welcome aboard this Ehm-err-aytes flight to Owk-lahnd, New Zee-lahnd, via Sydnuh, Austra-ee-a! Didja know that our cabin crew today come from eighteen diff'unt cunt-rees and speak twenty-four diff'unt lang-wee-jes? Wow!"

I felt sorry for the poor bastard who had to balance serving the scum-class passengers with translating Captain Billy-Bob Cody Peyton III's crap-waffling into Arabic…

But I'll repeat what I said. Emirates are the best. The end.

Initial Impressions of a Stolen Land

"Alone of all the races on earth, they seem to be free from the 'Grass is Greener on the other side of the fence' syndrome, and roundly proclaim that Australia is, in fact, the other side of that fence."
-   Douglas Adams

After the plane landed at Sydney Airport whilst I was listening to The Prodigy's 'Voodoo People', I made a rookie traveller error. I went for a piss after I disembarked from the plane, but before I had cleared immigration. As such, I found myself in a queue which took about an hour to clear. Stupid, stupid, stupid me.
Eventually, I got to the front, and despite being told by some that Australian immigration officials can be rather bullish at times, I encountered a bloke who was almost horizontal from being so laid back…
"Ya here on holiday, mate?" he smiled.
"Well, a working holiday – or so my visa says anyway."
He relaxed even more.
"Ah yeah, so it does."
STAMP.
"Welcome to Australia, mate!"
Having passed the Gestapo-style interrogation, and being deemed worthy to walk freely upon what the Eora Nation (as made famous by the legendary Pemulwuy) once called Warrang, I made my way into Sydney on the first double-decker train I had caught since my previous trip to the Netherlands in April. After changing trains at Town Hall, I ended up at the Backpackers HQ – a youth hostel located deep in the bowels of Sydney's backpacker ghetto (read: 'red light district') of King's Cross. Twenty hours of blissful sleep awaited me, but not before I travelled back into the city to open my Australian bank account.

And what an experience that turned out to be! I found myself at the Commonwealth Bank's Town Hall branch, or was it the best of an American hotel? I was greeted by a beaming woman in the foyer before I joined the queue for the tellers. Before I could get to them, though, I was served a selection of sweets by another greeter (can I call them that?), and was asked why I was at the bank by a third.
"Erm, I'm here to open my account…"
She beamed.
"Oh sir, you could have told the person on the door rather than having to wait in this long queue! Come, come!"
She whisked me off to a plush waiting area, complete with a leather sofa and a coffee machine.
"I'll just come and find somebody to help you. Please, help yourself to a coffee whilst you're waiting! You good for sweets?"
"Erm, yeah, sure. Need the coffee, though – I've just got off an Emirates A380 from London Gatwick!"
I began to wonder whether the plane had in fact gone down over Erbil, and what I was experiencing was the afterlife. After all, no business in the United Kingdom aimed at serving the masses of society would put in this level of service – never! I didn't have much time to ponder this – ten minutes later, my bank account was opened, and I had made my way back to the hostel. En route, I had stopped at the nearby Woolworths to pick up three uniquely Australian objects; a pack of crocodile jerky and a jar of Vegemite, which would

serve as my first meal in Australia, and a Telstra SIM card. Back at the hostel's office, I began to utilise a flat surface to help insert the latter into my phone, much to the chagrin of an older member of staff who, at the time, was sorting a large pile of clothes.

"Young man, I don't think you realise, but this is an office!"

"Well, that's why I'm doing something vaguely office-y with this paperclip," I instinctively rebuffed, my Higher National Diploma in Business Administration with Information Technology coming to the fore.

He shooed me out of his apparent domain; the pretty young receptionist, who was assisting me with my relative challenge, shrugging in my wake. SIM successfully inserted, I made my way to my room, where I slept for the next twenty hours.

I spent my first few weeks in Australia seeing the sights of Sydney, though I would never get to Bondi Beach – too mainstream for the likes of me, you know. Instead, I travelled by bus to Maroubra Bay to listen to the eponymous Edgar Froese track. Later, I surprised myself that not everyone in Woolloomooloo was called Bruce and claimed that Aristotle was a bugger for the bottle.

I also spent much of my time swimming in unheated outdoor pools around the city, wondering why everyone I passed en route to the pool were wearing thick winter coats and scarves in the twenty-degree heat. Much of the time, I ended up swimming at the North Sydney Olympic Pool – a fine establishment located in Milson's Point, just to the north-west of the Sydney Harbour Bridge, and next door to the equally-famous Luna Park. I nearly ended up applying for a job at the latter, but that's another story.

After a week in King's Cross, and procuring a bottle of sun-tan lotion that would last the entirety of my time in Australia, I moved north to a hostel in the up-market coastal suburb of Collaroy. There, I met a number of characters, including a Dutch guy named Willem who could solve a Rubik's cube in less than thirty seconds. But his is another tale.

In-between doing what Australians call 'cashies' – doing odd-jobs for cash-in-hand – I discovered sometime around then that a terrible event had occurred in the infamous hippie town of Nimbin. The local museum, the Bringabong gift shop and the Rainbow Café were all destroyed by a fire just a few days after I had landed in Australia. I figured that they needed all the help they could get from anybody – transient or otherwise – corresponding to the weird and wonderful, so I booked a one-way Greyhound bus ticket to the nearby middle-class liberal paradise of Byron Bay. This was twelve hours and virtually an entire political world away from northern Sydney, yet still a part of the state of New South Wales. Of course, there was one more thing I had to do in Sydney, and that wasn't running the local marathon that was going past the hostel…

August 30 2014 – Collaroy Beach YHA Hostel

Just had an interesting night: went to a psytrance event in Newtown, which was very enjoyable, especially since the DJs sampled a lot of Kraftwerk, Tangerine Dream and Orbital in the music. Oh, and a load of fit Aussie birds shunned their boyfriends and made a beeline for me, as they do.

As I moved through the rest of the Imperial Hotel, noticing a fair bit of male homosexual intercourse on the roof and a pair of lesbians making out in the gent's toilet, something in the back of my mind told me that something was wrong. Then I realised – the gay nightclub that I was partying in didn't have any cold taps in the bathrooms! No free water for this thirsty party animal, then! Oh, well.

Woo, psytrance! (Spot the author...)

A Random Online Conversation with Hamish

"How goes Aussie-land?"

"Australia's all right. I'm still looking for work, and I'm having trouble with the Medicare Vogons – they really are a bureaucratic bunch – but otherwise I'm fine.

Here's a tip – if you ever fly long-haul, fly Emirates if you can. They have this on-demand entertainment system in the backs of the seats, and they list the 'Essential Albums' in the music selection as being by Pink Floyd, Neil Young, Captain Beefheart, The Flaming Lips, Jimi Hendrix, The White Stripes, Santana, Led Zeppelin... suspiciously liberal for an Arab airline. Put it this way, it's strangely empowering listening to 'All Along the Watchtower' when flying over Erbil (yes, I did), and 'China Pig' when flying over Iran! Imagine this – an Arab gets on an Emirates plane, dons his headphones, and the entertainment system informs him that 'a squid eating dough in a polyethylene bag is fast n' bulbous...' well I know for certain it happened to some poor bugger in Dubai!"

"I like the sound of Emirates!"

"Oh, and the sleeper bus is a bitch. Short berths, pathetically small pillow and you have to store all of your on-board bags on your bunk. Just saying."

"I'll avoid them then. I'm in London right now; I listened to all of *Trout Mask Replica* in the Tate Modern – it kind of worked. Then, I walked to the

Houses of Parliament and listened to *The Terror* by The Flaming Lips, finishing it in a very trippy part of the Science Museum."

"Nice! In other news, I have two groovy roommates – a Malaysian guy called Jet and a Dutch guy called Willem. Willem reminds me of you, except he can solve a Rubik's cube in less than thirty seconds... And when I came back from dealing with the Medicare Vogons this afternoon, I had an interesting conversation:

Jet – 'How did you find out that I'm a stoner? Was it the smell coming from my locker?'

Me – 'Nah mate, you left your bong on the floor, you careless cunt! Also, how are you a stoner? I thought Malaysia imposed the death penalty for possession of cannabis...'

Jet – 'Yeah, but realistically, they only go after white guys...'

Good times!"

North to Nimbin

After a long chat with a lady from Fiji on the station concourse, I found myself sitting at the back of a Greyhound bus with the most legroom and the best WiFi I'd ever encountered on a public bus. With a compliment of around ten passengers, the bus manoeuvred out of Central Station on its long journey north to Brisbane. I looked forward to a decent sleep (well, decent considering I was on a bus), but the Akubra-hatted driver had other ideas. After he impressed the passengers by describing the vehicle's luxurious facilities and forgetting to activate the power sockets (which would be finally turned on when we got to Newcastle), Akubra Man proceeded to describe every roadside attraction in detail over the PA system. Twice over. Despite the fact that it was black outside.

"Right, folks. We are now passing over the Sydney Harbour Bridge. Did you know that the Sydney Harbour Bridge is held together by six million Australian-made hand-driven rivets? I'll repeat that, six million Australian-made hand-driven rivets..."

'Shut the fuck up!' I thought. 'I'm trying to listen to Hawkwind!'

Soon, though, the bus was rolling north up the Pacific Highway past brightly-lit Kenworth, Mack and Peterbilt tractor-units towing two trailers, and speeding towards Newcastle. The Hawkesbury River came and went in the darkness, as did the interestingly-named settlement of Mooney Mooney.

"Now on our right, you'll see a white light, then an orange light!" Akubra Man repeated.

"Far out!" I shouted from the back of the bus.

Making its way further up the Pacific Highway over the course of the night, the bus stopped at the roadhouses in Karuah and Macksville, where I took the time to sample various burgers and pies. By six-am the next day, after witnessing a glorious sunrise over the Big Prawn in Ballina, the bus hissed into the faux-hippie paradise of Byron Bay. Now, some people say that Nimbin today looks like Byron Bay in the seventies before all the celebrities moved in and made the place mainstream. But I don't know that. I wasn't there, you see.

Avoiding the German-speaking backpackers touting for the local youth hostels with their garish-yet-kitsch surfboards, I made my way to the beach, where I chilled out in the company of a pair of drunken tramps and waited for the tourist office to open so I could buy a bus ticket to Nimbin.

September 2 2014 – Byron Bay

Okay, so I've been in Byron Bay for three hours and some random Aborigine called Roads, who tells me he's from one of the desert mobs, tells me that I look weird and gives me the blessing of his nation. Even I found that weird...

The Nimbin Diaries, Pt. I

"You need to keep constant notes to pin down the Nimbin sensation. I lost mine after accidentally going one hash flapjack too far down the road to delirium."
-     Tom Parry, *Thumbs-Up Australia: Hitchhiking the Outback*

Nimbin Rocks

Pathway to Paradise

After fighting off the efforts of the leeches in the tourism office, who had repeatedly tried to sell me an expensive tour rather than a one-way bus ticket, I eventually boarded a rather cubic and faded breed of bus that one would associate with shuttling social deviants to and from privately-operated prisons, as opposed to teleporting near-broke backpackers to the epicentre of their fabled Shangri-La. That bus – a rather psychedelic number, complete with the driver's dog – had departed about an hour previous. Alas, it didn't offer one-way fares, hence the Ex-Penal Sort-Of Public Omnibus was for me.

After making a detour to pick up yet another faux-hippie at the Arts Factory, who was initially too stoned to remember she was actually going to Nimbin that day until someone was dispatched to collect her, we finally headed west out of Byron Bay. With Led Zeppelin's finest blasting on the speaker system, the bus creaked up the Bruxner Highway, passing through scenery which resembled a sub-tropical Ireland, and towns and villages which would become very familiar to me over the next eight months. Bangalow and Clunes pretty much flew by – well, at the flying speed of an obese goose anyway. The village of Bexhill and its open-air cathedral eased passed the windows. Some months later, I would visit the cathedral in the presence of a large watermelon I had purchased for two dollars from a roadside stall. The visitor's book had a contribution from a certain individual known as 'The Doctor' from 'Gallifrey'. It said "Wowza!"

The bus skirted the edge of the great metropolis of Lismore. This was not to be confused with the Lismore that I knew, that being a wee island just off the coast of Oban. No, this Lismore was home to the Tatts Hotel, where I would go on to open for one of my all-time music heroes. It was also home to the Thai Food Place, where I would discover the delicious dish known as the pork panang. Best of all, this Lismore was also home to Nimbin itself; it was within the extensive city limits.

The bus joined the Nimbin Road and headed north-west out of Lismore's near-endless suburbs. Soon, we were passing Goolmangar – 'where the cows come first'. I noticed a road branching off to a settlement called Jiggi – presumably a place where people get Jiggi with it. Coffee Camp, with its presumably hyperactive and homosexual population, came a few minutes later.

We briefly stopped for a photo opportunity near some of the purest holy monoliths in the country we now know as Australia – these were the Nimbin Rocks, which the Bundjalung people believe to be home of the *Nmbngee*, or 'Clever Men'. I would spend much of my time in the shadow of the rocks learning the truth about reality, but I didn't know it at the time.

The one thing on my mind at the time was that, after fantasising about this moment since I was in high school some five years previous, I had finally made it to Nimbin! The town that was settled by Caucasians in the 1840s, and deforested and farmed out by the 1960s, was the location of the Aquarius Festival in 1973. This was Australia's equivalent of Woodstock – and I mean that most literally. Music lovers, Gaia freaks celebrating the coming of the Age of Aquarius, and university students all swamped the town, and many decided not to go home, choosing to remain in and around Nimbin. These new arrivals brought alien concepts to the town; for example, some would end up submitting the first ever application of group title ownership of land in Australia. Oh, and before I forget to mention it, the festival was the first event in Australia that actually sought permission for the use of land from the Traditional Owners, in this case the Bundjalung people.

Since 1973, Nimbin has attracted thousands of people from the other side of the fence: writers, artists, drug dealers, musicians, young families escaping the humdrum of Sydney and Melbourne, actors, journeymen, environmentalists, vehicle-dwellers, communists, faux-hippie tourists, Rainbow Warrior associates, pikeys, pixies, permaculture enthusiasts, saints, sinners, all of them winners! Well, except for the hard-drug dealers and the middle-upper class faux hippies who think they know what and where it's at, of course.

And on the second of September 2014, the current crop was about to be joined by someone who would go on to become a legend of the Alternative Society. Someone who go on to introduce the local co-operative to the Rochdale Principles, help sow the seeds of a minor revolution, save the life of a local child, out-poet one of the weirdest people in the world and gain a certain reputation by appearing on the local radio station, had just arrived in town.

The bus driver informed us that we were still in New South Wales and, as such, New South Wales drug laws still applied in Nimbin. The bus proceeded to motor along Cullen Street at walking pace, the driver jokingly informing us that the police station was not a tourist attraction. After being chucked off the

Bogan Bus outside the Oasis Café, I picked up my bags and strode confidently up the hill to the Nimbin Rox Youth Hostel, almost disappointed by the fact that no-one in town had offered to sell me any drugs as soon as I had stepped off the bus.

September 2 2014 – Nimbin Rox YHA Hostel

So I was sitting with an Englishman and an Irishman in the garden at the youth hostel that I'm currently staying at, and coming from Scotland, I ask "So you're from England, I'm from Scotland and you're from Ireland. Is this some kind of joke?" The Irishman replies "Nope, da joke's on da poor feckers back home – dey're stuck over dere whilst we're sitting here in paradise!"

Gina

On the third of September 2014, like so many times over my life, I found myself in the right place at the right time. The right place being the HEMP (Help End Marijuana Prohibition) Embassy.

I struck up a friendly conversation with a middle-aged hippie lady whilst I was shopping for some hemp oil and a decent pipe and, after a few minutes chatting, she offered to buy me a cup of tea at the Embassy's café. After one of many good cups I would enjoy over the many months that followed that day, she quizzed me on everything from my hobbies to my experiences under the influence of LSD. Then she offered me a job.

It transpired that her name was Gina, or Junia as the denizens of Thailand pronounce her name. She was an artist; an ex-teacher whose father was an American MASH pilot. Her mother was a prominent Australian author/socialite; Gina would tell me stories about how her mother would attend balls with the Australian Governor-General of the day, as well as discuss the in-depth aspects of sacred geometry and the workings of the Skull and Bones Society. On top of this clash of cultures, the first language that Gina spoke during her younger days was Spanish, having spent the first years of her life in South America.

And thus, over that cup of tea, the trip truly began in earnest. Over the next eight months, I would live in the back of Gina's monastic Sprinter van with no electricity, running water or toilet in exchange for working the land, planting grevilleas and other such exotic plants, and helping to build a home-cum-art studio out of a shipping container. For me, it was a dream come true; Nick Rosen's *How to Live Off-Grid* was the book that got me through puberty, after all.

It would turn out to be eight of the greatest months of my life. But I didn't know it yet…

The First Day on the Land

On an ordinary bright day in early September 2014, you could have found me sitting at the bottom of the track leading up to the Nimbin Rox YHA; a smile creeping across my face. For you see, it was the first day I was to be working on a piece of land which would become my home for the next eight months.

I sat on the verge, admiring the handiwork that had gone into carving the Trishula and the words 'LORD SHIVA' into a nearby tree, complete with the good kind of swastika that didn't indicate genocide. Eventually, a rust bucket pulled around the corner and across the bridge over the river. It was a white Ford pickup truck, characterised by its high ground clearance, kangaroo bars, a powerful petrol engine under the bonnet, and a hard cover over the loading bay. Its raised air intake gave it the appearance of a snorkeler, not that uncommon on the coast at Byron Bay, which was why it came to be known as the *Albino Submarine*. And at the helm was, of course, Gina. She smiled as I opened the passenger door.

"Hello, my dear friend! I didn't expect to see you down here!"

"Yeah – there's not exactly that much space to turn at the top of the track. Thought I might as well save you the hassle. You all right?"

"Yes thanks!"

On the way to her property, we stopped briefly at the Nimbin Servo.

"Do you know how to check the oil?" she asked.

"Well, I should," I replied. "They teach us basic maintenance in the British driving test anyway."

"Really?"

"Yeah."

"Well, they should do it here in Australia too!"

After fuelling the truck and checking the oil, my reward being a macadamia bar, we motored onwards to her property. The foreman was already there, attacking a pine tree with a chainsaw; his then-fiancée watching on from the sidelines. It turned out that the tree was on the neighbour's land, but we wouldn't discover this for many months. Either way, that tree would become the source of many a good wood fire.

The neighbour at the time was Benny; a thirty-something chef and psytrance DJ who had recently been busted for driving under the influence. He was holding down the fort for a pair of gay guys, who were due to move up from Melbourne in a few months' time. He was an amiable fellow – well, apart from that time he was on the ice, but that's another story.

On that first day, things went well. The foreman spent the day carving up the pine tree, whilst I wandered around the land watering and mulching the plants; 'Tiptoe Through the Tulips' stuck in my head as I went about my business. The day passed very quickly indeed, and soon Gina returned me to the hostel with promises of future work.

Life was good.

September 4 2014 – Nimbin Rox YHA Hostel

I had this dream recently. In the dream, I got an urge to leave 'society', so I travelled to Nimbin, got blessed by an Aboriginal elder en route, checked into the local youth hostel, started chatting to a middle-aged hippie lady in the HEMP Embassy downtown, had tea and cake with her and got offered a job. This job entailed watering plants, moving logs, shovelling sawdust, admiring the view and smoking weed. My colleague and his friend would turn out to be the local psytrance DJs – I now have connections with the local electronic music scene.

I lied. It wasn't a dream. The last four days have blown the lid off what I've achieved across Europe over the course of four years. I must have died when my plane was flying over Erbil a few weeks ago – oh well, at least I'm living the dream!

A Random Text Conversation with Gina

":>...hope u have a great day....my fully kitted (tiny) container home is COMING IN .....by crane now next week....erk...eek...me too busy!....will invite u to housewarming party !!!!..have a lovely day!....look up Robyn Francis, Djanbung Gardens, Nimbin...they are having a fundraiser ... Towards starting a Nimbin co-op ...music etc.....at 2 pm this Sat...u can walk from where u are......I'm doing Permaculture for 1 wknd p.month....Other courses there might interest u too...
Love!
Junia"

"Cool!"

"Yes very good course if u want to go 'off grid' sooner rather than later.....!.....lots of people from everywhere, plans and optimistic activity.... Right now....reason= Bentley Blockade success (so far) in stopping the CSG moves into the area.
:>"

"That's good! You enjoy the rest of the day, and if you need any more work done, just give me a text :)"

Nimbin Rox Interlude

I had a blast at the YHA. When I wasn't working, I got to know Fisher and Ollie from England, Kevin from Germany, Roman from France and Rogério from Brazil, among other many other groovy people. I spent some of my time there listening to Nim-FM, notably a breakfast show aptly named *Wake the Fuck Up*:

"The bloody cops raided the town today, around eighty of 'em, armed to the teeth," complained the DJ one morning shortly after I arrived in town. "Apparently, they found a kilo of beneficial herb and arrested a bunch of innocents who weren't even carrying. It's a bloody disgrace – they could have spent their valuable resources going after the ice dealers... Fuck it – here's Motörhead with One Track Mind."

Through Gina, I also got to know a local lady named Tanya, and spent an evening at her place along with Luna, Forest and Namaste, her lovely children. Over the next few months, I would run errands for them such as taking Namaste to school in the *Albino Submarine*.

In the meantime, I was considering heading back to Sydney in order to earn some cash. But things got interesting...

A Random Text Conversation with Gina

"Sorry I didn't ring last night....slept from ystday arvo till 7.30 this a.m....

2pm fundraiser party /live music at Djanbung Permaculture farm/school gardens at 2pm today...for starting Nimbin food co-op
:>"

"Sounds good - might as well go to it :) Don't worry about not ringing – I was pretty tired as well!"

"I have a brand new Wolf tent (one man) u can look up at the stars......still unwrapped.... U could sleep in that on a couple pallettes....and inside Merc when it rains.....u being up there will help keep the wallabies away from the new trees....I'm going over about 11.30 this am to plant the 5 rosewoods....I could pick u up on the way... Pay u for an hour of helping me....then we'll go to Djanbung.....pick up my friend Tanya on the way....hope this suits u at such late notice!
Love!
Junia"

"Sounds good – when can you pick me up?"
"11.45 – 12.00 ok my dear friend?"
"Sounds good :)"
"cu then:>"

September 15 2014 – Nimbin Rox YHA Hostel

Right, I was going to write this status a day before the referendum, but since my boss gave me an offer to stay in her van in exchange for scaring the shit out of the local wallabies (the buggers are eating the trees I planted on her land) and watering the plants, I'll be off-grid for a while. Anyway...
Think about this. If you vote 'Yes' in the referendum, Scotland will be run by a fat bloke with a Braveheart complex, who will probably be voted out within a few months. If you vote 'No', Scotland will probably be run by those UKIP bigots by 2015 – as if the Tories aren't bad enough. So here's the choice; Braveheart or bigots – stupid or stupid and evil.
I say vote for the lesser of two evils: YES. And elect the Green Party already!

A Random Online Conversation with Hamish

"I remember you saying you wanted to vote Yes in the referendum – did you find a way from Australia? Postal vote?"

"I'm voting by proxy – my dad's voting on my behalf."

"Is he also Yes? In other words, do you trust him? Haha."

"Well, he told me he's not voting No..."

"Excellent! Have you seen the debate I'm having with a Unionist right now?"

"Not yet…"

"I'm loving the Hawkwind featuring Brian Blessed thing you sent me – it's amazing! It also reminds me of the referendum: 'you only have a few seconds to escape, use those seconds sensibly...'"

"Ha! Also, it's just occurred to me that I'm talking to you from THE FUTURE!"

"So, can you tell me the result of the referendum in advance?"

"I'm only 9 hours in the future, dickwad! Also in other news, my boss is buggering off for a few days, and she wants me to stay in her van whilst she's gone..."

"Awesome – pay rise?"

"Unsure. All I know is I'm going to go off-grid, live in a van and be a scuzzy pikey bastard!"

"Talking of cars, I drove along a crowded dual carriageway at 60 today – ahhhhhh!"

"70 is scary, trust me."

"Is it WiFi you use or 3G? And where/how do you get it?"

"Currently, WiFi at the Nimbin Rox YHA. Oh, and before you say anything, the van's unregistered, so I can't drive it anywhere."

"Aw, that's a shame. Is it 11pm over there?"

"Yeah, it's 11pm. More or less."

"What is bed time for you over there? About 11?"

"Yeah, but since it's my last night with WiFi, I can stay up a wee bit longer. There's fuck all to do before Friday. On Friday, there's drumming in the town, and on Saturday there's usually a doof happening."

"Doof?"

"Rave of dubious legality. That one I went to last week was just plain weird."

"I was at a club with Lewis last weekend, and a crazy Asian girl started picking my nose on the dancefloor. Picking snot out of my nose!?! So, what happened at your thing?"

"Imagine a load of Japanese people with dreads shouting 'JAH RASTAFARI!' whilst dancing to minimal techno under a tepee with a plumber named Trout..."

"I remember you saying. How long do you plan on staying in Nimbin?"

"No fooking idea. At least another 2 weeks now!"

"Making money pile up?"

"Not overly. Anyway, got to go, got woken up at 2am this morning by Sassenich pricks arriving, need bed badly. I can barely see the keyboard on my phone. Talk to you soon."

"Bye fow nows!"

A few days later, after moving into the van on the sixteenth of September (the tent plan was quickly and mutually shelved) …

"Heard what's happening in Glasgow? There's No voters stirring up trouble when they won... why?"

"Because they're assholes. Also, the wallabies are still a nuisance on the land, and they won't run off when I shout at them. So I run at them with a machete and scare them shitless! Also, assume that I have no internet or electricity until further notice. This is a VERY rare exception. And about the riots in Glasgow, they were covered in the Aussie news!"

"They weren't on the British news…"

"WTF?"

"However, I reckon there'll be another referendum soonish, say 15 years, since David Cameron just announced he's not going to keep his promises."

"Hopefully."

"I'm almost slightly glad he isn't keeping promises as that will give Scotland all the more reason to secede."

"Fair point. Got to go now, the annual agricultural show beckons... Hope you're all right!"

"Night then, or g'day, whichever side of this planet you inhabit!"

A Random Text Message from Gina

"U really impressed foreman today my dear friend.....he was amazed how into working the 'land' u were!....many thanks ....thanks in Gaelic?...I will remember it soon enough.....have a lovely gloaming
Love!
Junia"

The Nimbin Show and The Great Australian Beer Test

On the twentieth of September 2014, I went down to the Nimbin Show. After making a mockery of the chickens with afros, singing the *Schnappi Das Kleine Krokodil* song with Kevin and Ollie whilst feeling up a crocodile and betting on the duck races (hosted by none other than Michael J. 'Duck' Dundee), I retired to the comfort of the beer tent. The middies were cheap and plentiful, so I did my own taste testing...

- Tooheys (from New South Wales) – decent enough. Not something I would get regularly, though.
- Victoria Bitter (from, erm, Victoria?) – total shit. I would later find out that VB is the only beer one would find in many desert communities because it was the only beer that could survive the journey up from the brewery in Melbourne. Though this is probably because VB expires before it leaves the factory...
- XXXX (from Queensland) – all right, but puts you in mind of that old joke (Why is there a beer called Four-ex? Because Queenslanders can't spell 'beer'!).

I bought another middy of Tooheys – the lesser of the three evils – and listened to the band onstage playing Pink Floyd covers. Later that day, I met up with Gina, and I drove for the first time after passing my test back in Scotland two years previous. The show should have been memorable, but for me the drive was more so. Just goes to show how strange my mind is...

September 24 2014 – Gungas

I have reason to believe that I saved a man from going to prison yesterday. Twice. Here's why: The foreman came to my place, that being a van on the land on which I'm currently working, at 6.30 am yesterday morning. After dropping off some building supplies, he knocked on the van door.
"Scott, it's a big day today. We've got to go into Lismore to get some more supplies, but first, I'm buying you breakfast. Foreman's orders!"
He went off into Nimbin in his Subaru, leaving me to work the land until my next-door neighbour invited me in for a cup of tea.

A short time later, the boss' 1996 Ford pickup truck pulled up, with the foreman at the wheel; all-day breakfast pie, coffee and cheesecake slice waiting for me in the passenger seat. After a quick breakfast, we travelled to a well-known chain supermarket specialising in DIY equipment in Lismore.

That was where the foreman met his mother's ex-boyfriend, who used to abuse him and his family. The old guy never recognised him. The foreman later put it down to the fact that I was glaring at him that he never laid a finger on the old man. So I saved him from prison once.

We picked up a supply of wood, tied it down to the trailer securely with a tie-strap and set off towards The Channon, stopping at the local condom dispensary and a few other shops en route. On a hill, though, the tie-strap failed and we lost the load, and the foreman didn't notice.

"STOP THE TRUCK!" I screamed. "WE'RE LOSING THE FUCKING LOAD!"

He stopped the truck, and I quickly ran down the road and moved the bulk of the wood off the road, saving it in the process. Retracing our steps to see if we lost any wood (we did), we set off towards The Channon. The foreman informed me that I'd probably saved him $200, plus any legal costs and possibly prison time if he was indeed found liable of not securing the load properly and causing an accident.

A quick drink or two in The Channon Tavern and we went back to the foreman's encampment to pick up his fiancée. He decided to travel the last 15km back to Nimbin in his fiancée's Hyundai, leaving me to drive the truck. Under the influence. By myself. With a dangerously-secured load on the roof. Challenge accepted!

With the Hyundai up ahead with its hazards going, driving the truck back to my van was a breeze. After we unloaded the wood, the foreman broke down in tears, and admitted that he had been overworking. He also thanked me for saving his ass from prison twice in one day. He thanked me a lot.

I drove the foreman and his fiancée to our boss' room at the Grey Gum Lodge, where the foreman gave himself two weeks off.

I got paid $140 for 7 hours work yesterday, plus an extra $60 for saving the foreman's ass. This story's going to remain with me for a long time, I'll tell you that.

(After the foreman collapsed on Gina's bed, his fiancée and I went to the pizza shop in town to collect some much-needed sustenance. We waited for over an hour for the pizzas, so we chatted to pass the time. The foreman's fiancée subsequently realised that better partners than the foreman existed in the universe. Furthermore, it finally dawned on her that she was eleven years younger than he was, and he was in all likelihood only in it for the sex. She dumped him a few weeks later, took the Hyundai, and never saw him again. I never saw her again, for that matter.)

A Random Text Message to Gina

"Junia – some guys are currently unloading a red container and an old ice-cream van labelled 'The Nimbin Express' and 'The Nimbin Espresso' onto the land next door to yours... As I write this, they've just dumped it on the lower track in front of the Magna.

Thought you might like to know..."

(This would become the home of our new neighbours. Dave and Bonnie, along with their young children Coco and Luna, and Misha the malamute, would become some of the greatest neighbours that one could have. But their story is for another to tell...)

October 4 2014 – Gungas

My life's gone a bit Swiss Family Robinson at the moment. I have no amenities in my van – no water, electricity or Internet. I cook on an open fire pit. For entertainment, I write down my thoughts and opinions, or chase after wallabies. And a mouse, whom I've dubbed 'Gerald Gonzales', disturbs me at night.
Though I do have plenty of concessions. I obtain water from my next-door neighbour. My boss occasionally lets me use the Internet on her phone. I walk into town to use the free swimming pool, shower and toilet when the weather's nice, which it almost always is. Pity that they switched off the lights so I can't siphon electricity any more – oh well.
Also, I don't have to kill my own food. The availability of cheap bananas, bread and noodles, plus a substantial amount of hemp seeds provided by my boss, makes sure of that. And best of all, I've lost a fair bit of weight and my fitness is improving substantially.
Admittedly, my life is not for the average backpacker. But it's a satisfactory one, and beats the Scottish winter hands down :)

Sacred Geometry

"You know," I was saying to Gina. "I really hated maths in high school!"
Gina and I were sitting outside the container drinking tea, which had just been prepared over the wood fire.
She looked at me quizzically.
"Why is that, my dear friend?"
"Well, back in primary school, I was really good at maths. Like, really good – at several points in my life, I was the top in my entire school! Then, some years after I got into high school, they started introducing all this calculus bullshit and..."
"Wait," she interjected, smiling. "Calculus?"
"Yeah."
"I think I have a solution for that!"
"And what solution might that be?"
"Sacred geometry!"
She began to explain how sacred geometry ascribes symbolic and sacred meanings to certain geometric shapes proportions and how it could, in theory, be used to teach calculus, but I had to interject.
"Sorry Gina," I apologised. "I can understand how it can be used to teach calculus and all that, but my brain just cannot process the calculus itself!"
"Why not?"
"It's probably how it was taught to me. Also, the fact that I saw no need to be taught calculus at the time, and still don't to this day. I've probably got PTSD from it or something!"
She chuckled.

"I understand perfectly, my dear friend. I used to be a teacher myself!"

"What did you teach?"

"Computing. I had all these ideas for teaching programs that would make learning more fun, but they never came to fruition."

"What, you mean like *Maths Blaster*?"

"Yeah, but more for teenagers and adults. You know, like sacred geometry programs."

"Ah."

Eventually, I would come to understand sacred geometry during a good night at the Oasis, but it would pass five minutes later.

October 6 2014 – Gungas

I thought that being blessed by an Aboriginal elder would be the high point of my trip. I was wrong.

I thought that saving a man from prison would be the high point of my trip. Wrong again.

A few weeks ago, about 80 riot police carried out a series of raids on Nimbin over the course of three days. Fortunately, I was at the Nimbin Rox Youth Hostel out of town, and on the second day of the raids, I was chatting to a German hippie named Kevin.

"Something big's going to happen soon – I can feel it," I was saying.

"Like a protest?"

"Mmm. A big one. Something tells me MardiGrass (the big pro-cannabis protest/festival in May) is coming early..."

Turns out that Kevin had been in town a while, and had a number of friends who were pro-pot activists...

So there's going to be a big pro-pot rally in Nimbin this Saturday at 11am, and it's likely that I sparked the idea. Watch this space...

Nimbin's Inaugural Smoke-In

Gina couldn't make it to the rally. She went down the coast for a bit to see some of her friends, promising her safe return in three days. She eventually returned about three weeks later. That's Nimbin life for you…

Other than gardening, walking the three kilometres or so into town to use the free outdoor swimming pool and being bombarded by magpies on the road (I named one of them 'Bomber' after the Motörhead track…), I prepared for the rally by mounting an art canvas reading 'WEGALISE LEED!' on a wooden pole.

The rally day eventually came along. I woke up Terrence – an Anglophone Quebecer who was sleeping in the shed next door with his girlfriend at the time – and we prepared to hit the town. I set off a few minutes before him with my sign, truckers giving me encouraging honks and the thumbs up as they passed me on Gungas Road. They too must have favoured the outright legalisation of marijuana – it was Nimbin, after all…

Terrence and I, along with Kevin and a whole bunch of other people, all gathered at the HEMP Embassy. When eleven o'clock rolled around, we all marched down Cullen Street to the cop-shop to the sound of drums and had one hell of a good time! It would also be the first time I would encounter David Peace One Love, although I didn't know it at the time. More on him later…

A Random Text Conversation with Gina

"Owz the roamin' in the gloamin' goin'?.....me staying weekend with my Xman Of 22 yrs Jeremy ....may visit my mother in Canberra also....will let u know when I know de returno!
Been up at Nthn Beaches Newport with art 'colleague' old friends reunion...from Auroville while chainsaws cut down rainforest around us!!!! How are the trees?
Abbots new laws have brought out the chainsawzzzzzzzzzzz all over."

"Just got your messages – the trees are fine. Some wallaby activity – were scared off. Just been exchanging music with Terrence from next door – just listening to some Amon Düül II for the first time! Hope you are well :)"

The Fauna of Gungas

Gina frequently referred to Gungas as *National Geographic Land*, and I could see why. The wildlife variation and displays were just immense – flocks of fruit bats would come out in the evening, blotting out the sky whilst at the same time attempting to crap on my head. The bats were particular auspicious during Halloween, when I watched them fly overhead whilst listening to a version of Thriller slowed down from forty-five to thirty-three RPM. The flypast had started when I started the song, and ended as soon as Vincent Price laughed and the door slammed shut. You can say what you like about bats, but their choreography is astounding...
Lorikeets, of both the multicoloured and black varieties, added to the colour spectrum of the land. Kookaburras laughed at every opportunity. A species of bird I nicknamed the 'VCS3 Bird' owing to its distinct call regularly visited – to this day I have never been able to identify what species it was.

I mentioned earlier that the local magpies had a reputation for dive-bombing people during the Australian spring; the rare exception to this was the one that Gina sort-of tamed. Every day, it would come down to the ground level, drink out of a static water feature that Gina had placed, and eat some of our surplus food. It was a friendly wee thing; Gina would frequently talk to it whilst I would look on in mild amusement.

Landwise, I only saw two snakes on the property in Gungas – a goanna was living under my van and, as such, driving them away. On the road, however, the snakes were a different story. One day, as I was driving into Lismore, a carpet python successfully attempted suicide underneath the *Albino Submarine*, a forty-tonne Kenworth behind me turning the carcass into a traditional Chinese medicine. And the guidebooks say you don't often see snakes in Australia...

Funnily enough, the snakes don't attack you unless you're doing something totally daft. The marsh flies were a different story – easy to kill but painful if they bit you. Mosquitos and ants – some red and the size of your fingers – went for me as well. As I was shifting a log one afternoon, a giant red ant bit me on the foot and came back for more; the pain was comparable to being hit by a bullet. And to top it all off, speaking as one of those lucky bastards that Scottish ticks never go for, a tick bit me on the dick. The bad part was deciding whether to remove it using acetone or my lighter...

One day, a lorikeet brained itself after flying headfirst into a tree next to my van and, in the process of assisting it, Gina accidentally broke its neck. Of course, when you're in the possession a dead parrot, there's only one thing you can do. That is, you wish to make a complaint…

We ended up burying it with a strawberry, the last thing it ate. With any luck, the ex-parrot had fertilised the land just a little more.

Life was interesting then. As if you couldn't tell…

October 20 2014 – Gungas

So my boss and I took a 40-mile round-trip to the ALDI in Lismore today, and I found out that driving in an urban environment during rush hour in Australia is little different from doing the similar in the UK, what with bad drivers and buses signalling and pulling out in front of you when you're doing 30 miles an hour when you're only within emergency stopping distance of them. Albeit that everyone driving a truck is towing at least two trailers and under the influence.
Except me. I wasn't towing two trailers.

October 22 2014 – Gungas

A few weeks ago, I potentially saved a guy's ass from prison: tonight, my boss and I potentially saved a child's life.

Every day for the past few weeks, some of my neighbours have been shouting and swearing and, from what my boss and I can hear, beating the living shit out of their child. This time around, we could hear metal and glass being smashed and the child abruptly ceasing its screaming, so we called the cops. Instead of wasting their time on the harmless pot-smokers, for once the police got off their arses, went to the house and arrested the father, or at least have a word with him anyway. Turns out he was known to the police, or so the 000 operator blurted out. He didn't even put up a fight, possibly so that his partner wouldn't notice and 'spit the dummy', as we say in Australia. After the cops took him downtown – at least I think they did, he came downstairs to the door where the cops were waiting and the light shut off when they were still there – I posted a letter through their mailbox. This detailed my exact thoughts about them, offered an ultimatum – chill out and stop abusing kiddies or get the fuck out of town – and addressed it from 'the pissed-off residents of Gungas' (the village that I actually live in these days). Hopefully, the child will live (emphasis on 'live') in a better environment from now on thanks to the actions that we did tonight.

Child abuse is wrong. End of. If you know of a kid who is almost definitely being abused, phone the cops. And if you can, quote what they're actually saying – we had to ring 000 twice before they came out, and on the second time we quoted what they were saying. That helps a lot.

Seriously, stop child abuse.

28

Tahuti Falls and the Doctor Fish

To this day, I cannot remember the exact time that this particular story happened, but it was an interesting experience, so I might as well share it with you good people.

The days were blurring in October 2014. Nimbin, which is approximately the same latitude south of the equator as New Delhi is north, was experiencing a heatwave. The temperature soared to forty-five degrees in the daytime, dropping to a relatively-cool thirty at night. My van had the ambience of a Mexican kitchen – the heat was so intense that Gerald Gonzales had packed his bags, yelled ¡Ándale! ¡Arriba! and buggered off, presumably into the jaws of something dangerous as I never saw him again. I didn't need the crate of Hahn Premium Light I kept under the passenger seat in the van's cab; the act of merely moving around reminded one of being drunk.

And on top of the heat, Gina was running out of hard currency. The foreman (remember him?), owed Gina a few dollars, so I was dispatched in the *Albino Submarine* to the foreman's encampment to collect her bounty.

Under the luminous heavy sun which burned all within its dominion, I drove up the Tuntable Creek road at minimal speed; every ounce of concentration that remained in my heat-warped mind was trying to counter the extreme heat in the un-air-conditioned cab of the *Albino Submarine*. As I was driving down the foreman's track, I hit a tree stump growing out of the track and knocked off the back of the exhaust. Thankfully, the foreman had a chainsaw, and we cut the fuck out of the offending article to prevent any future accidents. After I accrued fifty dollars in a mix of hard cash and petrol, and using static electricity to bring a drowned marsh fly back to life in a pseudo-Satanic ritual for shits and giggles, the foreman and I drove into The Channon to pick up a six-pack of cider from the general store. We then drove up to Tahuti Falls – a swimming hole surrounded by a forest which wouldn't look out of place in a softcore scene of a major blockbuster. It was packed with families – not my first choice of company, but when the temperature hits forty you want to be submerged in something cold, whatever the cost. Besides, there weren't any tourists there, just one traveller – me. The foreman's friends showed up – they had the same heat-beating ideology – and as we drunk our cider in the cool of the river they quizzed me about life in Scotland.

"So how hot is it in Scotland during the summer, mate?"

"Erm, like, twenty…"

"TWENTY! Ha! How the hell are ya coping with the Aussie heat?"

I looked around.

"Swimming hole."

As the people made their way home, the foreman and I drove back towards his encampment. As we were making our way down his track, he asked me to stop.

"Turn left up this side track."

"Why?"

"You'll fucking love it!"

I had no fear – blame the heat of the day. I found myself driving past a house that wouldn't look out of place in a Stephen King adaptation, towards its great, murky-looking dam.

The foreman jumped out of the ute and into the dam.

"Come in up to your neck, and stay perfectly still!"

"Why?"

"You'll find out!"

I obeyed his instructions, and made my way into what felt like a decent bath. Then I felt a wee nip on my left leg. Then another one on my arse. And another one on my neck…

"I know what they are! They're those fish you see in the foot spas!" Doctor fish!

"Damn skippy!"

"Wait – aren't they supposed to spread, like, bad shit like HIV and Hep-C?"

"Yeah, nah, that's bullshit. Not these ones anyway 'cause, ya know, they're wild. Not exposed to any nasty chemicals. Gotta say though, they like you – they're going bat shit crazy, eh!"

"Must be because of my eczema."

"Yeah, probably mate."

After we had cleaned ourselves, I dropped the foreman off at his encampment. It would be the last time I would see him – he moved to Jindabyne in the Snowy Mountains to live his passion of snowboarding. Gina didn't overly miss him – he was a dick. But he was a well-meaning dick.

A Random Online Conversation with Hamish

"How are you? And how's Aussie? And out of curiosity, have you just started summer time? Our clocks just went back."

"Fucking awesome! Clocks went forward, yeah, at least here in New South Wales. Australia still rules, or at least Nimbin does! How's Scotland? Right now, out here it's 40+C and sunny – I'm on the same latitude south as New Delhi is north…"

"Scotland's awesome. Apparently, John Cooper Clarke was in Glasgow tonight, but I found out too late. My new flatmate was there though. Also, it's about 5 degrees here. Do you have the Skype thing working down under? We should Skype sometime – not now though I'm seriously tired. You should also catch up with *Doctor Who* – this season's been amazing so far."

"I'm going to say this only once. I can't catch up on *Doctor Who*. Don't talk to me about it until end of June 2015. By all means, talk about anything else, I'm just going to wait until I can catch up with it properly. Also, I have no WiFi, so no Skype. Sorry. Rant over."

"Ah shit – I was going to tell you all about that amazing finale cliff-hanger where the Doctor is discovered wanking off Davros in a portaloo TARDIS… In all seriousness though, I'm not going to spoil this series for you – it's the best the show has been since the days of Eccleston. Anyway, I thought it got broadcast in Australia on the same day or one day after, but I guess you don't have TV. Also, let us know if you ever get WiFi – it would be good to Skype call you sometime."

October 26 2014 – Gungas

So there's a heatwave, it's going to peak at 45C (!!!) today, there's a total fire ban so I can't cook any food, and I've got to heave a great big tarpaulin over a shipping container. Cue the desert rock...

(This was about the time that I went more or less feral. On top of living in the van, I wandered around wearing little more than Speedos and sandals – not that anyone cared in the hippie capital of Australia. I bathed frequently in every river I came across because the swimming pool was perpetually occupied by pissing children, and I didn't know what I was doing half the time and why I was doing it. Though it could have just been the side-effects of dehydration...)

A Random Text Conversation with Gina

"Still on here organizing etc ...going into town for 1pm appt tmw....also friend Denis coming over tomorrow to look at electrics ....his lovely fiancé my friend Anna is coming back from Thailand in 2 weeks.... She was a tourist guide in Krabi... He is a Swiss sailor.... Who lives here now
Nimbin Poetry reading 7.30 pm at Oasis this Thu....fun
I'm returning with a block of ice and some steaks for dinner.... Then back to Nimbin for a trip to Rainbow Power Company on Alternative Way.....if u want to come I'll be there in 5 mins...;>"
"Cool – see you then :)"
"Recommend covering steaks completely with oil before cooking ;)"

The Anti-Fracking Rally

It should be obvious to you, the reader, by now that Nimbin is a place where they do not suffer idiots gladly. Idiots, in the case of this chapter, being the people who vote for right-wing politicians who think that obtaining coal-seam gas through hydraulic fracturing is the way forward in life. Despite the fact that all but two people in Nimbin either vote for the Greens or the HEMP Party, the voting habits of the metropolitan area of Lismore as a whole were roughly split between the Greens and the right-wing National Party, with the Nats having a slight advantage and, at the time, the incumbent member of the State Parliament.

With a large percentage of the population routinely voting for the Green Party, great movements were to be expected. And they happened! Before I got on the scene, tensions were unfolding; Metgasco had obtained a licence to start drilling at an old dairy property in Bentley, a small village fifteen kilometres outside of Lismore. And of course, seeing as it was on the doorstep of the hippies, things snowballed. A camp was set up on the site several weeks before any fracking could take place; in the end, thousands of freaks, turned-on farmers and indigenous peoples alike had gathered to protect the land in an event that would come to be known as the Bentley Blockade. At one point, the government had plans to send in as many as eight hundred police officers to the site, but the scandal would have just been too great. Eventually, the government suspended Metgasco's licence to drill at Bentley in May 2014, much to the jubilation of the Blockaders.

It was a good start, but it wasn't good enough. Fracking was destroying the land and, in turn, livelihoods all over Australia after all. And it wasn't if the landowners had much of a say – under Australian law, a landowner only has ownership of the top few inches of his or her land. Anything below that, the government technically 'owns', and thus they can hand over contracts willy-nilly. So imagine, if you will, a company like Metgasco, Cuadrilla or Halliburton turning up on your doorstep and saying "Hello! We're here to dig up your garden [and pollute the water table with our chemicals, destroying the livelihoods of everyone in the area…]! Here's a cheque for a thousand dollars – we'll start work right away [you have no say in this matter]!"

And that's why the 'Lock the Gate' movement started. All over the Northern Rivers, one could see the yellow triangular signs indicating that trespass, specifically by coal and gas companies, was a criminal offence, complete with websites to be referred to regarding the anti-CSG movement. Towards the end of my trip, I liberated a spare sign and brought it back to Arran with me – at the time of writing, it resides in my shed.

Fast forward to the first of November 2014, and a major anti-fracking rally was about to start in the centre of Lismore. Gina and I had just arrived in the *Albino Submarine*, parking at the rally's start point at the Riverside Park.

And what an atmosphere it was! Marquees had been set up to feed and educate the protestors – including the famous Rainbow Chai Tent – a band on the stage was playing a slightly modified version of Woody Guthrie's 'This Land Is Your Land', the artist Benny Zable was dancing around in his gas mask suit covered in climate change propaganda, peaceful murals were draped from the side of vehicles, and the people were loving every second. Officially, the rally began with a group of Bundjalung dancers, complete with regalia, welcoming us all to the protest with a traditional dance. They were cheered on by a group of people holding up a sign saying 'TEACHER'S FOR A GASFIELD-FREE WORLD'. Evidently, they didn't teach English grammar.

At one point, the MC called upon the people from the east, south, west and north in turn to raise their hands and pledge to protect the land.

"Now I want the people from the north to raise their hands!"

"Ey up, t'north?" I muttered.

Gina chucked.

"Not that far north, mate!" smiled a nearby Nimbinite who looked and sounded like an Australian Lemmy.

Eventually, the rally got underway. Some of the organisers had handed out poetic verses we could recite en route, but apart from one group of pensioners the rest of us had decided to revert to some more primal chants:

"NO COAL-SEAM GAS! NO COAL-SEAM GAS!"

"HEY HEY! HO HO! THOMAS GEORGE HAS GOT TO GO!"

"WE WANT ABBOTT OUT! WE WANT ABBOTT OUT!"

It was an interesting rally, which took us all over the centre of Lismore. To my amusement, a goat had got in on the protest too – its owner had decided to dress it up in a high-visibility vest and bring it along with him. It was popular until it started shitting on the people behind it, and even then it was still popular.

"See that?" I said to a fellow protester, pointing at the ground. "That is a much better fuel source than CSG!"

She chuckled.

Eventually, after passing the regional office for the National Party where the chanting peaked, the rally was over. An MC on the stage subsequently informed that ten thousand people had turned out for this rally. One-quarter of the population of metropolitan Lismore. Needless to say, we were all very pleased with ourselves. Well, except Gina – she was too busy being thirsty than stopping to feel proud. After grabbing a hot dog each, we hightailed it back to the *Albino Submarine* to indulge in some very warm water – a side effect from leaving it in the cab on a burning hot November day. Thirst just about quenched, we drove home, where a sign saying 'NIMBIN – 98.9% SAY GASFIELD FREE!' had been modified to say 'NIMBIN – 100.9% SAY GASFIELD FREE!'.

"Just your common Stalin-esque tactic!" Gina's friend Thorsten Jones would later comment.

November 7 2014 – Gungas

It has just dawned on me that when I was sleeping on the bus from Sydney to Byron Bay over two months ago, I passed over the Harwood Bridge to a village called Harwood, which I believe is on Harwood Island. The influences of my actions sure get to a lot of places...

November 11 2014 – New Tattershalls Hotel, Lismore

Okay, so I was driving into Nimbin to fill up the truck, and I had the radio set to Nim-FM. Suddenly, the Madness track 'One Step Beyond' comes on, and I just can't stop grooving. When I get to the petrol station, I'm still grooving and shouting 'ONE STEP BEYOND!' at the top of my voice. Then I look to my right and see three kids in the back of a Mitsubishi looking at me with the most priceless confused stares I've ever seen... I think I ska'd them for life!

November 14 2014 – New Tattershalls Hotel, Lismore

So I was at this poetry reading at a pub in Lismore a few nights ago – one of the featured readers didn't show, so I went on stage and recited some John Cooper Clarke poems. The audience wet themselves laughing of course!
Turns out that one of the audience was Daevid Allen – the founder of the space-rock band Gong, which has influenced me for many years. Like me, he wasn't billed to recite, but he did so before I finished off the night.
I am definitely not the average backpacker...

A Random Online Conversation with Calum Paterson from Berneray

"Daevid Allen!? Excellent! That's something to put in the CV! He also founded the Soft Machine, who are top notch!"

"Yeah – he just showed up wearing a 1950s 'city gent' suit, a bowler hat and a paisley shirt. I didn't even recognise him until he went on stage and recited one of his poems... And to top it all off, he was pissing himself with laughter during my recitals!"

"You can't beat some John Cooper Clarke! That's excellent! Glad you're enjoying your time down under!"

"Thanks man! Hope to see you on Berneray in July!"

"Before you know it, it will be Berneray Week 2015! Oh, I also recommend you listen to Robert Wyatt! He was in the Soft Machine also! His voice will move you to tears! TEARS I SAY!"

"I've not listened to Soft Machine yet – I've only heard Gong and Planet Gong (i.e. Here and Now feat. Daevid Allen and Gilli Smyth). I still can't get my head round the fact that I made the guy who did the guitar solo on 'Allez Ali Baba Black Sheep – Have You any Bullshit: Mama Maya Mantram' piss himself laughing when I was reciting 'Kung Fu International' and 'I Married a Monster from Outer Space'..."

"Haha! You can't beat a bit of Kung Fu International! The Soft Machine are good, they are very much like Pink Floyd in their Syd Barrett years, as a matter of fact, they usually played together in the same clubs (Middle Earth, UFO and whatnot). But yeah, Robert Wyatt is quite moving – his solo stuff! He was a drummer for the Soft Machine but then broke his back so moved on to weirder stuff!"

"Cool – I'll check them out next time I have WiFi!"

"The Poet" by Louise Moriaty

A short poem written about my performance on stage at the Tatts that night:

"Got them eating out the palm of his hand
Stand it up and rocking the house, this educated man!
Quality stories with humour for the crass
This guy pulls poetry perfection out of his ass!
Loves to shock them and get their blood moving
Doesn't leave until the house is grooving!"

November 14 2014 – Gungas

So I was driving back from Lismore to Nimbin, and the cops appeared behind me flashing the blues just outside Goolmangar. Presuming that they were for me due to a broken light, I pulled over expecting the worst – I had a file and a crowbar within easy reach in the truck after all...
Then they overtook me at 120k and sped off after turning off the lights! The sergeant's coffee must have been going cold or something...

November 18 2014 – Gungas

So I was talking to this elderly couple from Lancashire at the Grey Gum Lodge a few days ago during yet another heatwave. I asked them why they had come to Nimbin, because they didn't look very alternative. The reply: "we heard it were quirky!"
They then asked me whether it was true what they heard: that everyone gets drunk every hour of every day, so obviously I replied "Yes. The higher classes like their gin and tonic, but the lower classes prefer to get pissed on Bundaberg Rum." Then I gave them a smile, laughed and told them the truth – cannabis is more socially acceptable here than alcohol, much to their surprise.
"Nimbin without cannabis is like the North of England without pies," I explained. They understood.
You meet some strange characters sometimes.

A Random Text Conversation with Gina

"Hey hey hey.....looking into hiring or buying a woodchipper.... Mulch and woodchipp the copse....and around the trees on upper level and the area will be able to retain moisture....and understory will begin to flourish.;) And maybe get the foreman back to help if he's still around ....with his chainsaw....eg cut up the logs next door and bring them over....cut down some more trees drags them up and put them through the chipper and spread them all in the same day.... The chainsaw is the sort of work really he loves to do I think....
Also....haven't forgotten about lifting the cabin of course... looking for equipment to hire that might be good to finish excavating the holes for lifting the van.....see you this afternoon?...;)"
"Already done an hour of work – I've dug out the hole under your door, got the jack we bought in Lismore in it and attempted to lift the container. Doesn't seem to be working very well... Let me know when you want to be picked up :)"
"Ok.,.had breakfast at 4am them went back to sleep with phone off...oops....ready in 30 mins ;)"

(None of Gina's proposals materialised.)

Interlude – Don't Mess with Dehydration

I spent a fair bit of my time delivering groceries to Thorsten Jones; an ex-Captain of the New South Wales Rural Fire Service who lived in the cab of a ute on the sacred land in the shadow of the Nimbin Rocks. In return, Thorsten would tell me tales – sometimes about his own groovy life, sometimes about life and knowledge in general. He would tell me of his childhood in and around the German city of Heidelberg, of being taken to shoots in South Tyrol by his Nazi father and subsequently being taught how to use a gun at a young age, of how he was put under surveillance by the *Bundeskriminalamt* at the age of twelve as his cousin had joined the Red Army Faction, of that one time he managed to outwit a US Army patrol who had stopped him one day – the Army personnel had no knowledge of the German language and the young Thorsten, who possessed a staggering IQ, could speak decent English by the age of twelve and knew not to reveal it.

He would go on to tell me of his adult life; of how he became a taxi driver, of how he met an Australian woman and took her last name – Jones – when they married as to distance himself from the Nazis in his family, of how they sired a beautiful wee girl and emigrated to Australia.

This story particularly interested me. As the mother was Australian, the West German government had refused to issue a passport to Thorsten's daughter. Likewise, the Australian government had refused to issue a passport owing to the fact that Thorsten's daughter was born in West Germany. However, a grandmother of the girl was born in the United Kingdom, so under the rather-lax British laws, a passport was easy to come by. With that, they all got on the plane to Australia, stopping off for a few days in Singapore. Naturally, they got some odd stares from the immigration officer in Singapore, but they were eventually allowed to pass unhindered.

Thorsten would then go on to tell me of his Australian life; of how he ended up becoming divorced, of his life in the Australian Army and the eccentricity of being in the Reserves as part of a transport corps, of how he would leave and later join the firies.

"I was going to be promoted to Corporal!" he said. "Can you imagine – an ethnic German called Corporal Jones? I was already getting a lot of stick in the Army with my last name – people were coming up to me saying 'Don't panic! Don't panic!', and I had to remind them that I wasn't a corporal yet!"

I laughed. It was the 20th of November 2014, and we were chatting over a coffee or six. Rat, Thorsten's bat-shit Jack Russel was bouncing around eating marsh flies, panting with exhaustion from his activities during the heat of the day.

"Now that's a hot dog!" I commented.

Thorsten sniffed.

"More like a hot Rat."

The conversation changed.

"Now tell me," Thorsten was saying, "how many people died as a result of 9/11?"

"Well, if you count respiratory illnesses brought on by the attacks, and service animals, about three thousand..."

"Which I do, and you are indeed correct. Now, how many Rwandans died in the 1994 genocide?"

"Nearly a million…"

"And how many Armenians were slaughtered by the Turks during the First World War?"

"Ah, that was about a million, wasn't it?"

"Well, a million and a half. And how many people perished in the gas chambers in Nazi Germany?"

"About six million…"

"Right. Now, here's a little perspective for you. How many indigenous people did the Belgians wipe out in the Congo in the name of King Leopold II?"

"Not a clue…"

"It was about ten million, and yet few, if any, people talk about it. Now, here's a little more perspective. What was the estimated population of Australia before the coming of the white man?"

"No idea."

"Well, some scientists estimate that it was about seventeen million."

Perhaps this figure was a little embellished, but with Thorsten's high IQ, I was inclined to believe him. He carried on.

"Now, according to the last census, how many people registered their ethnicity as Aboriginal, Torres Strait Islander or indigenous?"

Silence.

"Seven hundred-thousand."

"You mean…?"

"Yes. The British Empire knocked off SIXTEEN MILLION, THREE HUNDRED-THOUSAND indigenous inhabitants in the country that we now know as Australia. Okay?"

Silence.

"And, of course, countless millions perished in the Americas, Africa and Asia over the course of colonisation by the white man – not just the British – and the subsequent wars for self-determination. Yet, the world only pays attention to the events that, whilst still being horrific, pale in comparison. Think about it."

I nodded solemnly, my last vestiges of British-ness disappearing in a poof of knowledge.

"Oh, and whilst we're on the subject, don't call the indigenous people 'Aborigines'. And definitely don't call them 'Abbos'! Okay?"

"Well, I know not to…"

"Yes, but do you know what those terms are short for?"

"No…"

"'Abnormal Originals'. You are aware of the term *terra nullius*, I suppose?"

"Yeah – that's the 'uninhabited land' thing, isn't it?"

"Correct, or as that great Australian leader Tony Abbott once put it, 'Australia was nothing but bush.' When the white man first came to this land, he wasn't exactly expecting to find multiple civilisations thriving here. Hence the term 'Abnormal'."

"Ah."

"And don't call them 'Australian' either. Many, if not most, indigenous people would rather die. Okay?"

"Well, I know Gilbert doesn't identify as Australian. It was the first thing he told me when I met him."

"Exactly."

We drunk our coffee until I got severely dehydrated from drinking too much of the black stuff. Consequently, I had to spend the night in an air-conditioned room at the Grey Gum Lodge, drinking six litres of water in the process. By the next day, however, I was back to normal. It was a good thing too, as I had to make an interesting journey…

November 21 2014 – Upper Coomera, Queensland

This day, the twenty-first of November in the year of our Lord two thousand and fourteen shall go down in history. For today, I have undertaken my first long haul journey (in British terms) whilst driving a motor vehicle. It is also the first time I have driven on a motorway. And across a time zone. My current location is commonly known as Skase-ville, also known as the Gold Coast. My mission: pick up a box.

And my advice: the Gold Coast is not the real Australia. I'm glad I'm going back to Nimbin this evening.

Gold Coast Interlude

It was a peaceful day on the Gold Coast. The diners at the Burleigh Heads Surf Club ate their forty-dollar-plus meals happily, oblivious to the fact that the Gold Coast did not accurately portray the real Australia. A party of fifty-somethings celebrated the birthday of one of their number.

The three diners at table seventeen, however, stood out like a homosexual in Saudi Arabia. One of the diners was a blonde lady who appeared to be in her late twenties or early thirties, wearing a shirt and shorts. Not an uncommon sight in these parts. Her male dining partner, on the other hand, looked suspiciously like a caveman wearing army camouflage and t-shirt referencing the Frank Zappa albums *Hot Rats* and *Weasels Ripped My Flesh*; his long wiry hair was partially naturally dreadlocked.

On the other side of the room, the industrial-strength speaker system suddenly belched out sounds of people chatting about goodness-knows-what at ear-splitting volume. The birthday party looked unimpressed. A few noise-sensitive diners made a beeline for the door. Then, in an act of heroism, the caveman abandoned his plate of oysters and chips, turned his head around and shouted in a dialect not of the Southern Hemisphere:

"TURN THOSE FUCKING SPEAKERS OFF!"

And suddenly, all was quiet. The diners at table seventeen, who referred to themselves as Scott, Gina and Helena – Gina's niece, paid up and left, never to be seen again.

(We also climbed up a hill to an interesting viewpoint in the Burleigh Head National Park – a group of tourists got me to take their photo before they went off, not taking in the view whatsoever!)

A Random Text Conversation with Thorsten

"Can you bring the multimeter along when you drop the water off? I'll be needing it the next cooler day ;)"

"I'm just about to get your stuff. Can you remind me what coffee you like & where to get your water?"

"Sorry, just been to the dunny ;) Good for coffee now. My daughter is bringing some later. Water from the HEMP Embassy. Go through the shop and down the backstairs off the verandah. Pass the toilet block on the left and go downhill and you'll see the concrete rainwater tank to the left of the back gate. Shop opens in 10 minutes or so."

"OK, thanks. I just bought you some coffee at the Emporium – you'll have more than enough now :)

"Thnx. Just talked to Salty in the office. He promised not to shoot you while you get water ;)"

"Thanks :)"
"He growls but rarely bites ;)"

November 24 2014 – Gungas

Before I left Scotland, some members of my family told me "Don't get mistaken for one of those Aborigines, what with your hair and build!" Sorry guys – I failed you today.
I was having a glass of ginger beer with my boss at a bar in Lismore, then suddenly a 40-something Aboriginal woman sits down on my left knee.
"Sorry – I thought you were my nephew," she apologised. "You look exactly like him because of the hair and the clothes! I'm Rose, by the way."
I laughed and introduced myself. She couldn't believe that I was from Scotland and not the Bundjalung Nation.
Sorry everyone. The Bundjalung people have claimed me as one of their own – oh well!

A Random Online Conversation with Hamish

"Also, did you know that there's a fucking massive street rave every Friday in Nimbin?"
"But is it in an abandoned underground tunnel like the one in Glasgow that I went to recently? I think not, I win!"
"No. You lose."
"So, it's in an abandoned underground tunnel, then?"
"It doesn't need to be. We have the satisfaction of outnumbering the Thought Police here!"
"I'm joking! Nimbin sounds awesome – just in a completely different way to Glasgow."
"Also, there's no electronics. Everyone brings drums – it's mostly drums, with some guitars, brass, Bundjalung percussion sticks, whatever. It's sort of like the desert rock scene every Friday here... U jelly?"
"I don't think the Glasgow police could be bothered with the rave, if they even knew about it."
"They could, trust me. I once went to a rave on Benbecula with a few friends, and the cops shut it down after a few hours."
"I experienced that sort of thing in Berlin's squatter dens – live stoner rock parties, that is. The cops in the Western Isles are very bored people."
"We have the climate for stoner rock parties – it's awesome listening to Kyuss when the temperature hits 45!"
"Try 'Sure 'Nuff 'n Yes I Do' – it's a perfect desert song."
"Can you has Engrish?"
"It's a Captain Beefheart song, motherfucker!"
"Oh."
"It's the first track on *Safe as Milk*."
"Ah. Oh, and listen to *The Endless River* by Pink Floyd – some hippie was blasting it out of a PA at a market yesterday – fucking awesome!"
"I've head bits of it – sounds decent. Apparently, the last thing they'll ever do but a decent ending."
"Cool! Got to go, 3G zapping battery & wallet..."
"Okdokie byee!"

The next day…

"I nearly rolled the truck just now – was going down a 30% steep driveway at a bad angle. Had to get the Thought Police out to winch me back to the level – should have seen the look on their faces when they saw it wasn't a hoax call! Anyway, they did it with NO QUESTIONS ASKED! No name, no occupation, no breathalyser, nothing!"

"Ah the joys of efficient, slightly corrupt policemen!"

Gina, Namaste and Tanya at the Nimbin Market, 30th November 2014

A Random Text Conversation with Thorsten

"Um, Gina just lit her gas burner and it exploded… no one's injured and the firies are en route…"

"Glad everyone is safe. Hope some eyebrows got burnt as a reminder that the red stuff hurts ;)"

Off The Rails – An Outing to Byron Bay

It was the seventh of December 2014. Daevid Allen, whom I had previously encountered at the Live Poets event in Lismore, was due to perform at the Railway Hotel (the Rails) in Byron Bay. So, I drove down from Nimbin, and I got chatting to David Hallett – the host of the Live Poets event in Lismore – whom I later discovered lived only a few doors down from me in Gungas. Also, that he was one of Australia's top poets. It transpired that the Divided Alien was going through chemotherapy at the time after being diagnosed with a cancerous cyst on his neck, but Hallett wanted me to meet someone.

Presently, a little old lady with a degree of senility was deposited next to me by her care-worker.

"Scott," Hallett smiled, "this is Gilli Smyth!"

Yes. It was Gilli Smyth – the space-whisperer and other co-founder of Gong! She needed help for the basic things, such as getting around, but on the stage she was immense – belting out Daevid Allen's poem 'Zero The Hero'. It was one of many days I would never forget…

A Random Online Conversation with Calum Paterson from Berneray

"Calum – I'm currently in the presence of Gilli Smyth... I am not fucking worthy!"

"Awesome! Gotta get out the John Cooper Clarke notes, man!"

"Can't, bro – David Hallett (one of Australia's most renowned poets) has forbidden me – we are in a family-friendly place right now. Oh well. Daevid Allen was meant to turn up, but he's having cancer treatment right now. Hopefully I'll see him on Wednesday in Lismore. Hope you're all right!"

"Out-poet Hallett! He is no match for 'Kung Fu International!' Oh man – I never knew Daevid Allen had cancer! How is Oz?"

"Oz is still as fantastic as ever. I never knew Daevid had cancer either. Also, Hallett hosted the poetry night when I made the Divided Alien piss his pants, so yes I've already out-poeted him and I'm going to do it again on Wednesday!"

"Awesome! Have you ever listened to The Fall? They are quite poetic in a way! Their singer is quite close to John Cooper Clarke!"

"Not yet..."

"Listen to 'Lucifer over Lancashire' – one of their many hits! They have been around since the late seventies and basically been releasing an album every year."

"Will do!"

A Japanese Family in Nimbin

It was the eighth of December 2014, and a Japanese family were meandering through the Peace Park in central Nimbin. Suddenly, they espied a group of people standing around a strangely-designed black and white circle, the centre of which bared the word 'IMAGINE'.

Naturally, being stereotypically Japanese, they produced their cameras and started taking photographs of a man who appeared to be the artist, who was probably called 'Bennyzable'; he was talking to the group about something called a 'johnlennon', whatever that was.

Suddenly, one of those strange 'Aborigines' that they had read about produced a bushel of goodness-knows-what, set it alight and blew at it through one of those 'did-jerry-do' things. When the bizarre ritual was over, the Aborigine started to speak in a language that had no resemblance to English, let alone Japanese. He would finally introduce himself in a language that sounded like a *gaijin* tongue, calling himself an 'unclelewiswalker', whatever that was.

Suddenly, without warning, the family was dragged into a human circle, who all started to sing a song. The Japanese family assumed that the song was called 'Imagine' – it was the most used word in the song, after all. The family began to freak out – they hadn't signed up for this experience. Presently, the caveman who was holding the mother's hand offered her what looked like a cigarette, but it was roughly half the length and girth of his arm. Literally.

She sniffed the air, and tried to formulate the *gaijin* word for what she smelt. "Mariana?" she asked.

"No, Scott!" the caveman grinned.

She looked confused.

"It's marijuana, yes," the one called Scott elaborated.

She contemplated the behemoth of a joint, took a toke and passed it on to her husband. After all, she had been told that it was the custom in these parts. The Japanese family ended up feeling calm, and began to appreciate their surroundings. One doubts though, that they will ever repeat the experience…

TIMBER!

During my time in Nimbin, I frequently visited Mount Nardi in the Nightcap National Park. The park was created in 1983 a year after the three-year-long Rainforest War – a great and successful attempt by local activists to stop tree-felling in the region. By 1989, UNESCO created World Heritage protection in the western part of the park, and with good reason. The park supports a rich diversity of species that includes more than forty species of mammals, twenty-seven reptiles, twenty-three frogs, over a hundred and forty bird species and over six hundred and fifty known plant species including numerous ferns and various orchids, as well a diverse variety of fungus and lichens. Oh, and many of these species are endangered.

It was a spectacular drive from the low altitudes of Nimbin up to the pinnacle of Mount Nardi, some seven hundred and ninety metres above sea level. I would drive up the Tuntable Falls Road in the *Albino Submarine*, heading straight passing the turnoffs for The Channon and Tuntable Falls and finding myself on a very steep, yet well-tarmacked single-track road, meandering past various home-made dwellings hidden in the forest en route before entering the National Park jurisdiction. Had the road not been a dead end, I would have been able to drive down the other side into Doon Doon, and thence towards Murwillumbah and onwards to Brisbane. Alas, I would soon find myself at the dead end at the local transmitter towers, which looked as alien as they come given the surroundings. At their dense subtropical base, endangered species of frog and snake abounded, along with a very common and edible fruit – the humble raspberry.

One rainy day, when I was driving back down to Gungas from Mount Nardi, I was stopped in my tracks by the presence of a small tree blocking the road. Evidently, it had been uprooted after I had driven up just a few minutes earlier. Instinctively, I applied the handbrake and killed the engine. Now, as I was trapped, I decided to methodically review my options:

- Move the tree. No – too big for one person.
- Engage four-wheel-drive, low range, and drive around the tree. No – too muddy. Plus, I could fall off the cliff-edge to the right…

- Check phone signal. Five bars and 3G, of course, but who would come to my aid? Gina didn't have the truck, Thorsten was asleep, but what about Max Stone, a.k.a Big Bong, the guy who repaired the *Albino Submarine*? Nah – I didn't have his number. Besides, he probably had more important things to do…
- Sound the horn. *Beep beep beep, BEEEEP, BEEEEP, BEEEEP, beep beep beep!* No response except the calls of a VCS3 bird. Nobody was working on the towers, and the few householders nearby were probably too stoned to understand Morse Code.

So, I sat down in the *Albino Submarine*'s cab, and decided to wait until another vehicle came along so I could shanghai the occupants into doing some ad-hoc forestry work. I realised that hanging around was a pretty shit move – more trees could be coming down for all I knew, but I deduced that I would be safer in the cab than out in the open. I didn't have to wait long – ten minutes later, I heard the sound of what would turn out to be a pair of battered tourist cars. I turned the hazards on, and got out of the cab. Despite what was now our collective predicament, I decided to have a little fun with the young-ish Australian tourists.

"What's going on here, mate?" asked a young man.

"Dis is toll road," I intoned in a vaguely Eastern European accent. "You pay me twenty dollar or no Mount Nardi for you."

"What?"

"I'm joking – this bloody tree just fell down just before I came down the hill. Can you help me move it?"

"Yeah – sure, mate!"

"Let's be quick, though – more could be coming!"

The young man summoned his fellow gym freaks and their bewildered girlfriends, and we soon got the tree out of the way.

"Right, if you give me another minute, I'm going to engage the four-wheel-drive on my ute so I can get round you."

"Yeah, sure."

A few minutes later, I had passed the tourists, disengaged the four-wheel-drive and was steadily making my way back to Gungas, safely out of the Dominion of Falling Trees.

A Trip to The Channon

It was about a week before Christmas, and the Christmas Market was on in The Channon. Not wanting to waste the ethanol in the *Albino Submarine*, I decided to thumb it. Despite it being the middle of the harsh Australian summer, Nimbin was experiencing a cold snap; it was overcast, and the temperature had plummeted to just fifteen degrees.

"I had to get the doona out for the first time since August!" the voices on Nim-FM complained. "This weather isn't right at all!"

Donning my raincoat for the first time in months, I walked to the Gungas Road/Tuntable Falls Road junction and stuck my thumb out, shivering in the autumnal drizzle. It would take me three rides to reach The Channon. My first took me to the top of the hill from the junction; the tubercular species of estate car having a three-speed automatic transmission with no kick-down, so we crawled up the hill in third gear at thirty kilometres an hour. I started walking after that, passing a naked lady squatting by the side of the road.

"Morning!" I smiled.

"Nope – just taking a shit!" she replied.

My second ride was unexpected – Xanda picked me up. Now, for those who don't know Xanda, he was – at least at the time, I think he still is at the time of publication – Nimbin's John Lennon impersonator/LSD guru. Though, if you ask me, they're one and the same...

Xanda dropped me off at a local commune, or MO – 'multiple-occupancy dwelling' – as they are known as in the local parlance. The commune had just spent the last few nights celebrating the anniversary of their founding; I was invited to this particular shindig at Nimbin's drumming circle the last Friday, but I couldn't find the place. A pity – I missed out on two days of sex and drugs.

I ended up having breakfast there – a nice big bowl of mystery meat. It was a fine change from my basic choice of hemp-infused noodles, Thai curry, canned tuna or pan-fried steak; all cooked on an open fire and served with 'Hausbrot Rye' bread. After breakfast, I made my way back to the road, where my last lift came from an old German hippie lady in a Peugeot, who picked me up partially because of my Neu! t-shirt.

You've got to support your family somehow...

I spent a few hours at the market and bought myself half a cow on a bun from that one community stand that does the cheap food at events such as this, exchanging banter with the bloke on the grill:

"Watcha having, mate?"

"Steak, please."

"Steak, eh?" He winked. "I can guess what you've been up to this morning!"

"Well, it involved a naked lady, but not in the regard I assume you're thinking of…"

After consuming my great-big bovine burger, I wandered round the market and ended up buying some very crispy chips from a pop-up *frituur* run by a Dutch-born eccentric.

"And now, here is your chippie. Careful, they're hot"

"*Dank je.*"

They were good, but not quite as good as the ones with the *speciaal* sauce I had feasted on at the Chipsy King on Damstraat in Amsterdam. The inside of my mouth resembling the burns unit at Lismore Base Hospital, I bought a litre of fresh sugar cane juice before thumbing it back home – again, taking three rides. My first came from a local man in a white van that took me a few kilometres along the road, a battered Land Cruiser took me another third of the way, and my last came from a saloon car occupied by two backpackers, who were excited that they would soon be in Nimbin for the first time.

Gina was only just waking up when I got home, and couldn't believe that I had got to The Channon and back without the ute. At least until I gave her some sugar cane juice anyway…

December 17 2014 – Gungas

Nice to hear Nim-FM playing Captain Beefheart's 'Big-Eyed Beans from Venus' when I was driving home just now – made my evening!

A Random Online Conversation with Hamish

"You realise they were playing Beefheart on the radio because it was the fourth anniversary of his death?"

"Erm, no…"

"He died Dec 17 2010. He actually has a really tragic story – he lost the ability to sing/speak because he had MS. Ended up killing him."

"I knew all that – I just forgot when he died. Also, I'm on WiFi – Skype?"

"Hell yeah!"

Two minutes later…

"Bloody Office Works not letting me on Skype. Connection would have died after an hour anyway."

"Are you giving up?"

"Yep."

"What are Office Works anyway?"

"Look them up. It's like Staples meets IKEA with free WiFi, tea and coffee. Also, hot chocolate, but it keeps running out – probably because I keep drinking it all and they're too cheap to buy any more!"

"I think some public WiFi blocks Skype as it's data-heavy."

"Yeah. Though this place does block certain websites as well…"

"Go back to the place where you Skyped me before."

"That café?"

"Yeah, what was it called?"

"The Bank. Can't afford the food right now, though…"

"Order a glass of tap water! Or just stand outside…"

"No electricity."

"I did that a lot in Amsterdam – sat outside nice restaurants and leeched the WiFi. Wait, by electricity, you mean battery?"

"Yeah."

"It would last 10/15 minutes, surely?"

"This is an iPhone. You should know…"

"I said 10/15 minutes!"

"And I said that this is an iPhone! (I'm such a cunt, aren't I?) Also, my boss is with me doing her artwork."

"Ah, fuck."

"And I have the keys to the truck."

"Ah."

December 24 2014 – Gungas

Having only a billycan and a fire since my boss accidentally blew up her LPG canister a few weeks ago, my Christmas Dinner shall consist as follows:
•Starter: Kangaroo broth with a hint of chilli, served with rye bread.
•Main course: Kangaroo Mi Goreng with local herbs.
•Dessert: Tim Tams and UHT milk.
Total cost for several people - $10 (about £5.20). And they say you spend a lot of money at Christmas...
Also, I haven't heard any bloody annoying Christmas songs this year - yay :)
Merry Christmas!

(A message to Hamish later that day…

"I just got invited to this party just outside the music shop, there's a space-rock band called the Lunatic Hill Mob playing who are bloody brilliant, and there were these folk about my age wondering what the hell this music was and why it was so good. So they took some photos and videos...")

Christmas in Gungas

I woke up to what seemed like an ordinary Nimbin summer's day. It was about thirty-six degrees outside, and the kookaburras and VCS3 birds were hooting like there was no tomorrow. Today, though, it was Christmas Day – it wasn't as celebrated among the denizens of Nimbin as the Summer Solstice, but it still had some significance. I wandered over to Gina's container, where the radio was playing 'Christmas in Jail'.

"Merry Christmas, Gina!" I smiled.

"Merry Christmas, Scott!" she replied. "Say, I have a clever idea! Why don't you go and fetch Thorsten over? He's pretty much alone over on the reservation…"

"Well, he's got Rat, hasn't he?"

"Yeah, I suppose. Bring them here anyway!"

So, I hopped into the *Albino Submarine* and made my way over to the reservation, nonplussed by the lack of traffic on the road. I ogled the few faux-hippies on the street, who were excited by the fact that they were in Nimbin for Christmas, despite the fact that the Summer Solstice was much more widely celebrated and renowned locally. After a few minutes, I arrived at the reservation, where Thorsten and Rat were acting their usual selves.

"Ho, ho, ho!" I grinned.

"Bah, humbug!" replied Thorsten. "Did Gina send you?"

"Yeah – she instructed me to kidnap you and take you to our place for Christmas Dinner…"

"Well, it's a noble move, but I can't. I'm not in the mood for a large meal today – must be something to do with my chronic fatigue. Besides, this idea of a big meal on Christmas Day is just a hangover from the midwinter conditions of the Northern Hemisphere – I don't know why the Caucasians around here haven't given up the idea. I mean, who in the right mind would want to eat a big meal in the middle of a hot summer's day?"

"Fair enough."

That afternoon, our friend Potsie – a Kiwi lass who lived in her car – and Socks, her slightly brainless Border Collie, showed up and we all feasted on the kilo of kangaroo mince I had purchased the previous day at the Nimbin Emporium. With Gina's container, Potsie's car and my Sprinter van surrounding an open fire, it was a true vehicle-dweller's Christmas Dinner.

After dinner, I made an announcement.

"And now," I theatrically intoned, "it's time to do the infamous Christmas washing up!"

With a flick of my wrist, our paper plates flew onto the open fire.

"And now, after so many microseconds, the washing up is complete!"

As I relaxed in the back of the van, my head sticking out the back, I got a phone call from my parents. I had sent them my phone number in the post a few weeks previous, and asked them to phone me at Christmas. I smiled, accepted the call, and put on a butch voice.

"Hello! You have reached the Nimbin Sex Line, THE place for hot, hippie action!"

They laughed. We talked for a while, my dad being especially curious as to how I met Daevid Allen. During the call, Socks decided to come and lick my face, prompting a bit of confusion from my parents.

That was the only time I directly spoke with my parents when I was in Australia. I just didn't see the need the rest of the time. Although I did message them a few days later…

A Random Online Conversation with My Parents
(a.k.a. Anally Fingered by a Personality Transplant Patient)

'Don't want to alarm you, but things aren't so good. I've been passing a LOT of blood in my stool (I've lost about a pint recently), so I admitted myself to the local A&E. The nurse tried charging me $120 to see the doctor until I started being German with her…
'You would charge me that if I was a citizen of, say Morocco, but since I am a citizen of the United Kingdom and there are reciprocal agreements between the health service here and the National Health Service back home, you will waive EVERY fee, with the exception of prescriptions – which I don't need yet – and the ambulance, which I also didn't need because I drove here in my truck.'

'Um...Ok...I'll just go and check...' she stammered.

She came back a few minutes later and admitted she was wrong.

Doctor came after 2 hours, anally fingered me, diagnosed a bad case of piles, prescribed me some anal cream and hopefully, since they're not painful unless I'm straining on the bog, they should be gone in a week. Had to pay around £20 for prescriptions, but it should kill the buggers off in one go, so it's all good!

Relax. I'm fine – the nurse who first saw me thought I was in better condition than most! Hope you are all fine too!"

"Thanks for letting us know. Fibre in your diet should help. Hope they go soon as they are not pleasant. Take care and keep in touch."

January 1 2015 – Nimbin

For the next eleven hours, I am one year in the future than most of you. Your argument is invalid.

Happy New Year from an illegal rave in Nimbin!

January 2 2015 – Hotel Cecil, Casino, New South Wales

I've been in the Northern Rivers for four months now, and since my house-building job has come to an end, it's time for me to get the train back to Sydney – it's $100 cheaper than the bus for some reason...

Hopefully, I can pick up some work there for a bit, then travel onwards into the desert by February... Should be back in Nimbin by the end of April, though!

(The trains in New South Wales really were that much cheaper than the bus, at least when I rode the rails out there. This is because, unlike the United Kingdom at the time, virtually all scheduled passenger trains in New South Wales were still owned and operated by the state. Just saying.)

Beating About the Bush

"Here is nothing to see, however, and not a soul to meet. You might walk for twenty miles along this track without being able to fix a point in your mind, unless you are a bushman. This is because of the everlasting, maddening sameness of the stunted trees – that monotony which makes a man long to break away and travel as far as trains can go, and sail as far as ship can sail – and farther."

-    Henry Lawson, *The Drover's Wife*

Somewhere along the Sturt Highway in south-western New South Wales...

Gina deposited me at the railway station in Casino, as opposed to the casino in the railway station, of which there were none. Leaving me in the presence of wrinklies, uglies, teddy bears and backpackers wearing 'Bringabong' singlets, I boarded an XPT of nineteen-eighties vintage which was to take me through the night back to Sydney.

I could go on forever about the XPT; how each individual rake had modified British Class 43 power cars mated with seven American carriages, how first class was almost completely identical to second class (even in terms of legroom) but twice the price, how it was capable of operating at a hundred and sixty kilometres per hour (i.e. about as fast as a commuter train in Britain...), but I'm not. Because most of you reading probably don't give a flying fuck about the operations of NSW Trainlink.

So, here's the human experience of the XPT. I ended up being squashed up against the window by a lady who intruded into my space with a combination of fat, bags and bags of fat; this meant that I couldn't get to the toilet until we reached Strathfield, but at least I slept until I witnessed a glorious sunrise over the Hawkesbury River.

I returned to the Collaroy Beach YHA, where I was surprised to see a few familiar faces from my previous visit, including Rubik's Cube Willem. After my experiences in Nimbin, though, I would eventually discover that city life was just not for me – at least not on this continent anyway.

One fine Sunday, I took a local train to Katoomba in the Blue Mountains, upon which the conductor painstakingly announced every few minutes that two carriages were closed due to 'safety reasons' and that anybody who entered them would be ejected from the train. I contemplated whether or not such an undertaking would happen when the train was moving…

Arriving at Katoomba, and baulking at the sight of the overcrowded municipal buses and expensive tourist buses, I walked to the nearby world-famous viewpoint. Subsequently, I was surrounded by Loud Americans in Hawaiian Shirts who had arrived on open-topped tour buses sporting British number plates in addition to their Australian ones, and complaining that "the Steelers game's on and we're missing it!" So, I walked a few minutes away from the official viewpoint and found a view that was almost exactly as great, except nobody was there. A few minutes more, and I found a café populated by locals that served excellent 'works burgers'. Satisfied with my lot, I pushed on to the town of Lithgow for shits and giggles, and shortly afterwards returned to Collaroy, passing such wonders as the 'Interactive 7D Mobile Cinema' (presumably showing Brockian Ultra-Cricket reruns) and the Gallipoli Mosque en route.

Despite travelling out of the city frequently and landing a 'cashie', I really needed to be back 'on country' after only a week after arriving back in Sydney. Admittedly, being harassed by the cops twice whilst I was on my way to see the town of Moss Vale in the Southern Highlands didn't exactly help things. So, after realising that I could be free at the moment I wanted to be, I started preparing for an epic adventure. I stocked up heavily on cheap cans of tuna from the ALDI in Dee Why, and wedged a three-litre bottle of water onto the outside of my bag. Together with a cheap A4 notepad bought for less than a dollar from a nearby branch of Office Works – the bedrock of many a hitchhiking sign – a basic roadmap of Australia on my phone and the spirit of Jack Kerouac in my soul, I was ready to hit the road and live out my fantasia. Mildura, here I come!

Donning a second-hand kilt that Gina gave to me in Nimbin (I have no idea what clan it was, so don't ask), I travelled by bus from Collaroy to the centre of Sydney, then a local train to Blacktown in the western suburbs. Here, I caught a free rail-replacement bus, which took me all the way through the Blue Mountains. After a heart-stopping moment where the bus nearly side-swiped a car as it left the car park at Zig Zag, I made it to Lithgow for the second time on this trip. There, I wrote out a sign for Bathurst and started thumbing it – I managed to get a lift from a local lady within the space of fifteen minutes. It was an interesting ride – we discussed the correct way to go about legalising drug use (i.e. fully legalise, regulate and tax all non-lethal drugs, decriminalise personal possession of everything else), as we zoomed past the 'Wang'-shaped towers of the recently-decommissioned Wallerawang power station.

She decided to drop me on the other side of town, where I could easily get a ride west. As I waited for my next ride, I was given a litre of pop and a job offer from a grinning Jacobite sympathiser and his family. I accepted the pop but declined the job – I wasn't exactly experienced with interior decoration.

"Ya know mate," he called as I left his house, "if you're looking for farm work, you'd be well off going to Orange. Plenty of work there this time of year!"

I was blinded by my own ambition to get to Mildura and would come to somewhat regret it later. But I do wonder sometimes, what if I did follow his advice? What if I did end up doing some farm work in Orange? Rather unfortunately, I'll never know. Instead, I wrote out a sign for Cowra. Must be a lot of cows there, I thought.

My second ride was with a local contractor, who took me to a small farming town called Blayney in his ute. An hour or so here, and I was picked up by a railwayman in his Holden saloon, in whose vehicle I finally left the Great Dividing Range and ended up in Cowra – a town of around ten thousand Bogans where one could head down to the Golden Arches and order steak and eggs for breakfast. Unfortunately, I got stranded here owing to the horse races in town – nobody was driving long-distance out of town for a while. I ended up staying at the Cowra Hotel – the local pub, the insides of my legs chafing like hell owing to the effects of kilt-wearing. But it felt good; I had only spent about ten dollars over the course of three hundred kilometres, plus another twenty or so for the room in the pub. I took what was to be the best shower on my trip in a shared bathroom – the ambience of which being straight out of another century – and fell asleep with a satisfactory smile on my face.

As I couldn't get out of town with thumb-power, I caught a NSW Trainlink bus to Cootamundra after spending a second night at the Cowra Hotel. With two hours to kill in the birthplace of the cricketer Sir Donald Bradman, the effects of maniacal boredom manifested themselves in the form of crude *South Park*-influenced graffiti in a local public shitter, complete with stickmen doing vaguely sexual things to the needle diagram next to the deposit slot.

From there, I travelled across the south-west of New South Wales on another Trainlink bus populated equally by a mix of backpackers, locals of the numerous small towns and villages en route and, other than Gina, the first Wiradjuri folk I had laid eyes on. Joining the Burley Griffin Way at Stockinbingal, the bus made its way west through the food bowl of Australia. After a few hours, the bus had reached the farming metropolis of Griffith – a planned city of just under twenty-thousand people designed by Walter Burley Griffin and Marion Mahony Griffin. In other words, Griffith is a scaled-down version of Canberra – albeit without the decriminalised ganja and the fucked-up politicians. During a piss break at the railway station, which was unexpectedly extended after someone left their luggage on the bus and caused a minor bomb scare, a bored five-year old child on the bus shouted 'LET'S GET THIS PARTY STARTED!', waking me up slightly and causing me to respond 'YEAH! – wait, what?'

The bus left Griffith and soon joined the Sturt Highway, named after the explorer Charles Sturt. Roughly following the course of the Murrumbidgee River, we arrived at a Caltex roadhouse opposite the Shear Outback Museum in Hay – a town I written on my hitchhiking sign with fool's optimism back in Cowra. The bus had an hour to kill here, so I ordered half a dozen dim sims and a medium-sized box of chips, the latter being large enough to feed a small family for two days. I spend the remainder of the break watching the antics of a minibus full of Sikhs heading for Adelaide.

Finally, the rest break was over, and a new driver took over. As we pulled out of Hay, he was almost concerned for our collective mortality…

"I highly recommend that you fasten your seatbelts," the driver intoned over the PA system. "As you may or may not be aware – I'm looking at you city-and-backpacking-types here – we are in the middle of the Outback. As such, there is a lot of wildlife out here on the Sturt, especially kangaroos. Often, I swerve to avoid them, but occasionally I end up hitting the bastards. I know this bus has 'roo bars, but in the event that we hit a 'roo and you're not wearing your seatbelt, you're going to end up flying through the bloody windscreen! Or even worse – you could even end up going into another person and, unless you know them, they bloody well won't like it! Also, it's a legal requirement that you fasten your seatbelts, so please do so anyway!"

Needless to say, none of us paid any heed.

As the bus travelled further and further west, the sounds of Kyuss and Queens of the Stone Age pounding my ears, I witnessed my first sight of true desolation. We were crossing a vast, treeless saltbush plain where the temperatures could soar to above forty-seven degrees in the summer, and plummet below minus-three in the winter. For many kilometres, there wasn't much to be seen apart from the asphalt, the sky and the roadside pylons, together with the occasional truck. The occasional inactive and stagnant irrigation canals by the roadside provided an indication that much of the farming industry along the highway had all but collapsed only a few years previous; the few remaining farmers having being placed on suicide watch. Well, I suppose that's what you get for growing rice on a semi-arid saltbush plain and allowing the bigger corporations to divert the Murray-Darling river for their own profiteering agenda. According to *National Geographic*, between 2006 and 2008, the rice production dropped by ninety-nine percent. It really is *Mad Max* times down there; albeit without the physical bloodshed and the cool vehicles. Just saying.

As the bus drove into the sunset on the open plain, I fell asleep whilst listening to Electric Moon on my Walkman. Eventually, I reached Mildura, a town in northern Victoria known for its agriculture and casual labour opportunities. There was something I wasn't banking on – that the only good hostel in town was booked for two months solid. Then again, I wasn't banking on the fact that I would meet a guy that I had previously met at a rave in the Netherlands that last April. It's a small world indeed…

I stayed for one night on the communal sofa before making my way back to Nimbin – but not before a dip in the paddling pool. It was nice when a lass who normally worked as a stripper at Seventh Heaven in Glasgow declared an international pool orgy when I was relaxing in it. Well, it was her birthday after all. I didn't participate, but I had yet another civil conversation whilst bollock-naked. That's why some people call me the Virgin Sex God…

After twenty-four hours or so in this land of temptation, I made my way back to the Trainlink bus stop at the inactive railway station; the pedestrian crossings on Deakin Avenue blinking and clinking away in the night. I sat freezing my arse off for the first time since August, watching possums race up trees by the side of the Murray, and being mistaken for a Wiradjuri man by a sister who was looking for a smoke. It wouldn't be the last time I would be mistaken for a Koori man – when I got back to Nimbin, Bundjalung women would give me lifts up the road because they thought that I was a brother…

Good times!

I made my way back to Nimbin via the three-am bus back to Cootamundra, making my way into the sunrise as I once again crossed the saltbush plains; the repetitive, sequencer-driven Berlin School sounds of Free System Projekt pulsing through my in-ear buds. From Cootamundra, I caught an XPT train to Sydney, the arrival of which was delayed by an hour owing to the fact that a drunken signalman had let a two-kilometre-long freight train run in front of it at Junee. I contemplated hopping onto the freight train – it was only moving at fifteen kilometres an hour – but I stupidly decided against it.

On board the XPT, after procuring a pie from the buffet, I listened in to an interesting conversation coming from the seats in front of me. A speechless faux-bohemian woman was listening in awe to a female road train driver from northern Queensland who was discussing her life's work (and the associated perils, which frequently came from the menfolk of this speed-riddled, ninety-hour-week lifestyle) and her relationship with her Chinese husband. She talked at length of the sexism elicited by the male truckers along the road and her witty comebacks – I was just as awed as the faux-bohemian, but I decided not to join in with the conversation. It was, as the indigenous folks say, 'women's business.'

In central Sydney, I spent a night at the Central YHA hostel, which cost more per night than the pub in Cowra. Judging by the spotless duty-free bags strewn across the dormitory, my roommates were fresh off the plane from Copenhagen Airport; a place I knew well thanks to spending a weekend in and around Freetown Christiania back in 2013 and becoming an honorary community member owing to my part in the Global Marijuana March. I never saw my roommates awake – I had fallen asleep after the thousand-plus kilometre journey from Mildura. That being said, I was woken up by the three-am all-male snorers duet, and proceeded to douse a particular offender's face with water.

The next morning, I checked out relatively early and sat in a nearby park for several hours before I caught another XPT in the early afternoon. I travelled up to Casino in the presence of a flu-filled tramp who didn't have the gumption to politely move when I needed to get from my window seat to the loo, and a Koori woman who periodically shouted into her mobile phone in her native language and later fell asleep after turning her reading light on. I caught the connecting bus to Lismore – arriving on Molesworth Street at around three in the morning – and finally thumbed it back to Nimbin after spending the rest of the night in a roadside ditch just off the Nimbin Road. Well, the worse experience, the better the story – don't you think so? It's like I've always said; misfortune accompanies fortune. There was also another reason why I went back…

January 16 2015 – Lismore

Big news. I've returned to Nimbin – turns out the project that I've been working on nearly went down the pan since I left for Mildura. Also, there was no suitable accommodation in Mildura – the one good hostel was booked solid until April, whilst the backpackers at the other staged a mass-walkout due to bad management. So I left, headed back north and was welcomed back to Nimbin a hero! Also, I've got in the Nimbin GoodTimes for the second time – pics later...
Since I've achieved all but one of my realistic goals for Australia, the last one is to be undertaken in Nimbin in May, I'll probably remain in Nimbin for the remainder of my trip. However, one of my boss's close friends, who owns a sculpture park, has requested my services. She's coming up to visit in March, and intends to take me back down to Wollombi for a month. So watch this space...

(It didn't happen.)

A Random Online Conversation with Hamish

"Captain Beefheart's birthday today! Or as he may say it, 'the anniversary that day I flopped like a boot to the ground and sent her back my naval to feed to the Mirror Man…' Anyway, it sounds like you're having fun! Why not explore further into Australia before heading back to Nimbin?"

"Ha, yeah! I was listening to *Trout Mask Replica* on the train up to Casino… good times! I'm not exploring further due to lack of funds and declining lack of initiative to cross the desert. The Sturt Highway was bad enough, and that was only a few hours. It's like Lincolnshire on steroids, with fewer people. Also, read my latest post."

"Ah, I see your post. So you may get some more exploring done anyway? I also listened to *Trout Mask Replica* yesterday. There's a line at the end of Sugar 'N Spikes: 'Goin' t' see the navy-blue vicar, Paul Peter 'n misses wray flicker…' How did he know my dad was a man of God?"

The Nimbin Diaries: Pt. II

"Deep down, what is experience of drugs if not this: to erase limits, to reject divisions, to put away all prohibitions, and then ask oneself the question, what has become of knowledge?"
-     Michel Foucault

The author in January 2015...

January 18 2015 – Nimbin

So I'm at the Echidna Dreaming Festival in Nimbin, which is a 2 day celebration of Aboriginal culture. Notable things that have happened.
•I've been mistaken for a Koori for the fifth time this trip – this time by one of the local Elders... I've been telling some of my friends this and they've mostly replied 'Mate, you're a white Koori!' or something like that.
•It's around 2pm, and the festival has been suspended due to excess heat...
•The trip to Canberra may be back on – my boss promised to visit her mother, and Invasion Day (or Australia Day as it is more commonly known) is coming up on the 26th and we both want to show support the Aborigines at the yearly protests. There is a growing indigenous sovereignty movement down here – on the basis that the Aborigines are not recognised in the Australian constitution, and the government has granted them vast amounts of land, some nations have declared independence and/or burned anything that regards them as Australian. Big things are afoot...
We've agreed on the fact that if we do go down, I'll do all the driving both ways, and we'll travel at night. Watch this space...
So right now, I'm chilling in the Rainbow Chai Tent at the currently-suspended Echidna Dreaming Festival in a temperature exceeding 38 degrees. From what I can glean from the BBC, I seem to be better off over here!

(Again, another trip that didn't happen.)

The Lillian Rock Ayahuasca Fiasco

It was the evening of the twenty-second of January 2015. Gina, Xanda and I were drinking tea with Forest – a mutual friend of Xanda who lived on an MO to the north of Nimbin near a settlement called Lillian Rock. Unfortunately for me, I had picked up the flu from that dickhead tramp on the XPT, and it had left me a wheezing wreck of a man. A fellow freak who originally hailed from Shropshire had advised me to increase my intake of fruit and caffeine, so I convinced Forest to buy me a cup of tea at the Oasis Café in exchange for giving him a lift home. With Xanda riding around in the cargo bay of the *Albino Submarine*, Gina on the back seat and Forest in the front to guide me, I motored north towards the settlement of Blue Knob. From there, Forest directed me up a series of back roads to his house on the MO near Lillian Rock, where a potent copse of giant San Pedro cacti lined the track, stalks raised as high as the arms of a raver on MDMA welcoming us in a psychedelic salute. By this time, it was raining heavily, so Gina and I decided to stay the night. Or rather, Poseidon had decided this for us. As Forest collected some cacti to prepare a quantity of mescaline, I had a look around the house. Something interesting soon caught my eye.

"Hey, Forest!" I shouted.

"What?"

"See this Oberheim sequencer – is it yours?"

"Yeah!"

"You've got taste, man!"

Forest grinned as he skinned the hallucinogenic cacti in the kitchen. By this time, Xanda had prepared a spread of food and Gina was making me try Forest's selection of wigs on. It was turning out to be a good night, apart from the fact that I still had the flu and, as such, refused to partake in some fresh mescaline. Also, Xanda was becoming slightly hypocritical. You see, over the past few months, Xanda had claimed that he respected women more than anyone. What I saw him demonstrate over the next twenty-four hours, however, was quite the contrary. I would not, and even if I did I could not, accomplish such disrespect towards women if I was granted ten thousand years on the eternal wheel. He constantly talked down Gina and frequently told her to shut up that night – by which I mean every second sentence which came out of his mouth. Okay, so it's nowhere near as bad as beating the shit out of her, but I suppose that the hypocrisy was getting to me a bit more than the disrespect that night.

Nevertheless, I was concerned for Gina. When I dozed off that night on a convenient bed on Forest's veranda, I didn't so much as doze off, more had a degree of consciousness as I dreamt, keeping an eye on Gina and her welfare. Nevertheless, I dreamt that I was on a Megabus on the west coast of the United States.

The first thing I did when I woke up the next morning was liberate Xanda's chocolate chips and cheese in retaliation for his blatant sexism. The rain was easing off by then, so I roused Gina, engage the differential to activate the four-wheel-drive on the *Albino Submarine* and motored back to Gungas. I cursed Xanda for his sexism, but it worked too well. A week later, he was diagnosed with septicaemia in his legs. It was a few months before I saw him again, by which time he was fine and well. With any luck, he's learnt not to disrespect the womenfolk of this world.

January 25 2015 – Gungas

Well, there goes one of my great muses. Edgar Froese, the founder of Tangerine Dream, the composer of the first song I can ever remember (Rubycon Pt 2), is gone. If it wasn't for his works, I would probably never have picked up the synthesiser. In fact, I was just composing some Tangerine Dream-esqe music when I found out he died...
You will be sorely missed.

A Random Online Conversation with Hamish

"Was at a 60s night at a good wee Glasgow club and they played BEEFHEART... twice! The line 'hey hey hey all you young girls, whatever you do' never felt more real...
I also recently saw an Australian film called *Charlie's Country* about the struggles of an indigenous Australian man against the white settler's laws destroying his culture, set in the modern day. It was very harrowing – I didn't realise just how bad race issues are over there."

"Well Hamish, let's put it this way. In a remote community in Western Australia, a hell-hole (what desert folk call a paddy-wagon) picks up a drunk indigenous man. The holding area in the back doesn't have air-con. It's 200km to the jail. The hell-hole breaks down en route. It takes a few hours for a tow-truck to be despatched to the patch of desert, where it's 45+ degrees outside. It takes another two hours to get to the jail. The police open the back for the first time since they picked up the drunk guy, and are 'surprised' to find him dead. They paid scant attention to him, they gave him no food or water and they left him in an area where the localised temperature was approaching 70 for five hours.
The year? Two-thousand-and-fourteen.
Let's put this another way. Australia lets each of its states and territories enforce apartheid – each state can, in theory, enforce legislation that prevents the blacks from voting. Actually, my friend Thorsten once described it as 'benefits for some, but not others'. So essentially, all humans are equal, but some are more equal than others.
The indigenous people weren't even recognised as human by the census until about 1968 – before then they were counted as 'livestock' – and they still aren't recognised as the original people in the constitution.
And again. The population of Australia before the coming of the white man was estimated at seventeen million, at least according to my friend Thorsten. The current indigenous population is around seven-hundred thousand. That's right. The British are responsible for the genocide of over sixteen million innocent people on this continent alone. And now you see why I don't want to pay any money which ultimately goes to the mostly-white authorities to travel to the middle of the desert to see a completely and utterly bastardised monolith. I can see the holiest monoliths in Australia which HAVEN'T been bastardised from my bed – literally, all I have to do is open my eyes in the morning, and

there they are, outside my window across town. And I'm one of the few Europeans who is actually allowed onto the sacred land because Thorsten lives there and I deliver his groceries.

So yes. Australia does have a race problem. Thanks for noticing!"

A Random Text Conversation with Thorsten

"Bring a USB drive with 1gig of free space when you drop my gas cartridges off. Then I can give you *2001* ;)"

A few days later…

"Did ya check your generator re which wave form it puts out?"
"I did – it's a 600w modified sine wave inverter. Also, I've seen half of *2001* – I don't believe it was made in '68..."
"You're right. It was made in '67. Following a conversation between Arthur and Stanley in 64 about finally making a good sci-fi movie :p"
"Though I did plug my phone into the generator once, and now every time I plug the phone into any socket the touch-screen buggers up if I touch it in certain places. Sometimes it thinks I'm touching it in six different places – handy for making compositions on GarageBand but bad for everything else..."
"As I said. Most generators put out square wave and produce surges. Not good for electronics."

A Random Text Conversation with Gina

"I'm at Grey Gum Lodge for the night....zzzz"
"Cool! I cooked the spag bol – added some hemp powder to the meat before cooking, best thing I've eaten for a while! Also, it's drumming night tonight :)"
"Nice 1 :)"

February 3 2015 – Gungas

For some unknown reason, Nim-FM has been playing a lot of bad pop music these past few days. Although this morning, I've been hearing Goa trance, Faithless, Neil Young and Queens of the Stone Age. I think they've made up for it!

Internet Haikus

A haiku selection that I recited at the Live Poets event at the New Tattershalls Hotel on the eleventh of February 2015, to an audience which included Daevid Allen shortly after he found out that his cancer was terminal and elected to cease his chemotherapy.

"Here are some haikus
That describe the internet

Very, very well.

My Little Pony:
How did a little girls' show
Get so popular?

Saw a video
About some creepy kid who
Said, "Is this real life?"

The Lonely Island
Sing a bunch of silly songs
Like 'I'm On a Boat.'

I've said this about
One million times, and again:
I DON'T like mudkips.

If you start hearing
'Never gonna give you up,'
Then you've been Rickrolled.

The "All Your Base" meme
Is just the result of a
Bad translation job.

Even in the bleak,
Dark parts of the Internet,
Rule 34 stands.

The only thing I
Hate about online porn is
There's not more of it.

If you ever go
To shock websites, please beware.
NO BARFING ALLOWED

Face it: Al Gore did
NOT invent the Internet.
What made you think that?!

In Conclusion:

The internet is
A very creepy place where
You should not click links."

Daevid Allen, performing I Am an Old Man *at his final Tatts appearance on the 11ᵗʰ of February 2015*

February 13 2015 – Gungas

It's been exactly six months into my Australian odyssey, with around four more to go. It's also Friday the Thirteenth today. To celebrate, I got pulled over by the Highway Patrol on the Blue Knob road for a spot breath and drug test – my first. Unluckily for him, he pulled over the only sober motorist in Nimbin... Scott 1, Thought Police 0!
Friday the Thirteenth has always been good to me for some reason – I must be devil spawn or something... oh well!

The Moment I Realised That I May Not Be as White as Some...

To this day, I cannot exactly confirm the reason why I got pulled over, but I can hazard a good guess as to why. You see, I was driving the *Albino Submarine* – a decrepit ute that had seen nearly twenty years of service around Australia judging by the maintenance logbook. And like Rose – the Bundjalung woman who thought I was her nephew – once said, she thought that I was her nephew based upon the quality of the clothes I was wearing, my hairstyle and, to a lesser extent, the colour of my skin.

In other words, I got pulled over for driving while black. Or, to put it in layman's terms, I was racially targeted by a Highway Patrol officer.

I knew I was going to get pulled over as soon as I saw the patrol car heading in the opposite direction brake suddenly to make a U-turn. I was hoping to get back into the centre of Nimbin in full sight of the hippies – all of whom were very much opposed to what was about to happen to me, and would possibly come to my aid in the event that shit kicked off. Alas, my plan was to no avail. I pulled over off the road outside the Bush Theatre on the north side of town, turned off the Orbital album I was listening to and calmly removed the key from the ignition. That way, I knew he couldn't bust me on trumped-up charges for not being in adequate control of the vehicle. For example, if I got my phone out, he would have had no excuse to bust me for using a phone at the wheel.

The grim-faced officer came up to the open window, and asked to see my driver's licence. Naturally, I complied.

"Where's your New South Wales licence?" he suddenly demanded.

"What?"

"Where's your New South Wales licence, boy?"

I had done some research before my trip, and knew that driving on a British licence was perfectly acceptable for the duration of my stay. I assumed that this agent of the Thought Police had asked me this question again as he was looking for an excuse to put some penalty points on my licence. Well, assuming I had an Australian one anyway – the Australians can't put penalty points on British licences.

"I'm British – I'm here on holiday!"

He eventually accepted this fact. Luckily for me, he didn't ask for my passport – it was back in the van. He didn't ask about the contents of the ute either, for some weird reason. No mention of the sixteen buckets of gravel in the back, nor any concern of the file and crowbar on the rear passenger seat. Then again, the latter were out of my reach. Additionally, as per the local law, the officer had a gun, which at this point was a little unnerving for me, it being perilously close to my face.

Unluckily for me, however, he still tried extract every other single little detail from me, looking for that one excuse to haul me off to the cop shop, or at least the drug bus parked at the south end of town.

"Is this vehicle yours?"

"No – it's my friend Gina's."

"Is it insured? Do you have permission to drive this vehicle?"

"Yes."

Like most countries, but not the United Kingdom, third party insurance that covers the other party in the event of an accident is included in the road tax in Australia. A side effect of this is that anyone may drive any vehicle that they are licenced for, so long as they have the owner's permission. For some reason though, the officer didn't ask for Gina's phone number.

He paused.

"Right. I'm going to do a breath test," he said, holding up a small machine. "I want you to slowly count to ten."

I complied. The result came back as zero.

"Okay. Now I'm going to check to see if you have any drugs in your system. For legal reasons, I have to inform you that I'll be testing for cannabis and methamphetamines. Have you taken any of these substances recently?"

"No," I replied honestly.

I had heard of this test around town. There was a fifty percent chance that it would come back wrong, and no other country in the world had adopted this test at the time due to its inaccuracies. After all, many non-drug users were coming back positive on the test, and at the time, virtually all of the ice-users had come back negative. Many people who ate hemp – then an illegal action at the time – were coming back positive too. And I, who was living on a diet of hemp powder-infused noodles at the time, was quite literally bricking it. I would later find out that one can fudge the test by sucking on a Fisherman's Friend…

I swabbed my tongue with the apparatus that the officer had provided, and watched as he made his way back to the patrol car with the apparatus and my driver's licence in hand. It only took a few minutes for the results to come back, but it felt so much longer. After what felt like an eternity, he came back.

"How was it?" I asked.

He looked disappointed.

"It came back negative!" he answered.

He began to hand me back my licence, but at the last second, he snatched it away quickly from my outstretched hand.

"Were you scared?" he sneered.

"No – I'm just hungry," I replied. "It's past my lunchtime, and I've got a chicken curry on the boil…"

He finally handed me back my licence, and let my go on my less-than-merry way home.

It is only now as I document my travels that two thoughts occur to me. The first thought is the fact that many people of colour have to deal with this shit – and worse! – on a day-to-day basis, and despite the fact that I myself got DWBed, I still couldn't begin to imagine what every other poor bastard who experiences this kind of thing must be going through.

The second thought is this. Am I white? Well, of course not, but I'm a darker shade of pink than some people.

I mean, I was born on the island of Britannia Major, but I know for a fact that many of my recent ancestors were immigrants. Some came from Ireland, others from Italy, but what went on in the ports and shipwreck coasts where the clans Conneally and Luciani started their journeys to Britannia Major? Why do I pick up other languages better than many other British people?

And why were Australia's indigenous population mistaking me for one of their own? Why were indigenous people offering me lifts on the basis that I was a brother? Why was I invited to the Echidna Dreaming Festival – essentially a bona fide indigenous corroboree?

To this day, I haven't a clue about anything anymore. But these days, if I get asked about my nationality, race, or country of origin, I just respond 'human' or 'Pirnmill'. I mean, borders? Nations? What concepts! They only exist because everyone else believe they exist…

Oh, and a week or so after the incident, another Highway Patrol car did a U-turn and switched on the blues as I was driving back to Gungas with Gina sitting beside me. I was subsequently pulled over by Australia's equivalent of Sergeant Wilson from *Dad's Army*.

"Hello!" Wilson said cheerfully. "Sorry to pull you over – this is just a routine check. May I see your licence please?"

I showed my British licence.

"Are you here on holiday, sir?"

"Well, a working holiday, or so my visa says anyway. Right now, I'm just helping out my friend here."

"Ah, I see. Well, you wouldn't mind doing a quick breath test for me just now?"

"Of course not!"

Again, a reading of zero.

"Once again, sorry to disturb you," Wilson smiled. "Enjoy the rest of your day!"

"You too!"

Nice fellow.

February 14 2015 – Lismore Base Hospital

Ah, Valentine's Day. The day for lovey stuff. I've never had a girlfriend, but that's not bothering me.

What's bothering me is that I'm in the ED at Lismore Base Hospital having been admitted with chest pain, breathing difficulties and the constant feeling that I may pass out at any moment; I'm currently awaiting the result of an X-ray – my first – and a blood test. I have been stressed a lot recently – probably brought it on[1]. We'll see.

Admittedly, though, I never thought I would miss the taste of bad creme caramel pudding - what they served me here reminds me of the stuff they used to do at South Crosland Junior School!

Leeches!

Xanda's then-compound

It was the twenty-sixth of February 2015, and I was helping Xanda move house. At the time, he was living in a surreal compound just outside Tuntable Falls – he was residing in a tent covered by a tarpaulin as some hard-core backpackers are known to do, which was located next to an early Volkswagen Type 2 which was, unfortunately, rusted out.

Xanda's tent had flooded for some reason or another, and so he was moving his stuff into a secure locker just outside Nimbin. I went to his compound, parking the *Albino Submarine* some way away as the track turned into an undrivable footpath. Between my parking spot and the compound, Xanda and I pushed wheelbarrows the hundred metres or so back and forth, rescuing his flooded goods.

That's when I noticed them.

---

[1] It did – it was probably just a bad panic attack.

That day, I was wearing sandals and not much else. As I looked down at my feet, I saw a great mass of squirming black objects.

Leeches.

It was as if the earth was rising up to swallow my feet. At first, I was scared shitless, especially when I saw the fat bastards move about in a concertina motion across the floor, forming an upside-down U-shape in the air as they did. But then, two thoughts dawned on me – firstly, the joke was on them because my feet were riddled with athlete's foot! Secondly, how the fuck did Xanda survive in this environment?

"You noticed the leeches, eh?" Xanda was saying.

"Yeah! Never encountered them before!"

"You got any salt?"

"No…"

"Best way to get rid of 'em. But they can do you good – I mean, look at that tumour on the side of your left foot."

The tumour Xanda had noticed had randomly developed in February 2012 whilst I was on a trip to Oban. I finally had half of it removed in April 2014 after a series of misdiagnoses – thankfully, the surgeons at Crosshouse Hospital chopped off the bit that hurt and grew. The six local anaesthetics I had to endure, though, were the most painful thing I had encountered until that giant red ant bit me several chapters ago.

"What about it?" I asked.

"Well, put some leeches on it. They'll shrink it!"

I put a leech on it as a test, and it seemed to work. Unfortunately, just I was discovering the medicinal value of leeches, we had packed up everything. And a good thing too – I was beginning to feel a wee bit woozy from the blood loss. After I deposited Xanda and what was left of his belongings, I drove into Lismore to pick up some groceries (which was the plan for the rest of the day anyway), and wasted no time feasting on red meat. I really needed the iron…

February 28 2015 – Sphinx Rock Café, Mount Burrell

You know when you're in Australia when you're driving along, and suddenly there's a dingo laying in the middle of the road outside the police station and it's trying to outstare the traffic...

(I later found out that the popular television programme *I'm a Celebrity – Get Me Out of Here!* is filmed around Mount Burrell after accidentally watching a clip and recognising the calls of a VCS3 bird. I presume they chose this area as it's only a few kilometres down the road from Nimbin where one may easily obtain some fresh bud for five dollars a gram, but that's none of my business.)

March 1 2015 – The Rails, Byron Bay

Just spent the morning driving to a village called Harwood, home of the Harwood Sugar Refinery, Harwood Bridge, Harwood Roadhouse, Harwood Hall and the sadly defunct Church of Harwood. All this is located in a town called Maclean, where all the street signs are in Gàidhlig. Pics to come...

Now I'm in Byron Bay awaiting the 'Writers at the Rails' afternoon - a discussion featuring the poet David Hallett, possibly the space-rockers Daevid Allen and Gilli Smyth, and of course, yours truly. Until then, the local Hare Krishnas are providing some interesting entertainment...

(Daevid Allen showed up and did his last ever public performance that day. He recited three poems: his famous 'Devil's Avocado' poem, a poem about chemotherapy and why he had elected to die with dignity, and finished off with 'I'm Sorry' – a poem I would later set to music and uploaded to YouTube.
It was a legendary day.
And I was there.
In the front row.
As a support act.)

An Ode to McDonalds

This is a poem I recited when I was supporting Daevid Allen at his final public performance:

"Greaseball burgers and a salty crisp fry,
It's no bloody wonder that these fat-asses die!
No matter how tasty a Big Mac can be,
T'will lengthen your waist line in inches by three.
And just when you think you are done for the day,
They make you come back for a free McSundae
With McFlurries, McJaggers, and even McStraws,
Obesity is no fucking wonder! Because,
No matter how much we all hate to say,
It's certain the "Arches" will just have to stay."

The Lucid Dream Sequence

I briefly met Daevid Allen one final time before I motored back to Gungas in the *Albino Submarine*. Leaving via the back roads out of Byron Bay, Kraftwerk's *Computer World* and *Techno Pop* blaring from the stereo, I briefly stopped outside the Tatts in Lismore to see if I could pick up the WiFi connection. Alas, it was a Sunday and the place was closed. Not that it was essential.

I fell asleep quickly that night and proceeded to have a strange sequence of lucid dreams; the weirdness increasing with each dream. Now, I had dreamt some strange dreams in recent times, including a dream where Xanda was yelling that I couldn't use a bunch of metal poles to prop up Gina's container as they were holy to the Bundjalung people. But this sequence took the biscuit. In the first part of the sequence, I dreamt that I was driving from a vaguely futuristic Copenhagen to Malmö in a Nissan Leaf. Except that Copenhagen didn't look like Copenhagen, the Øresund Bridge didn't look like the Øresund Bridge, and Malmö didn't look like Malmö. But I knew I was driving from Copenhagen to Malmö. It felt right.

In the second part of the sequence, I was on my way to visit my grandmother in a snowy, Scandinavian-ish landscape, trekking cross-country through the trees. She was living in what appeared to be a giant grey cube, off the grid, with a toy boy for company. For some reason, the cube had American-standard power sockets.

For the third part, I'll leave you to read what I posted on social media the morning after the dream.

"It was the third part of my most lucid dream sequence to date. For some reason, I was throwing a strange metallic object the size of a coin – which looked suspiciously like the spinning top from Inception – at random people in a strange interpretation of London's Victoria train station, causing them to float over to me and merge with me. After merging with at least three different people, I looked in a mirror. I had the colour and looks of a half-caste Aborigine with deep scars down my face. The merger with those people affected my personality – many of the core values which I believed in were eradicated in a heartbeat. A voice in my head broke whatever concentration I had on myself.

"Throw the object at anyone wearing yellow."

So I threw the metallic object at a slightly chubby woman, aged around 35-40, with short hair, gargantuan breasts and nice ass, wearing a yellow singlet. Like the others, she floats up to me, but she stopped merging with me as soon as our genitals touched.

And suddenly, we were naked and locked together in love's embrace on the floor of Victoria Station. As we moved as one, I could feel the moist warmth pulsing down below. Her legs locked around mine as if to seal the deal. I could feel her oversized belly touching mine. I could feel her full oversized breasts pushing upwards onto me like a water bed mid-ripple. I could feel her warm, husky breath on my temple; my lips on her cheeks. Her cheap perfume wafted past my nose, providing fragrant nectar to fuel my love-making.

And we kept making sweet, passionate love until the next part of the dream sequence took me away from her and the onlookers – we were still at 'Victoria'...

It wasn't the first time that such a dream sequence has happened to me, but it was the most lucid. I saw, felt, heard, even smelt and tasted every single little detail in the dream." I still haven't kissed or shagged a girl in the real world. But I know how it feels...

To quote Dali; "I don't need drugs – I AM drugs!" All you need is a screwed-up third eye and a bottle of Hahn Premium Light before bed…

I would finally have my first kiss at an underground techno night at the Glasgow School of Art that November. Until then, I had a more pressing issue – what's up with my pineal gland?

As we all know, the pineal gland is that part of your brain that produces *N,N-Dimethyltryptamine*, or DMT. Thanks to my pineal gland presumably working overtime, I was having strange thoughts:

'Am I a peace-bringing Messiah? Am I the start of a new, realistic peace-loving generation? Was that vision that I had that time in Amsterdam true – am I a monk? Will these visions end if I ever get a girlfriend? I bloody hope not! Then again, I've probably been reading too much Raymond E. Feist and Robert A. Heinlein…'

I had a chat with Gina soon after, and she told me to visit her friend Johnny Allen at the intentional international community of Auroville if I ever got to India. I eventually got there and met him in January 2018, nearly three years after Gina told me to travel there, but that's a story for another book...

A Random Online Conversation with Hamish

"Wow, your post was very beautifully written. Reminds me of the surrealist author Haruki Murakami. He often writes dream sequences and frankly detailed sex scenes. I think I've had such dreams however I can't remember any right now. Tell Lewis about this – he loves this sort of stuff."

"He casually mentioned he does, but failed to elaborate..."

A Random Conversation with the Neighbours

"Hey Scott!"
The voice came from Bonnie, who lived on the compound next door. A tall, relatively young lass, she was as lean a post despite giving birth to two children within the past ten years. She was playing with Coco by the fence that divided our two properties; they were reluctant to put it up, but Misha the malamute had regrettably developed a reputation for chasing wallabies.
I wandered over.
"Oh, hi Bonnie! You all right?"
"Yeah, thanks! Yourself?"
"Yeah, I'm grand!"
Coco beamed up at me.
"I'm four years old!" she proudly exclaimed.
I bent down to her level.
"Are you now?" I smiled. "Well Coco, I'm five times your age! So how old am I?"
She looked confused at this, her introduction to the four-times-table. Bonnie leant down and whispered something in her ear.
"Twenty."
"Well done!" I clapped. "Now run off and play, you little scamp!"
I turned to Bonnie.
"She'll learn her times-tables soon enough! Though admittedly, I was a genius at maths – at least until they introduced calculus in high school. But you know, by the time I was three, I was reading 'Joseph and the Amazing Technicolour Dreamcoat' off the side of a bus. I mean, I can't remember that day, but my mother was stunned!"
Bonnie's eyes widened slightly.
"So, how's life in Gungas treating you anyway? Dave told me he got the job in Lismore!"
"Yeah, he did! Gungas is all right. The big problem for us though, is we can't seem to get any phone signal! We have to drive to the top of the road just to get anything!"
"What network are you on?"
"Optus."

"Ah. I'm on Telstra, and I'm getting 3G down here. Just"

"Oh, really? You think I should switch?"

"Well, I recommend getting a Telstra SIM and keeping the old one just in case. But that does mean you can get internet without driving anywhere!"

There's nothing like a bit of friendly neighbourhood advice is there?

The Fermentation Festival

During my time in Australia, I had managed to get Gina interested in brewing her own beer – the Hahn was going down too fast, and we were both looking for a cheaper method of getting drunk. One day, on a routine trip to Lismore, Gina purchased an array of alcohol-making equipment, and as someone who had experience in brewing, I instructed her on every part of the process. Soon, we had twenty-three litres of lager brewing in a vat on Gina's porch, much to her ecstatic delight. Unfortunately, she didn't stack the bottles right in her ice box, so half of them spilled out. We ended up using the spillage as pickling vinegar.

From there, our collective interest peaked. On the seventh of March 2015, Gina and I attended the Fermentation Festival in Blue Knob; a gathering where people from across the Northern Rivers and beyond came to sell and share fermented products, edible or otherwise, and knowledge of their preparation. The highlight of this gathering was a raffle; the top prize being a hamper containing, amongst other things, a certain organic fertiliser that was being promoted at the festival, homemade kimchi, a loaf of bread prepared through the process of fermentation, various beverages, and a copy of *The Art of Fermentation* by Sandor Ellix Katz. Gina bought a ticket – which cost all of one dollar – and we waited until the end of the day for the raffle to be drawn.

"Okay folks!" shouted the MC. "It's time to draw the raffle!"

I started having a strange thought.

'Gina's going to win!' I prophesised.

A hand made its way into the ticket bowl, and pulled out the lucky name. The MC frowned.

"Erm, Guna from Tulsi Lane, Gungas?"

"It's Gina, moron!" I shouted.

I pushed a red-faced, ecstatic Gina to the front of the marquee, where she received her bounty to rapturous applause.

It took us a while to leave the festival, what with Gina being congratulated at every opportunity by the rest of the festival patrons. As I secured the hamper in the back seat of the *Albino Submarine*, I finally got a word in.

"Congratulations, Gina!"

"Thank you, Scott! I didn't think I would win!"

"I sort of did. You know, that gut feeling. Some people call it feyness or telepathy."

"Ah."

"Now, as this is your hamper, I'm not going to ask for any food from it. However, I do request that I transcribe a recipe or two from the book. You know, as to better my alcohol-making skills."

She smiled at my modesty.

"Sure, of course, my dear friend!"

I started studying *The Art of Fermentation* almost as soon as we got back to Gungas. That day, I started work on my first mead – a product I now make in time for Berneray Week. Albeit I don't use cheap jam and some old honey I found in the van any more…

A Random Online Conversation with My Mother

Hi Scott. Just to let you know *[names redacted]* have been sent down for 7 and 6 years for raping someone in York. Not clever, eh?"

"Hell no! Just heard about it – first status update that cropped up in my feed. Also, I got a phone call from Grandma and Bernd – apparently the family wants to meet up in Huddersfield for my 21st. Well, I know Andrew and Peter do anyway. I say go for it!

"We can't, really. We're probably looking at the end August or the beginning of September as we'll have finished the cèilidhs by then."

March 14 2015 – Sphinx Rock Café, Mount Burrell

A very sad day for me as I mourn the loss of another two of my heroes – Daevid Allen and Terry Pratchett.
I had the good fortune to meet, know and eventually out-poet the former on a spectacular level, something which every fan knows is very hard to do. I've got a hell of a legacy to fulfil now… Whether you're riding around the sky in a big green flying teapot, OR JUST TALKING IN CAPITAL LETTERS, you guys will be very much missed.
Rest in peace, chaps.

Daevid Allen – A Personal Account

This is a piece of free poetry I knocked out to be performed at a special Live Poets event in Lismore, which was to commemorate the life and work of Daevid Allen. However, Gina was under the illusion that the event was to be held in Nimbin and, as such, didn't put any ethanol into the *Albino Submarine* that day – I found out this information after we had set off and travelled into Nimbin.

And so, many years late, here's what I wrote.

"I can't remember that exact day, all those years ago, when my dad first came up to me and asked, completely out of the blue:
"Hey Scott, have you discovered Gong yet?"
And I replied, "Um, no..."
Curiosity taking hold, I went onto YouTube, looked up Gong and decided to listen to a track called 'Flying Teapot'... now, to a lad who had been raised on such psychedelic establishments as Hawkwind and Tangerine Dream, this Gong band sounded pretty fucking groovy to say the least!
Little did I know that this discovery would be the start of a long journey. A journey that, over the next few years, would see me taking a trip in a Flying Teapot on the long yearly pilgrimage to the wee island of Berneray, discovering an Angels Egg in an abandoned bunker on the Isle of Arran, listening to You on the long college commute, and partaking in some Camembert Electrique with a girl named Aisha in an Irish youth hostel whilst en route to my ancestral home near Tralee.
Alas, before I could discover more about Daevid Allen, I found myself on an Emirates A380, heading for the other side of the world. Fast forward a few months, and you could have find me in a hotel in a town named after one of my favourite Scottish islands, awaiting a night of poetry. And who should walk in the door but an old, cosmic-looking gentleman, and I thought to myself "Aw, it's nice that the old people are being alternative!"
Little did I know that it was the Divided Alien himself until he went up on stage, and thus I subsequently discovered his fantastic whimsical poetry... After this performance, I discovered that a friend on Berneray was a Soft Machine fan, a massive fan to say the least! And thus, I started enjoying them too, in addition to the little-known supergroup Spirits Burning.

I had the good fortune to see Bert Camembert twice more – not recognising him again on the second occasion until he introduced himself to me. And that's something I still can't believe – the madman responsible for the guitar solo on 'Allez Ali Baba Black Sheep, Have you Any Bullshit: Mama Maya Mantram' shook my hand.
The conversation we had was equally astounding:
"Hello, I'm Daevid Allen!"
I looked him up and down, bug-eyed, wondering what to say. I could have quoted Gong. I could have told him how much of an influence he was on my own musical abilities. Instead, I did something a lot better, something my father would be proud of:
I managed to summarise everything in just four words:
"We are not worthy!"
To which the great man smiled, chuckled and responded:
"Bullshit. Total and utter bullshit!"

Then the Writers at the Rails event in Byron Bay came around, and I saw him for the third, and final, time. I never realised until I came to Australia that there were so many fans of his poetry, some of whom were younger than me! But alas, his poems were said, I flashed him one last smile, and left without a word. All that I needed to say I had already said. At least I recognised him that time!

Yes, my friends, Daevid Allen may be riding around in a big green flying teapot in the sky, or living in a great big castle in the clouds, but it is obvious that his burning spirit still lives on in our inner temples.
Hey, as the great man said once in the early seventies: "You can kill my body, baby, but you can't kill me!"

Rest in peace, Christopher Daevid Allen."

Interlude – Another Lucid Dream Sequence

My lucid dreams are pissing around with me again.
In the first part of this particular dream sequence, I found myself in the clouds. In an open room. With a bed. And in it, a perfectly-formed goddess. But there was something odd about her – it wasn't the fact that her breasts were out, it was the fact that there was a strange white void in the upper middle.
She smiled at my lack of expression.
"Fuck my tits, and I will give birth to a new world!"
Still expressionless, with the Gong track 'Castle in the Clouds' playing faintly in the background, I succumbed to the inevitable. Slowly, as the deed was being done, a Nirvana-like state washed over me; I ascended to an astral projection, no longer feeling, but watching over the scene.
Shortly, the deed was done, and I watched the void grow, swallow everything in the room and send me into the next part of the dream sequence...
No drink or drugs were consumed in the making of this dream – I merely fell asleep listening to Global Communication...

Bottle Kids!

Gina and I regularly drove the thirty kilometres or so into Lismore for the basic essentials – food, beer, banking, and cheap ethanol for the *Albino Submarine*. One day, as we were parked up at the ALDI, Gina remembered to buy something important and ducked back into the supermarket. I sat in the cab of the *Albino Submarine* sipping a two-litre bottle of cheap strawberry milkshake, one of my few vices at the time, listening in to a local radio station of dubious legitimacy that exclusively played psychedelic chillout music. It was bliss.

Across the car park, however, was a car playing thumping dance music with the volume at eleven. And suddenly, out of nowhere, a group of pre-pubescent kids rocked up on their kick scooters screaming 'PAAR-TAY! PAAR-TAY!' I began to wonder whether if they had liberated their parents' alcohol supply. Or judging by the way they were sounding, could have it been their ice dens? Either way, they became bored very quickly after the doof-mobile motored away, so they started throwing bottles which formerly contained goodness-knows-what at the only other vehicle in the car park, which just so happened to be the *Albino Submarine*. Thankfully, these unwanted projectiles didn't break the back window – the bottles just landed in the cargo bay.

I was powerless to do anything – what was I going to do, project milkshake in their general vicinity? I had visions of mowing them down on the pavement outside the Hungry Jack's next door, their little brittle cadavers mangled by the *Albino Submarine's* 'roo bars, blood on the cracked windscreen, scooters crushed under the wheels. Then I envisioned my arrest at the hands of the New South Wales Police Force, my anus continuously violated under the blind eye of the ghastly administration of a Serco-operated prison, the families of the deceased and many other Australians calling for the re-introduction of the death penalty. So, I left them be and, rather thankfully, they buggered off.

Parents of the universe, hear my call. Don't give your children alcohol. Or crystal meth. It probably won't end well.

On Alcohol

It is well known amongst the denizens of the world that Australia has an alcohol culture of a certain repute. Let's put it this way, beer is pretty much considered a *de facto* currency alongside the Australian dollar. If you get offered a beer and decline it out of politeness, like what I did during the AFL Grand Final whilst talking with Benny, you'll find that a beer is thrust into your right hand anyway, along with a joint on your left. In some establishments, wine – especially the dregs which are sold as 'goon' to backpackers looking for a cheap way to get blooted – is cheaper than bottled water.

But here's the thing that surprised this particular traveller. In Australia, unlike Scotland, supermarkets are generally not allowed to sell alcohol. The few which did had a limited selection of wines and spirits, surrounded on three sides by view-proof dividers, that could only be processed on one checkout which, as one would predict, would have queues that normally would put off all but the most hardened and polite Brit. This has resulted in the major Australian supermarkets opening subsidiary bottle shops, in most cases next door to the food outlets, in order to get around the law.

Ah, yes. Bottle shops. So-called because they're shops which sell, um, bottles. No Australian in the right mind (i.e. one who cannot generally master words with more than two syllables) would have called them 'container emporiums'. The bottle shop is indeed ubiquitous in Australia. In addition to the rule-bending chains, a great many are independently owned, and are often attached to pubs. Some of them, such as one that Gina and I would regularly visit in Lismore, are drive-through. Literally. You don't even have to leave your vehicle.

One day, Gina and I pulled up next to the checkout at the Northern Rivers Hotel. Being inside a building, I killed the *Albino Submarine's* engine as not to asphyxiate everyone.

"Erm, a crate of Hahn Premium Light and a bottle of Kopparberg, please! Oh, and a pack of beef jerky!"

Bounty duly loaded, we motored back to Nimbin, where we attended a poetry night at the Oasis Café, a lovely part of the world with decent food and local wizards who would get stoned and play chess in the shadow of 'Starbuds' and Bob Marley posters. If this gem of a place existed elsewhere in the world, it would surely be shut down.

After ordering the meal of the day, Gina and I sat down, where I took the opportunity to crack open the Kopparberg. Big mistake.

"Can't you read the sign?!" shrieked one of the poets.

'Sorry, who the fuck are you?' I thought.

"'No Alcohol Needed!'"

"Obviously, English isn't her first language," I muttered to Gina sarcastically after Little Miss Conceited had flounced away. "Needed does not equal permitted – it just means that drinking is discouraged. I know that marijuana is more socially acceptable than alcohol here, and I agree with the concept, but all I'm doing is having a cider with my evening meal! I mean, I'm drinking responsibly, I'm not on the vodka or the goon, so why is she attacking me?"

"Maybe she likes the sound of her own voice!" Gina whispered back. "I mean, it's poetry night, after all…"

I put the Kopparberg into a wee paper bag, and proceeded to surreptitiously drink the rest of it with my meal, enjoying the poetry in the process.

Gina herself didn't have a problem with alcohol in the way that many Nimbinites did. On the contrary; as I pointed out to a mutual friend of ours I met some years later, she didn't have a drinking problem, more like she had the occasional problem when she was on the drink. Case in point; one evening, we were down the pub in Nimbin. She had drunk a few pints of Guinness, and was referring to me as her 'soulmate'.

"I'm not your soulmate, Gina," I responded.

Big fucking mistake. Gina got angrier and angrier, until she just about screamed "I WANT YOU OUT!!!" But at least I got things under control. Just.

"Whoa, hang on there," I said calmly. "Let's all calm down, and talk this out like responsible adults. I have no intent on harming you or upsetting you."

She calmed down significantly. We talked for a while; I forget what I said after that point, I can only remember that I was trying hard not to throw up by using all my willpower to keep the situation under control. The drive home was silent, and so was much of the next morning. In the end, I wrote a letter to her and left it outside her door. In it, I explained that my interpretation of the word 'soulmate' came from that one episode of *The Simpsons* where Homer eats a hallucinogenic chilli and meets a talking space coyote, and I didn't mean to upset her or cause offence. In the end, she forgave me, and I was allowed to stay.

March 28 2015 – Gungas

Fun fact: Tree frogs are endangered. They are also very punk. I opened the door of my van one day and three fell on my arm. As they hopped off, one of them took the opportunity to try and piss on my phone – without success. You could almost hear it go 'WHAAA!' as it tried to evade my wrath...

The Dunoon Story

"Hey man!"

A voice was calling to me from an open car window outside the Peace Park one sunny afternoon.

"Well done, you just found the only sober person in town!" I responded. "You all right?"

"How do I get to Dunoon from here?"

Well, fly to Glasgow, get a train to Gourock, then the ferry over, I thought, but then I remembered. The Dunoon that people knew around here was a small village located a few kilometres beyond The Channon, and was renowned for its production of macadamia nuts.

"Just keep going down this road and follow the signs," I responded. "Keep an eye out – you're going to have to make a few turns with little warning."

"Thanks! Wait, did you say you were sober? In Nimbin of all places?"

"Aye…"

"Fucks sake mate! You want a joint?"

He tossed a fatty out through the window and sped off before I could respond, proving to me that he wasn't an undercover cop trying to catch me out.

A Random Online Conversation with My Mother

"Hi Scott. Thanks for your package. It was lovely to hear from you. When you talk about driving, we keep needing someone for home delivery. I was talking to the CEO of Co-op Food and asked him what the chances were of getting a 4-wheel-drive van as ours has broken down a few times. I got a call from the fleet manager this week saying the money has been approved to build us a brand new all-wheel-drive van! Not bad eh?"

"Not bad at all!"

Yet another interlude

Things were interesting around this time. I spent my days working, running errands for Gina and Thorsten, meeting friends old and new at the Friday-night drumming circle in town and attending MOB (MardiGrass Organising Body) meetings in order to get the year's MardiGrass festival significantly planned. I attended an equinox feast with another few weird folk next to the Aquarius Society building, fetching a supply of camping gas from the servo in exchange for some of the best food I had consumed in months.

I watched a 'straight' family who were on holiday shooing away some of Nimbin's famous semi-feral chickens outside the Pot o' Gold café on Cullen Street, and laughing at the chickens extracting their revenge by jumping on the table. I laughed harder at the three-legged chihuahua who stood upside-down on its front legs in order to pee on a lamppost!

Occasionally, I would go down the pool and spend up to three hours doing lengths. Often, a group of local eight-to-eleven-year-olds would come and play Marco Polo…

"Marco!"

"Polo!"

"Marco!"

"Polo!"

"Marco!"

"Wanker!"

"Marco!"

"Fuck you!"

…before they were chucked out of the pool by the bloke responsible for the cleaning on the basis that they were unaccompanied. Occasionally, the police would buzz the pool in a helicopter, searching for marijuana ("This is an ACTUAL swimming pool, ya daft bastards!" I would shout at the misguided pork chopper). One day, I met my friend Lewis' neighbours from Rutherglen in the pool – sadly, they hadn't met him.

After a chat with Michael Balderstone – the head of the HEMP Party and Nimbin's unofficial mayor – I found out the best tactic to scare away a police helicopter is to point a didgeridoo at it.

"They'll think it's an RPG and shoot right off!" he was saying.

"I can imagine the headlines – 'ISIS INFILTERATES HIPPIE SCUM!'" I laughed.

"Well, they may as well already have at the rate the cops raid the town, mate!"

One day, Gina and I went to Lismore to see a special screening of *Frackman* – a film about one man taking on the fracking wells – and met the Frackman (Dayne Pratzky) himself, along with his girlfriend and the director. We were given petition letters that we could send to the Australian Parliament, and Gina wanted to fill her letter in there and then.

"Hey Scott, do you have a pen I can borrow?"

I didn't.

"I don't, sorry. Pen Island might have one."

"Pen Island?"

"Yeah – don't you get the joke? Move the gap!"

She sat quietly for a few minutes, pondering what I just said.

"Oh, PENIS!" she suddenly squeaked stridently.

The Mayor of Lismore, who was sitting directly in front of us, turned her head round. Gina and I made ourselves as small as possible, and didn't talk for the rest of the screening.

After a visit to the nearby settlement of Bishop's Creek, I made friends with a young couple named Andre and Melissa and their rescue dogs, all of whom had just moved up from Melbourne. I would see them regularly in town until I left.

I also started volunteering with and getting free food from The Five Loaves – a Christian group who go around the food outlets in Lismore and give food to the hungry, hungry hippies. I used to put up the tables and deliver food in the *Albino Submarine* to those who couldn't get into town. Strangely, vegetarianism and veganism is such the norm in Nimbin that even the down-and-outers wouldn't go for the free and plentiful meat sashimi on offer. Except for the Japanese Rastafarian community, of course.

There was no shortage of culture provided by sources other than the poetry nights at the Oasis Café, which I would often attend with Tanya, and the Friday night drumming sessions in town, where I would frequently meet Potsie and Socks. I spent my afternoons listening to the familiar intellectual left-wing tones of Phillip Adams on *Late Night Live* – a 'little wireless program' on ABC Radio

National. I also made regular visits to the Zee Book Exchange – an oasis where I could get away from what I originally got away from.

One day, I went busking at the Nimbin Market with a Tibetan singing bowl and a girl named Fairee, and before we got asked to move on the basis of 'sonic attack', I had an interesting conversation with a stereotypically-Australian eight-year-old wearing an Akubra hat.

"Where ya from mate?" he was asking.

"Scotland," I replied.

"Aw, awa' an suck mah bawb, ya wee fanny!" he suddenly exclaimed.

I laughed at his fluency of braw patter. Turns out he played a lot of online multi-player video games where Scots gamers like to congregate, and he had picked up the lingo from them…

So, yes. Life was, for the most part, decent indeed.

April 14 2015 – Gungas

Hello. I'm still alive. This is not a test.

I've paid for some Internet for once, so unfortunately, I'll be online more often...

Things are holding steady here in the Bin. The meth dealer across the valley has stopped abusing his kids - he's bought them a dirt bike to make up for it... Sigh.

Oh, and I'M NOT FAT ANYMORE! I've figured I've lost between 7 and 10 stone since I arrived in Australia. Several months working outdoors under the Australian sun have left me a tanned, hairy bag of bones and muscle. Coincidently, there are so many girls checking me out at the pool...

The temperature's finally reasonable. It gets to around 26 in the daytime, but drops below 10 at night. Good thing too – I was bamboo-cutting for 6 hours the other day with a bunch of groovy people in exchange for a MardiGrass crew pass – that was fun!

The only thing bugging me is that it's going to be costly for me to get to Berneray this year – Citylink wants to charge me £42 each way from Glasgow to Uig! Relax guys – I'm still coming up!

I've had to watch my finances for a bit – last month my total expenditure came to just $20 (about £10 or so), and it would have been half that if I didn't buy a T-shirt on 'fire sale' discount at the revitalised Bringabong. Good thing too, considering where I'm going...

People sometimes ask me whether I'm going to go to New Zealand/Bali/Thailand after Australia. Regrettably, I'm not going to any of these places this time. Where I am going however, is Malaysia (a state where hippies are illegal), then Brunei (a state where alcohol is illegal), then Dubai (again), then I'll probably be home sometime in June, ready for my yearly trip to Eigg.

See you all in a few(ish) weeks!

A Random Online Conversation with Hamish

"I'm at a cafe in Nimbin, and they're playing LCD Soundsystem's 45:33 part 3!"

"Wanna Skype?"

"Nah – connection's too shite. I'm here because AirAsia X just fucked with me. They cancelled my flight to Malaysia. They have offered me a full refund, though, so I'm going to use it to fly from the Gold Coast instead of Sydney. Shit happens."

"So you'll get your connections back to the UK all the same? I forgot to say how awesome it was that 45:33 was playing, did you have anything to do with that?"

"No, they just played it... Also, I just watched a skin-flick called *9 Songs*, and Franz Ferdinand appear as themselves in it... You've gotta check it out man!"

"I must check out that film... Also, I met Seasick Steve yesterday and it happened to be Record Store Day, damn he throws an amazing gig for an OAP!"

"You met Seasick Steve?! Excellent! But you never met and out-poeted Daevid Allen..."

"Lewis was there and out-DIY guitared Steve – he told him how he once made a guitar out of a walking stick and other random shit. Anyways, I'm off to a new one-day festival happening on Arran tomorrow."

"Deoch an Dorus? Lewis told me about it..."

April 24 2015 - Gungas

A date for your diaries, ladies and gentlemen...
On Tuesday the 28th of April, if you tune in to Nim-FM from around 20:00 AEST (11:00 BST), you just might hear a familiar voice discussing music...
(If you have problems connecting to the Internet broadcast on the Nim-FM website, use a proxy...)
That is all.

April 28 2015 – Nim-FM Studios

I am live on Nim-FM. I repeat, I AM ON NIM-FM!!!

(Ah, yes. *The Magic Carpet: Adventures in Communication* with David Peace One Love and – for a few weeks – Scott from Scotland. One of the finest things I did in Australia was get on the community radio and play music that people wanted to hear. I started with Fatboy Slim, moved on to Hawkwind, Kraftwerk, Kyuss and Amon Düül II amongst many other purveyors of actual music, and would end the night with some of Tangerine Dream's finest Berlin School. It wouldn't be the last time that I would get to be on Nim-FM – by the time that day rolled around, some were calling me the John Peel of Nimbin...)

A Random Online Conversation with Hamish

"Get Nim-FM on – I'm broadcasting LIVE!!! And I've mentioned you at least once..."

"I'm trying to get it. I hope you have a recording of your broadcast?"

"No idea..."

"Get one! Put it on that mp3 stick you got from that Office Works place or your iPhone, and I can hear it in a few weeks."

"I'm using my iPhone for other things..."

"Well, ask the station for a copy. Just find a way!"

A few minutes later and I was playing a the slowed-down version of Thriller, which Hamish had introduced me to some months earlier…

"Right, I'm tuned in… I LOVE YOU! Haha! Have you played any Beefheart yet?"

"Not yet…"

"Right now, I'm moonwalking in my kitchen in super slow motion! You realise your probably the first person ever to play Thriller slowed down on the radio, don't you?"

"Got a message for the people of Nimbin?"

"Yeah - they're radio's actually worth listening to, unlike over here!"

"Well, the unofficial motto of Nim-FM is 'All Other Stations Are Shit!'"

Another few minutes…

"Fantastic, Scott! I'd love to hear a bit of Beefheart later on – I've had Moonlight on Vermont stuck in my head all morning!"

Another few minutes…

"Right, that's it stuck in your head for the next week!"

"No, that's it stuck in my head forever! 'Come out to show 'em, gimme that old time religion!'"

By this time, David Peace One Love and I were discussing a popular and sensitive topic; the impending execution of Myuran Sukumaran and Andrew Chan – the two Australians on death row in Indonesia for drug-trafficking as part of the Bali Nine. As we discussed their impending demise and the reaction across Australia, Hamish sent in a 'listener's comment':

"'I think Death penalty is a crazy thing, if you think of the way it can encourage some crimes to become a thrill-seeking addiction. As risking your neck is an additive behaviour this is especially prevalent in the U.S. System.' Hamish, if you're going to send in comments to the station, structure your sentences, mate!"

"He's got a fair point, though," David Peace One Love commented. "People would do this sort of thing just for the adrenaline rush. If you remove the prohibition, you remove the demand."

"Couldn't agree more with you guys," Hamish responded. "What is deemed as criminal behaviour is always a result of past trauma or, in non-destructive cases, simply the result of seeing past the plastic corrupt laws which often make so little sense. The former group – murderers, rapists etc – should be helped to understand their crimes and given the chance to live the full human experience rather than being pointlessly punished and not learning anything."

Hamish and I continued to talk online as the music and chat kept going live on air.

"And talking of songs before their time, listen to Beefheart's 'Telephone', where he basically describes modern smartphones and directly referenced Twitter: 'And I strangled and I ripped the cord, and I saw the bone, and I heard these tweetin' things, 'n twinkling lights, 'n there was nobody home. Where are all those nerve endings coming out of the bone? Telephone! Telephone!"

"Cool. Playing 'Kingdom' by Callum now..."

"Amazing – I just phoned Callum while it was on!"

I played John Cooper Clarke's 'Beasley Street', dedicating the track to one of my fellow Live Poets from the jungles of Lillian Rock.

"Watch *Shy Bairns Get Nowt*," Hamish messaged. "It captures that same northern English poverty. And talking of John Cooper Clarke, have you ever listened to the Beefheart inspired punk band The Fall? They're from the same parts and time as John Cooper Clarke and focus on similar themes of working class poverty."

I moved onto the Neu! track 'Hero.'

"Oh, and as for punk, I reckon it was invented about five different times, which is why it became such a thing. The Stooges, The Monks, Neu! and a few others came up with the principals. Actually, I could argue that the first punk was George Orwell as his simplistic rebellious writing style is very punk. But I do love this Neu! track!

"One day, I'm going to introduce you to Calum Paterson," I correctly prophesied. "I know him from Berneray, but he lives near you in Glasgow. He's into the same shit as both of us – he's been trying to get me into The Fall for months."

"If you want to get into The Fall, listen to their song 'I Am Damo Suzuki' – it sounds like a Can song on more drugs than normal, flirting with gothic punk."

Time really flew that evening, and soon one in the morning had rolled around. Alas, our collective plea earlier in the evening, along with the then-trending Twitter hashtag #IStandForMercy did little to change President Joko Widodo's mind. Sukumaran and Chan were executed on the twenty-ninth of April 2015 at 00:25 Indonesia Central Time. Their funerals were held just over a week later, and the MardiGrass festival started with a two-minutes silence for not only them, but also the other victims of the so-called War on Drugs.

The First Moments of MardiGrass

MardiGrass rolled around like a stoned hippie knocking over an octobong. As I listened to Nim-FM, which was playing a psytrance song laced with *Futurama* samples to celebrate the coming of the yearly cannabis harvest festival, I donned my kilt and jester's hat, ready for the greatest freakout of my life.

Unfortunately, the rain pissed from the sky. And pissed. And pissed some more. It broke briefly – the first was just long enough for me to visit Potsie and Socks at the car park in town.

"Happy MardiGrass, Scott!" Potsie grinned.

"Happy MardiGrass – the fuck's a giraffe doing over there?"

"What giraffe? Are you stoned, bru?"

"Yes, but that's not the point – there's a fucking giraffe standing over there!"

And sure enough, sauntering through the car park, was a young girl on her way to school in a giraffe onesie. Evidently, the Nimbin School was having a nonuniform day in celebration of, or at least solidarity with, the MardiGrass festival. Socks, forgoing her sheepdog training, wandered over for a sniff.

"I wonder what the kids will be learning about today," I mused.

"My guess is that they'll learn that cannabis is a beneficial plant that shouldn't have been made illegal," Potsie replied.

By now, the sky was about to break again, so I bid Potsie adieu and made a beeline for the shelter of the HEMP Embassy.

May 1 2015 – Nimbin

Ye gods. I waited six years to go to the MardiGrass festival. I put in six hours of work cutting bamboo for one of the stages in exchange for a crew pass. And on the first day, it rained so hard that the State Emergency Service advised people in the Northern Rivers region (i.e. me) to stay indoors.
Still, at least I briefly met some of the feature speakers from the 'Hemposium'. Oh, and the rain let up enough for the Mayday Rally – that was fun!

(We marched on the cop shop from the other side of the road – 'a distance of four-point-two-zero metres' according to local legend Max Stone, aka 'Big Bong'…)

A Random Conversation from a Secret Location during MardiGrass

We had regrouped at the table after the threat of an imminent police raid and the sudden appearance of a Prime7 news team. Collapsing back down onto the sofas, we began to pass around bongs filled with BC Bud and Blue Cheese, and vaporisers filled with some of the most potent hash oil known to man. Outside, the same Hare Krishnas I had met in Byron Bay back in March were singing and dancing over the cacophony of backpackers, faux-hippies, POLITE volunteers, police officers and the Cypress Hill tracks blasting out of our stereo system like there was no tomorrow.

"So tell me about Britain, mate," one of the numerous drug dealers was saying to me.

"Like what?"

"Well, you know Wales? Is it part of England?"

I sighed.

"If you went there and said that, they would pump you full of Viagra and make you fuck a sheep!"

"Ah."

Silence.

"So, where did you say you were from anyways?"

"Scotland."

"Really? You don't sound very Scottish…"

"Well, my dad's from Lancashire and my mother's from Yorkshire. I grew up in Scotland, though."

"Ah. I've always wanted to know – is Yorkshire a city?"

I sighed.

"If you went there and said that, they would pump you full of Viagra and make you fuck a sheep!"

"Ah, okay."
Silence.

May 4 2015 – Nimbin

The best way to experience MardiGrass – volunteer. It was one hell of a party, plus I got to help carry the Big Joint through Nimbin!
Oh, and I'm probably going to be on Nim-FM again on Tuesday from around 2000 AEST (1100 BST) – turns out my last performance got universal acclaim...

(That night, me and a bunch of my friends got together and did a jam session live on the radio which I later uploaded to YouTube – searching for the Yellow Crystal Warrior Session should help you find it if you fancy a gander...
I would have one final crack on Nim-FM on May 12, the day before I left...)

A Random Online Conversation with My Mother

"Hi Scott. Sorry I missed you on the radio. Will you be bringing a copy of your interview home with you? Thanks for the pictures. Is the white truck the one you've been driving or sleeping in? Glad you've been enjoying yourself. Take care and see you soon."

"Actually, that was the second time I was on the radio, and my third time will be next week. And yes, I'll be bringing home copies of all of my shows! The truck is what I've been driving – I reckon I've done many thousands of kilometres now... If you're at home next Tuesday at 11am your time, you can hear my third show!"

Preparing to Leave Paradise

"Gina?"
We were in Office Works once again; Gina working on her art. I was working on something too.
"Yes?"
"I need to ask you a question, and I would like you to take your time in answering it."
She looked up from her artwork.
I took a deep breath.
"I've been working at your place for eight months now, and it has been an utterly fantastic experience. However, I admit that it's not all been plain sailing, especially in recent times, and I'll freely admit that some of these faults are mine and mine alone. Let's assume that, in five years or so, I have learnt from my mistakes, and am a much better human being than I am today."
"Okay, I can definitely believe that."
"Now, think carefully about what I am about to say. Sleep on it before you give me an answer, if you so like. Would you like to see me return to Australia?"
A smile crept over her face.
"YES!"

"Okay, well then, will you be my reference if I apply for a second-year visa a few years from now?"

"Of course, my dear friend!"

Now, an Australian working holiday visa is a once-in-a-lifetime thing – literally, and the visa is only valid for one year. However, by working in some postcode areas for at least three months (such as the one covering Lismore and Nimbin) doing something related to agriculture, construction or mining, I would be entitled to a second visa. As Gina returned to her artwork, I began to fill out some forms, cross-checking them with the latest rules posted by the Australian government on the internet.

Good thing I did.

"Oh, SHIT!" I exclaimed.

"What is it?"

"Listen to this – 'As of May the 1st 2015, WWOOFing will no longer entitle you to a second-year visa!'"

I shook my head in despair, chuckling slightly at my misfortune.

"Eight months…and they killed it just a few days just as I was about to leave Australia!"

"So, what will you do?"

"Pass it off as either building or gardening – that is assuming I ever come back. I still haven't made up my mind about that – I was just trying to keep my options open!"

"Ah."

We filled out the forms anyway, just in case. My opinion of the Australian government at an all-time low, I was thankful that it was a few short days until I would be on the plane home.

May 13 2015 – Gold Coast International Airport, Queensland

I HAVE LEFT NIMBIN, AND AM SLOWLY HEADING FOR ARRAN.
Now that I have your attention, I have left Nimbin, and am slowly heading for Arran. It's been one hell of a journey, even though I've barely left Nimbin, and it's not over yet. I'm going to spend some time in Kuala Lumpur, then Brunei, then the Emirates before returning to the UK.
I'll see you all soon!

Interlude – AirAsia X

They are generally crap. But it's still one of the best budget airlines in the world…

I was originally going to fly from Sydney to Kuala Lumpur, but they cancelled (and refunded, thankfully) my flight. Being in Nimbin at the time, I decided to fly from Goldie instead.

Once again crossing the Queensland border in the *Albino Submarine*, Gina deposited me at the terminal, hugged me one last time and left me to my own devices. I spent a few hours in the company of an Indian student named Robin who was flying back to Kolkata via Kuala Lumpur, chatting with him when I wasn't reading a copy of Raymond E. Feist's *Silverthorn* or falling asleep.

A few hours later, after procuring a burger from Hungry Jack's, clearing immigration and getting my water confiscated ("I filled it airside!"), I found myself in the sky over central Australia. I was perched on a tiny seat with less digital entertainment than legroom, sandwiched in-between a Bogan and a cheerful-looking Malaysian man who otherwise kept silent. The Bogan used every opportunity available to demand copious amounts of wine from the Kraftwerk impersonators who served as stewards and stewardesses on our flight, who by and large had next-to-no command of the English language. Presumably, though, they would save our arses if the Airbus A330-300 went down in the Java Sea.

I do recommend one thing; the cheap and filling *nasi lemak* which I finally got after the stewardess completely mangled the pronunciation of my name ("My. Name. Is. Scott. Harwood. And. I. Pre. Ordered. The. *Pak. Nasser's. Nasi. Lemak.*"). Maybe she was surprised that the white devil didn't pre-order the roast chicken...

I took a sleeping pill that Gina had given me, and stuck on a Goa trance mix on my Walkman. Soon, it was four in the morning, and the plane was descending on a spot of land about an hour by road from Malaysia's former capital.

A Random Online Conversation with My Friend Lewis

"IMMA FIRING MALAYSIA!! BWAAA!"
"lol."
"Seriously though, this country is bloody cheap. It costs £3 for a return bus ticket from the airport to the city, 40 pence for a decent meal, 4 quid for a night in a backpacker's hostel..."
"Ha! That's not bad."
"Shame I'm leaving tomorrow. Oh yeah, and everyone speaks English!"
"Awesome, shame you have to go so soon."
"Look on the bright side - I'll be back in Scotland in a few days!"
"Nice!"
"It's 6am on Thursday here!"
"You're from the future."
"Still got 6 hours before I can check in to my hostel, so I'm using the electricity and WiFi at the airport. And yes – I'm in the future. Problem?"
"Try and create a temporal paradox."
"Too tired, man..."
"Ha! Did you meet any girls on your travels? Did you kiss anyone?"
"Not in this reality. Though tell me this – have you ever had a lucid dream where all 5 of your major senses are working? Because I had one back on the 1st of March."
"Scott! That was a perfect opportunity! You had an exotic accent out there. Girls love that sort of thing."
"I still haven't kissed or shagged a girl in this reality. But I know how it fucking feels."
"I had a dream like that the other night."
"?!"
"I'm not going to go into details, Scott."
"By the way, Australia is a very sexist place, and it works both ways."

"Really, in what way?"

"Well, let's say that a guy 'roots' a girl. In the morning, the girl often tells the guy to wash her car or do something else that's manly on the sole basis that he's a guy. Common story, at least that's what my friend Thorsten tells me. To which his response would have been something like 'And you're a girl, so on that basis, get in the kitchen and make me some breakfast, bitch!' Not seriously of course, just making a point."

"Ha!"

"Also, Australia is an unbelievably racist place. They still have a form of apartheid."

"Have what?"

"Apartheid."

"I shall Google it..."

"'facepalm' 'double facepalm'"

"Ah right. Seriously?"

"Yep."

"Sorry Scott, but this really isn't the best time."

"Yeah, it's like 23:20 your time or something..."

"Yep. I'm kind of doing things virtually with a female friend as well."

"Ah."

"Sorry..."

"No matter. I'll be seeing you soon anyway!"

"See you soon."

May 14 2015 – Kuala Lumpur International Airport

Hmm. 4G WiFi by Yes. Prog rock seems to have come a long way in this part of the universe...

Nasi Lemak Galore! (One Night in Malaysia)

"Even with our cultural differences, everyone sits down in the morning — or throughout the day — to tuck into a plate of nasi lemak. With that one dish, we're truly united despite our differences."
-    The Malay Mail

On the motorway coming into Kuala Lumpur. Spot the Petronas Twin Towers...

Malaysia was always one of those places I had no desire to visit but would end up going there anyway. I disembarked from the plane at around four in the morning, picked my way through the mass of Indians sleeping on the floor, and found myself in a lengthy, but civil, queue for immigration. Eventually, I made my way to the front of the queue, and was fingerprinted by a beaming lady in a hijab who had obviously drunk too much coffee.

"Would it help if I pressed down on the scanner harder?" I asked.

She chuckled at my pathetic attempt at a dad joke, and warmly welcomed me into Malaysia.

After avoiding the taxi touts after immigration and customs that one immediately expects after landing at an Asian airport, I withdrew a few hundred *ringgit* from a nearby ATM and made my way to the main airport bus station via a short trip on the *KLIA Ekspres*, being too cheap to pay for the train into Kuala Lumpur itself. I mean, why spend the equivalent of fourteen pounds for a return train ticket when you can spend three on a bus with a much better view?

Killing some time before sunrise, I spent a few hours on the airport's free WiFi, occasionally glancing up to watch a glorified golf cart shuttle the well-off to and from the Sama-Sama Hotel. Finally, I decided it was time to make my way into the city. I meandered through a short tunnel and emerged in the airport's bus station where, thankfully for my thirsty self, there was a small shop selling cheap cans of aloe vera juice and coconut water. But even in the sanctuary of the shop, I was still being accosted by touts.

"You want bus ticket?"

"Nope."

"Oh, you're just buying drinks."

"Yep." Now fuck off, I thought.

He had the decency to fuck off, leaving me to purchase several tasty beverages at a ridiculously cheap price. Striding past the touts, I made my way to the legitimate *Kaunter Tiket Bas*, and a few short minutes later I found myself on a plush Airport Coach that was substantially more comfortable than the plane I flew in on. I chuckled as the driver lit a cigarette underneath a *Dilarang Merokok* (No Smoking) sign on the station concourse, knowing that the next thirty-six hours or so were going to be a blast.

I chatted briefly with a Dutch-born Australian couple sitting opposite me who had just got off a flight from Sydney, before settling back into my seat and sticking Edgar Froese's *Epsilon in Malaysian Pale* on – it seemed appropriate considering where I was. As I did, the poster boy for the tobacco industry of Western Peninsula Malaysia boarded the bus, and soon I found myself on the *Yang di-Pertuan Agong's* Highway, heading for the beating heart of Malaysia's former capital city.

It was my first time landside in Asia and, true to my presumptions at the airport, I was loving every second. This was despite the fact that I was on a motorway that resembled the M62 in England, albeit with lusher tropical vegetation, magnificent mosques, commercial palm oil plantations, near-naked Nepali guest-workers labouring in rice paddies, and skyscrapers being built next to said paddy fields. It dawned on me that I was passing Putrajaya – Malaysia's administrative capital.

Here's a random fact about Malaysia. The sole official and national language is Malay, even though only 50.1% of the population are Malays; the rest largely hold Chinese or Indian languages as their native tongue. As a result of British pillage and rape (read: colonisation), and the fact that the Malaysian government discourages the use of non-standard Malay dialects used by the 49.9%, most Malaysian nationals are conversant in English – or at least *Manglish*. Nevertheless, I was surprised when the bus passed an English-language billboard for a private primary school ("Giving your children the best start in life!") with a cute little cartoon of all these kiddies playing together, complete with girls wearing hijabs in this largely Islamic country.

I especially loved it when we hit a traffic jam and every single traffic rule was immediately violated. The four-lane highway became at least seven. The motorcycle lane (not a hard shoulder…) became, simply, a lane. Stone-faced *eksekutifs* in Porsche Cayennes mingled shoulder-to-shoulder with families and commuters in Protons and Peroduas; the drivers of which having one driving hand on their telephones, the other in their bowls of *nasi lemak*, their knees doing the steering work. Police cars escorted school and works buses through the bedlam. Sooner than I had expected, though, the bus arrived at KL Sentral, where I caught the driverless metro one stop to Pasar Seni in Kuala Lumpur's Chinatown. Admiring my surroundings, I checked into the Hotel China Town 2 – a youth hostel with air-con, excellent WiFi, clean Western loos and the best showers I would encounter since the pub in Cowra. In other words, after literally shitting in a hole in the ground covered by a toilet seat for the best part of eight months, heaven.

I smiled at the girl at the reception.

"Hello! I'd like to check in, please!"

"Okay, your name, *tuan*?"

"Scott Harwood."

"Okay. Do you have your passport?"

"Well, let's put it this way. If I didn't, I wouldn't be allowed into Malaysia!" She chuckled.

"I suppose not!"

The only other Westerner at the hostel was an Austrian man named Klaus who faultlessly apologised for his 'bad' English; the other guests being either Chinese or Thai. I didn't spend much time chatting, though; being in a country where everything was roughly four times cheaper than in Australia, the world was my oyster. I spent the rest of that day feasting in local hawker centres – where I got the biggest portions of pork I'd ever seen for just six *ringgit* (at the time, about one pound) – and the local 7/11. Of course, being a white guy who is over six feet tall and built like a brick shithouse, I stood out from the crowd. And thanks to Malaysia's multi-ethnic, multi-lingual population, I was being bombarded by hawkers who were shouting in every Asian honorific under the sun:

"Taxi, *sahib*?"

"You like, *tuan*?"

"Come to my stall, *babu*! You want DVD?"

I was mildly surprised – almost glad even – that people noticed me. The few other Western tourists in the area were armed with backpacks and giant bulbous cameras round their necks. I, on the other hand, was meandering around wearing a Neu! t-shirt and military-grade trousers; in other words, the standard gear I would wear for a hike up Beinn Bharrain back home. Nevertheless, a great many salespeople tried and failed to sell me crap clothing and illegal pornography.

Looking north along Jalan Pentaling

I fell asleep at around eight in the evening, and was woken up by two Chinese people shouting outside my room a few hours later. I couldn't get back to sleep, so after testing Malaysia's internet firewall with a free proxy website, I watched *Ren and Stimpy* on my phone until I had to go back to the airport and check in for my next flight to Brunei.

Now, Malaysia has its bad sides, such as freedom of speech issues and the death penalty for possession of cannabis. But I have to say, the people are amazing, the food is out of this world, and I spent less than twenty pounds in-between flights. And that was for everything – the bus there and back, all my food and a private room. Well, it was meant to be a two-person dorm, but my Thai roommate moved out...

The first thing I saw when I left the Hotel Chinatown 2 was a rat which resembled Templeton from *Charlotte's Web*, having the girth and velocity of a medium-sized dog. Presumably, it too had been feasting on the rich leftovers of the many street-hawkers. Nevertheless, the sight of something so fast and bulbous didn't put me off my food; after obtaining some *nasi lemak* at the 7/11, I made my way back to the Pasar Seni metro station. Returning to the airport by way of the metro to Sentral and then the Airport Coach, the sounds of Amon Düül II pulsing in my ears, I grabbed another cheap platter of *nasi lemak* from the food court and checked in for my Royal Brunei Airlines flight to that world-famous megapolis known as Bandar Seri Begawan.

"And you're booked through to London Heathrow with us!" twittered the effeminate bloke behind the desk. "Don't worry about your bags when you get to Brunei or Dubai, they will meet you on arrival in London."

"Hopefully…" I smiled.

He giggled, and immediately placed me in an exit row on my first leg to Brunei, gave me two seats to myself on the second leg to Dubai, and an entire row of three seats on the last leg to London.

Royal Brunei Airlines is one of those halal airlines – no alcohol or pork is served as per Sharia law and they play a prayer to Allah to 'guide us on this journey and relieve the burden we have placed on our families by our absence' over the TV system. As the only Westerner on the plane from KL to Brunei, I should have been wierded out by the rest of the passengers murmuring the Takbīr in the cabin, which by now was resembling a Black Sabbath concert judging by the headbanging going on, but I wasn't. Because I'm a pretty weird guy. Also, I was too tired to care.

Stupidly, I forgot to pack any food in KL, and I was still hungry after the in-flight meal. Thankfully, my Buddhist seatmate – who didn't have the gumption to order the vegetarian food when he booked his ticket – offered me some decent meaty portions. Luckily, he didn't slip any poison into it, and I was content for a few more hours.

After about an hour, the chief stewardess cheerily announced that we were coming in to land at Bandar Seri Begawan International Airport. Not wavering from her upbeat attitude, she announced that Brunei imposes Sharia law, and as such, possession of narcotics carried the death penalty in Brunei. Thing is, I had tiny metal bong on me – a souvenir from Gina – and it was a wee bit dirty despite the fact that I disinfected it five times prior to leaving Nimbin...

As only one of two transit passengers off that flight – the other being a Filipino lady heading for the Gulf – the bored security staff found my disassembled bong.

"What is this?" one enquired.

"It's my water pipe," I replied.

"What is it used for?"

"Smoking tobacco."

He handed it back to me, and pointed the way towards my onward flight to Dubai. I briefly visited the toilet to wipe the shit stain from my pants, and settled in for the six-hour layover.

Other than the adrenaline rush at security, my brief stay in Brunei was boring. At the time, there was nowhere selling food in the airport, but there was a mosque that played the call-to-prayer and the resulting sermon over the airport PA system, which had the tone of a kazoo that had just been flushed down the toilet.

I entertained myself by chatting with a Kiwi lass who taught English to migrant oil-workers, and using the WiFi – subsequently finding out that the blues legend B.B. King had died that day.

I also chatted with Hamish for a bit.

"I'm currently in BSB – going to board the flight to London in 25 mins!"

"BSB?"

"Bandar Seri Begawan, the capital of Brunei. You know, for a country with a lot of petrodollars, their airport is a wee bit shit – there's nowhere selling food, and just one little trinket shop. Although Royal Brunei gave me two seats, an exit row and a bloody good curry!"

"I thought you boarded hours ago, or was that the plane to Brunei?"

"That was the Brunei plane, yeah."

"Ah, so you were in Kuala Lumpur a few days."

"Yep – it was cool! Remind me to go back there one day..."

"How conservative is Malaysia for a South East Asian country?"

"The state religion is Islam, so possession of cannabis carries the death penalty, and you see these massive mosques everywhere. Pork and booze are OK and socially acceptable, though."

"Cool, is there like a similar church ratio over here?"

"Hard to say. The country's around 65% Islam, most of the rest are Buddhists, Hindus or Christians. They allow for freedom of religion."

"Oh, I see. Nice country."

"It's very multicultural at least."

"Is it the UAE you refuel in? Or Saudi?"

"It's the UAE."

"Good."

"As I was saying, the Malays make up just over 50% of the population. Most of the rest are Chinese, Indian or indigenous."

"I bet their version of UKIP loves that! Have you slept yet?"

"I haven't slept since 1am..."

"1am whose time?"

"Mine."

"What time is it now?"

"1818."

"Ah I see so you'll sleep in Saudi."

"I'm not going to Saudi. Shit, my flight's about to be called and I need a piss..."

"UAE then! Get on the plane!"

"I've got some pills, so I'll sleep on the Dubai-London leg."

"Well I'd best leave you now. We'll talk when you get to London."

The one photo I took when I was in Brunei…

The Royal Brunei Airlines Boeing 787 was a world away. I had so much room and good food, the hijab-clad stewardesses kept bringing me the surplus juice from Business Class, and to top it all off it was 'Sci-Fi Season' on the entertainment system. I would discover the latter sometime into the journey – in the meantime, I took a second sleeping pill that Gina had provided me, and slept until the henna-clad lady sharing the row of seats with me lightly shook me awake so she could get past me to the shitter.

The plane had a layover in Dubai for an hour and a half, where we were all made to disembark and pass through security as the plane was refuelled and towed from the arrival area to the departure area. Having passed through Dubai on my way out to Australia, I knew the whole rigmarole; security check (where they failed to find my bong), a long walk to the gate, and being manually searched and security-wanded by a spotty adolescent before getting on the plane. Although this chap seemed rather friendly.

"How are you doing? Where are you from?"

"Scotland."

"Ah, Scotland! Yes! Good whisky!"

"Aye, that's us!"

He let me keep my (empty) water bottle and my lighter, and I strode back onto the plane as a new code-switching crew were doing the introductory announcements.

"*As-salaam alaeikum, erm, selamat, tuan-tuan dan puan-puan,* ladies and gentlemen, welcome…"

I settled back in my now-empty row, smiling at the prospect of seeing my family and friends for the first time in a year.

After a memorable moment where I listened to '3am Eternal' by The KLF as we were flying over central Europe at three in the morning, I finally got back to London very content indeed! There's only been a few countries where I've been subjected to little more than a brief 'hello' and 'thank you' at immigration. England is one of those countries, or at least Heathrow Airport is. But if you're as weird as I am, you can make these experiences somewhat fun, especially at six in the morning…

"Where have you just come from, sir?" asked the bored border guard.

"Bandar Seri Begawan."

He did a double-take.

"Where?"

"I believe that it's the capital of the Nation of Brunei, the Abode of Peace."

"Ah. Have you been travelling around the region?"

"You could say that…"

He let me in with no further questions.

I should mention at this time that only two people knew that I was coming home at this time – my friends Hamish and Lewis. After getting the Tube back to Victoria, changing at South Kensington en route, I boarded a Megabus back to Glasgow. Ten hours later, I wound up at Hamish's flat; his flat-coat retriever, Bòidheach, was especially excited for not having seen me in a year. The dog's face was expressionless, but his wagging tail and body indicated that he very much recognised a friend that he hadn't seen for so long.

"What are you looking at, you mad bastard?" I asked Bòidheach. "It's like you haven't seen me for a year or something!"

I got into the flat, and Hamish released the dog from his grip. I adopted a tone that I often saw Thorsten use with Rat.

"Yes, it's so exciting isn't it?" I cooed as Bòidheach clambered all over me in the hallway. "Oh yes, your friend's back after so, so long!"

In the end, Bòidheach rolled over onto his back, whereupon I gave his belly a good tickle. At that point, I went into the kitchen and finally took my bags off.

Twenty minutes later, I re-emerged in the hallway to find out that Bòidheach was still rolling around and laughing, and hadn't even noticed I had been gone during that time. He certainly wasn't the thinking monkey's peanut, but damn he was hilarious!

After a night in Glasgow, I made my way home, surprising my family to the desired effect that I had planned for months.

May 18 2015 – Pirnmill

Surprise! I'm back on Arran early! And thus, my first epic trans-global voyage has ended. It is probably correct for me at this time to thank the vast number of people who made my trip what it is. However, I'm not going to name names on the basis that I may miss out some people and, as such, piss them off. So, those of you out there who have assisted me during my journey, both in the UK and Australia, thank you all!
Give me a few days and I'll have my pictures uploaded.

A Random Online Conversation with Callum McPherson

"Hey! I know this is waaay overdue, but just wanted to say thank you for playing my song 'Kingdom' on your radio show! I still haven't heard the recording of the programme (Hamish won't send it to me, gave up on pestering haha) but that's the first time I've ever been on the radio – thought Hamish was pulling my leg at first when he told me!"

"Thanks! Both the versions that you put up were played – the YouTube version was the one I played when I first co-hosted the show, and David Peace One Love (the host – he's following you on SoundCloud now) played the SoundCloud version on his daytime show the next week – I didn't find that out until I got back to Arran! So yep – your music's getting airtime! I'll go and pester Hamish for you about getting a copy of the show… Also, I followed you on SoundCloud – I set up an account so people could download my own stuff for free."

"I didn't realise that – thanks so much! On reflection, I think I prefer the original YouTube version to the SoundCloud version – might make a third, final version that incorporates elements of both... I'm also working on a new version of 'Glory' and hoping to make a music video for it over the summer. Oh, and yes please do pester Hamish, though I believe he is essay-writing over the next few days so perhaps wait till after then, haha!"

A Random Online Message from Gina

"Would love to read anything you have written...how was the trip to the island with the beaches that was passed off as Thailand???...Thorsten is doing triple grandfather duty on the coast ...and there has been some trouble at the reservation with power challengers trying to get rid of Thorsten because they want to develop the place... But Uncle Cecil loves Thorsten and wants him to

stay....I too am staying here FOREVER....I love it.....thank you for protecting me!....and the letters !!!!!...I need to... In fact if you can HELP ME write another letter ...!...We need to write another one to the crazy dog abusing people next door which live next to the screaming child abusing people in that big house across the creek...poor dog sounds like an unhinged gate......Love!....
all the best...do well...have fun...I found a field full of big boulders just like I had pictured in my mind very nearby....I will float them over to complete the picture..."

Musings on Epic Voyage I

My trip to Australia was the first time that I had spent more than three weeks on the road; by and large, it was the best trip I had ever had so far in my life. However, it wasn't all fun and games, as you can deduce from my accounts of being DWBed and hospitalised. During January 2015, you may remember that I left Nimbin for a few weeks, hoping I would be away for a few months. You see, had I stayed in Nimbin longer, it was almost certain that certain rifts would open between Gina and I, much like any other persons kept close together for an extended period of time. But overall, I think it worked out. I forgive Gina for the few bad things she did to me, and I hope she can forgive me for my own naïve transgressions.

Australia itself is an interesting place. It's just a shame that there's so much casual racism, fracking, shit government authorities and oppression of indigenous people. And yet, there's 'mateship', the 'fair go', and the inane ability of many Australians to help out a fellow human in need. And if you ever find yourself in Australia, and you want the latter without so much of the former, then Nimbin is definitely the place to be. I speak from personal experience.

Now, I need to thank a bunch of people for making my first Epic Voyage a roaring success! I didn't name them on social media, so I'm going to try and name them now…

First, I want to thank the Bundjalung Nation for allowing me to visit their great country. They were the traditional and legitimate inhabitants of what we ignorant white devils know as the Northern Rivers region in the past, continue to be in the present, and hopefully will still be in the future.

I also want to thank:
- Thorsten and Rat for providing wisdom when there was none.
- The POLITE/HEMP Embassy crowd for allowing me to come to their meetings and cut bamboo for MardiGrass.
- David Peace One Love for letting me have a decent crack on Nim-FM 102.3.
- Dave, Bonnie, Coco, Luna, and Misha the malamute for being the best neighbours one could hope for.
- David Hallett for his poetry events and expertise.
- The late cosmic revolutionaries Daevid Allen and Gilli Smyth for influencing me over the years, and being really cool when I finally met them. Rest in peace, guys.
- The Thai Food Place in Lismore for some of the best grub I've ever had.
- Tanya and her family, Potsie and Socks, James, Xanda, Terrence, Jethro, Ben, Tamara, William, Hamish the Cool Guy, Kevin, Fisher, Johnny Ganja, Helena, Forest, Aaron, Adam, Willem, Sam, Jet, Andre, Melissa, Jack, Dayne 'Frackman' Pratzky, the business owners of Nimbin, the Nimbin Drumming Circle, the Lunatic Hill Mob and, you know what, virtually everyone else I encountered for being a bunch of really cool guys.

- And most of all, I'd like to thank Gina for putting me up (and putting up with me, and steering me further left, and making me aware of the Skull and Bones Society…) for eight of the greatest months of my life. Very little of this could be done without you, so thank you!

EPIC VOYAGE II: NEPAL

Team 'Unnati A' at Shree Dirgha Pradip Higher Secondary School, Khalte.
Left to right; George Graham, Ram Kafle, Olivia Johnson, Bibek 'Pasa' Maharjan, myself, Aashika Budhathoki.
The building on the left where the children are gathered is an active classroom…

A Man's Gotta Do What A Kathmandu

"I want to try, I want to be me
I want to get high, I want to see
I want to fly, I want to be free…"
- Hawkwind – *Kadu Flyer*

Scotland gives power to Nepali proletariat!

It was September 2015, five months after I had returned from Australia. I was working at the Co-op in Brodick with my parents, and was transferred to the night shift after nearly being sacked during the summer – too many complaints from certain ninnies whose IQs were below that of room temperature. I found the night shift to be much more free and easy, but even as my work picked up, I was still being threatened with remarks that suggested my future employment could well be insecure.

Needless to say, I was pissed off. It didn't help that the Co-op didn't give me the time off to go off on my yearly trip to the isle of Eigg back in June, so I missed out on a good night of sex, drugs and Shooglenifty. So the travel bug biting so hard it was cutting off the essential blood supply to my brain. Again.

One morning, after coming home from work, I was browsing on my phone and an advert appealed to me.

Do you like to travel? Damn skippy.

Do you like to volunteer? Well, I used to volunteer in the ArCaS charity shop of my own volition, so I suppose so.

Would you like to volunteer abroad for three months with all expenses paid? We'll even give you a basic allowance! Where do I sign?

The advert was for a youth-led development agency called Restless Development. It was one of the many development agencies which are part of the International Citizen Service – an overseas volunteering programme for eighteen to twenty-five-year olds which was funded by the British Government's Department for International Development.
I did some more research, and found out that although they mostly worked in Africa, I could also be sent to India or Nepal. They don't look for skills or

qualifications from prospective volunteers – just ambition and willing to travel. So I applied to volunteer.

Armed with nothing but my desire to visit Nepal and India (and prior experience in Australia, and qualifications…), I was summoned to an all-day interview in central London – all travel expenses paid even at this stage in the journey…

"In your opinion, what's your best personal quality?" asked the young lady tasked with interviewing me at the one-to-one stage.

"Stamina."

"Stamina?"

"Aye."

"Why do you say that?"

I leant in close and lowered my voice slightly.

"Because I've just spent twenty-four hours travelling by bus, ferry, train and overnight coach from an offshore island in Scotland to get here, and I'm still reasonably fit for interview…"

When the interviewer burst out into a fit of laughter that pretty much sent her into orgasm, I knew I was going to be sent somewhere, but alas, we still had the group activities to do.

During the group activities that day, I was still feeling just as bold as I was during the one-to-one interview. We were tasked with building a bridge that could support the weight of a stapler, yet be tall enough to let a stapler pass underneath. I took one look at the instruction sheet, and took off my shoes.

"What are you doing?" someone asked.

"See this sheet? It doesn't say on it that we ONLY have to use the materials provided. When you're out in the middle of nowhere and you're in a spot of bother, you have to be resourceful. Now take off your shoes – we're building a bridge!"

I later found out that I came in the top five of the thirty or so people there for the interview. I presume that the interviewers must have looked down at my shoes.

I tied the interview in with a bus trip to Amsterdam, which was a rather jolted affair involving a bus fresh off a commuter service from Kent, a young driver who had never driven on the European continent before, a scare in Dover after it transpired that a passenger had checked in but failed to board the bus in London ("Is there a Mohammed Abdul Touré on board? No? Oh, shit…"), an unscheduled rest break just outside Ghyvelde in northern France after the driver failed to switch off the tachograph whilst we were on the ferry, and myself having to provide navigation for the driver around the housing schemes of the Dutch city of Breda ("My GPS has failed and I've got the map upside-down!"). But that's another story.

Whilst on my way home from Amsterdam and staying at my friend Hamish's flat in Glasgow, I found out that I was selected to go to Nepal in January 2016 with twenty other restless young individuals, whom I would later meet and get to know at a pre-trip weekend briefing in York.

Unless you've been living under a rock, you'll know that Nepal has more than its fair share of problems. Nepal is one of the poorest countries in the world, with around half of the population living on fewer than two pictures of George Washington's head per day. The infrastructure leaves a lot to be desired – more than one-third of Nepal's population live at least a two-hour-walk away from the nearest all-season road. In many places, the electricity is only operational for a few hours a day.

Oh yes, and an earthquake measuring 7.8 on the Richter scale struck Nepal on the twenty-fifth of April 2015, killing nearly nine-thousand people, injuring twenty-two-thousand others and causing an estimated ten billion dollars-worth of damage. Half of Nepal's gross domestic product.

The Restless Development placement I was on would be the first to go to Nepal since the earthquake. Well, I like a challenge.

Some of us would become ill. Some of us would become homesick. Some of us would never assimilate into the local culture. But all of us would make friends that would last forever. We would be made to feel as family. Some of us would even find love in a strange kind of way, or at least they think they would.

What you are about to read is what I went through over the three months of the voyage…

January 4 2016 – on a train to from Ardrossan to Glasgow

I HAVE LEFT ARRAN, AND AM HEADING FOR NEPAL!
Now that I have your attention, I have left Arran and am heading for Nepal! It's been several months of blood, toil, tears, sweat and failure to properly document my previous oriental escapade, but I'm finally heading back east thanks to the combined efforts of many generous people :)
I'll be staying a night in Glasgow, then getting a night bus to London tomorrow in time to get an evening flight to Delhi on Wednesday. Yes – I know Delhi's in India, but I have to go there to head onwards to Kathmandu...
See you in three months!

Anti-Cunt Navigation

When I finally arrived in London, I was once again pissed off with the authoritarian snootiness of the staff on the sleeper bus and vowed never to use it again. I would later jump for joy when I found out that the sleeper bus would be withdrawn in May 2017…

Before I made my way to the airport, I was going to head out to Chorleywood to visit my aunt. However, it was only six in the morning, so I decided to go for breakfast at the Golden Arches at Victoria first. Hungry, lagged and bleary-eyed from the bus journey, I took my place in the queue.

"So are you just gonna ignore me?"

I looked to my right, and saw an American in better physical condition than me pestering for money.

"I only have US dollars."

'This is Victoria,' I thought. 'Every second building is a fucking exchange office. Also, if you're desperate for food, go skipping behind a supermarket like I would do…'

I wasn't in the mood or financial gain to pander to his idiocy. So I responded how I usually deal with idiots these days. Socially. In broken Gàidhlig.

"*Chan eil Beurla agam.*" (I don't speak English.)

"What?"

"*Chan eil…* I no speak much English."

"So what language do you speak?"

"*Dè?*" (What?)

"What. Is. Your. Language?"

"Um, *a' Gàidhlig. A bheil Gàidhlig agad?*" (Gàidhlig. Have you the Gàidhlig?)

"Uh…"

"*Chan eil? Chan eil Gàidhlig agad?*" (No? No Gàidhlig?)

By then, he was backing away, leaving me free to whisper my order in English to a bemused cashier. Alas, it wouldn't be the last time I would have to deal with morons in Gàidhlig on this trip.

After I finished my breakfast in peace, and witnessed the fool going through every person in the queue begging them to buy him breakfast, I caught a Tube train along the Victoria Line to King's Cross-St. Pancras. Needless to say, a big beardy bastard with a rucksack should not be travelling on the Tube at rush hour, but I did so anyway. I stood out from the peak-time commuters, some of whom were in all likelihood scared shitless by my presence. I mean, everyone still remembers 7/7…

At King's Cross, I transferred onto a near-empty Metropolitan Line train for the long trip out to Chorleywood; the sounds of 808 State's *Newbuild* blasting through my in-ear buds as we raced a Jubilee Line train near Swiss Cottage. However, when I got out there, I was greeted by some sad, but not totally unexpected, news…

January 6 2016 – my aunt's house in Chorleywood

Hi everyone.

It is with great sadness that I have to announce that my grandmother, Francesca Margarita Maria (Frances) Harwood – whom some of you know as the founder of the charity ArCaS – recently passed away in her sleep at Lamlash Hospital after a short battle with cancer. My family and I are coping well, and would like to thank our friends, relatives and other associates for their continued support during this difficult time.

Regarding my impending trip to Nepal, I have decided to continue with it. One of my grandmother's final lucid requests to me was to carry on with the trip regardless, and as such I'm going to honour her request. After all, compared to family affairs, undertaking a development project in an underdeveloped nation is for the greater good in the world. Besides, I raised nearly £1000 on the premise that I would head out to Nepal…

Again, thank you all for your continued support. My family and I really appreciate it.

The Deranged Flight of Merlin Mahadeva
and His Marginal Detention in Delhi

"No hurry, no worry."
- An Indian road sign, possibly the motto of the airport security in Delhi also…

Of course, it was a sad day. But my grandmother wanted me to do this thing, and I was going to honour her request. After all, she had devoted much of her life to helping others in need – it was only fitting that I should do the same at this point. Besides, if I pulled out, I would in all likelihood regret it for the rest of my life.

I ate a beef sandwich that my aunt had prepared – the last time I would eat beef until April for fairly obvious reasons – and made my way back to the station. Catching a Chiltern train to Harrow-on-the-Hill, I transferred back onto the Tube to reach the Piccadilly Line at Rayners Lane. Here, I boarded another Tube train and was almost immediately forced off it because there was a signal failure at the station. Three minutes later, the station dosgbody had duct-taped the faulty sixties-era wiring back into place, and I re-boarded the train after it had pointlessly reversed a hundred metres up the line and came back again. Eventually, I reached Acton Town, where I transferred onto a Heathrow-bound Tube train and disembarked at the wrong station – Terminals 2 & 3 as opposed to Terminal 4. Thankfully, there was a free shuttle service provided by Heathrow Express, and I was soon on the right track – no pun intended.

I ascended in a noiseless lift to the terminal floor, and as the door opened I was immediately surrounded by a great mass of men in *thobe* and *ghutra* shouting at the Saudia check-in representatives and, for an extreme minority, their burkha-clad wives. Walking past the Great Umrah Bazaar of Heathrow, I met up with my cohorts; most of whom had brought two large suitcases in contrast to my one medium-sized rucksack. I wouldn't have even considered taking just one suitcase to a rural region of one of the poorest nations on Earth, but each to their own, I suppose.

Alas, Restless Development had bungled. We all had our tickets ready to hand to the friendly Sikh at the check-in desk, except for Hannah – a then-dreadlocked eighteen-year-old girl who would join me at the Isle of Eigg Anniversary Cèilidh that June. It turned out that Restless Development had forgotten to purchase her flight ticket in advance, so they sheepishly had to purchase one at the airport on the day. Luckily for her, she got to travel in Business Class for the outward journey – the Scum Class cabin being full. Whilst on my placement, I had a lucid dream where she and I were in the Business Class lounge in Delhi, and I was telling her that I forgave her as the towering butter sculptures looked down on both of us scuzzy bastards. For now, though, I had no idea that she was being pampered, and the fact wouldn't dawn on me until we got to Kathmandu. I wasn't jealous though – after I got 'upgraded' whilst flying from Malaysia to England on Royal Brunei Airlines a few months previous, I had discovered that I couldn't sleep on a lie-flat surface on a moving aircraft. I put that down to being used to sleeping upright on the number of overnight bus journeys I had taken in my lifetime.

At Heathrow, we checked in, cleared security and were contemplating the idea of buying cigars to take to Nepal. Needless to say, we dismissed the idea as being ridiculous. An hour or so later, we were taking off on a Jet Airways flight heading for Delhi, thinking that whoever was responsible for naming this particular airline deserved a Nobel Prize for Literature. I subsequently proceeded to get drunk on the free and seemingly-infinite supply of whisky despite the fact that the legal drinking age where the airline was registered was twenty-five, causing me to fall asleep whilst watching *Minions* and, in an act of extreme stupidity, accidentally order the Western food after one of my cohorts shook me awake for the food call.

After falling asleep again, I was violently woken by the plane succumbing to the effects of turbulence; my cohorts were screaming as the stewardess repeated "Return to your seats! Return to your seats!" over the PA system. Albeit this was probably more of an effort to reassure herself that the Boeing 777 wasn't going to go down over Iraqi Kurdistan.

"Where am I? The fucking String Road?" I mumbled drunkenly.

I looked over at Ryan, one of my cohorts. It was his first time flying, and the experience was slowly killing him. I looked harder at his uneaten *gulab jamun,* sweating away its sweet syrupy contents.

"Hey man, are you going to eat that?"

No response.

I ate his dessert, leaned back and put some Mr. Bungle on as we tumbled onwards over Iran and Pakistan, mentally searching the deserts below for Techno Allah. I smiled at my screaming cohorts in an attempt to remind them that misfortune accompanies fortune; to no avail, of course. I tuned out the pre-recorded announcements reminding us in Hindi and English that "the Cap'n has switched on the seat belt sign," and accepted whatever fate was going to throw at me that day.

After nine jarring hours in the air, we had landed at Delhi's Indira Gandhi International Airport, where we would transfer to our flight to Kathmandu. Now, I don't mention the phrase 'Kill Me' a lot, but when you're jet-lagged, drunk, grieving for your recently-deceased grandmother and have to pass through airport security in India, then you'll end up doing so. For a start, they implement *purdah* in the queues – ladies get through in no time, gents not so. And there were a number of ladies in the gents' queue and vice versa – no signs indicated the fact that the queues were segregated. So at this stage you're confused – you're even more so when they solve the queue problem by starting another, longer queue and placing you in it. Ahead of me was a pissed-off English businessman mouthing off the Sikhs with guns – at least until I commanded his attention and gave him two words that Thorsten Jones had taught me in Nimbin: "That's India."

The fun didn't end there. I had forgotten to take out a lighter from my carry-on bag when I was packing, denied that it existed when it went through the scanner, and was briefly detained by an angry bastard with a submachine gun whilst my bag was searched. Thankfully, I was let go before any more damage was done to my sanity. As I would later comment in braw Scots to Bibek – my Nepali counterpart in Khalte: "Aw, Indian military can suck mah bawb!"

After all that, I just wanted to get the hell out of Delhi on our connecting flight to Kathmandu, but we had a little time to kill. As my cohorts discovered a relic of British colonialism in the airport (a branch of WHSmith that accepted pictures of the Queen's head as payment), I did a little observing. Specifically, I noticed that many of the Indians awaiting their own departure were male, young-ish, dressed in rustic garb and were either happy or apprehensive. This to me meant only one thing – they were en route to the Gulf to earn more money in a month than they could ever earn in a year, be exploited, or both. One of my many tasks as part of the Restless Development placement would be to convince the young population to stay in and around their communities, so as said communities could develop to a point where the capitalism-fuelled exodus would dry up. This got me thinking; Arran was suffering a gradual decline of the younger community – in fact, I myself had left the community for extended periods, and still do to this day. I felt about as hypocritical as an evangelist in a whorehouse! But then I realised – Pirnmill, with the average age of the population varying between forty and sixty (depending on whether I'm living in the village at the time), didn't exactly have that many opportunities for young people in the first place. Nepal, on the other hand, would have a plethora of young people willing to do what seemed right. This thought would re-occur to me many times over the next few months, and each time I would feel guilty before arriving at the same conclusion; I would be doing much better in Nepal than I would on Arran.

We spent another hour or so in Delhi before our second Jet Airways plane departed for Kathmandu. As the plane took off, I listened to the Hawkwind song 'Kadu Flyer', smiling in the knowledge that I would shortly be in the land of Buddha and *daal bhaat*. In fact, I would have some of the best *daal bhaat* of my life on that very plane journey whilst viewing the high peaks of the Himalayas glistening away like one of Charlie Sheen's wet dreams. Well, I could see them when Ryan wasn't passed out on the window anyway.

Just over an hour after departing from Delhi, the plane was touching down on Kathmandu – the sounds of 'Semi-Multicoloured Caucasian' by Captain Beefheart and The Magic Band playing through my Walkman as we descended upon the city skyline. Upon disembarking, a suspiciously modern bus whisked us to a building that resembled a bus station in the north of England, specifically the one in Preston. After breezing through passport control, a shouty Nepali man who didn't have the patience for the English language divided us into separate queues so that we could pass through a selection of antique security scanners that made the Ford Model T appear as modern as a Tesla. The machine screamed as I passed through it (I had forgotten to remove my belt for the *nth* time), but the bored security experts merely waved me through. To them, I seemed the type that would buy the local drugs rather than import the bad stuff from the Golden Triangle.

We waited for over an hour for our bags to emerge in the most chaotic facility in all Asia; a plane from Doha had landed and was causing a logistical nightmare on the tarmac. Then, we had to clear customs. I was the first to go through, managing to bring in a few kilos of pre-packed sausage under the watchful eye of the patient young lady who decided not to rifle through my rucksack, instead briefly checking my ticket and welcoming me to the Federal Democratic Republic of Nepal. I walked passed many of the taxi touts, and stopped before I got outside to make sure that the other Europeans had successfully cleared customs. During this time, I struck up a conversation in Nepali with two optimistic taxi drivers and, lo and behold, they stopped trying to sell me shit! In the end, I got bored of waiting, so I made my way outside and met our team leaders, a ragtag group of porters and a friendly stray dog. I was starting to believe that the dog was an avatar of Ganesh owing to my significantly jet-lagged state, but that was just me.

Gradually, the other Europeans successfully cleared the hurdles (or distinct lack thereof) at customs, and we made our way up a hill where our bus was waiting. Overloading this, the first of many buses we would hire in Nepal, we had to pay the porters who had carried our luggage to the bus and strapped it to the roof. But how?

"I only have pounds!"

"I have a few euros!"

"I've got some dollars!"

"I have some Indian rupees…" Ryan eventually chimed in.

"Good – they're legal tender up here!" I told him.

"How much should I give them?"

"Well, there's five of them, so give them five hundred."

Ryan looked vaguely nervous at the prospect.

"Relax – you will be reimbursed," said one of the team leaders reassuringly.

Ryan enthusiastically handed each porter – one of whom had a severe speech impediment – the equivalent of a quid each for fifteen minutes' labour, and we set off onto the chaos of the Kathmandu Ring Road, grinning with jet-lagged excitement. Our first destination? The Hotel Shivam Plaza, just over a kilometre up the road.

January 8 2016 – Hotel Shivam Plaza, Kathmandu

So I woke up this morning to the sounds of animals and spirituality, and the smells of incense and curry.
I feel like I'm back in Nimbin!

Namaste, Nepal!

A Random Message to Hamish

"I took a walk through Kadu today to find a working ATM, and took a trip into myself. I saw my own reality, fantasia and madness wherever I looked. And it was fucking amazing. As were the pot fumes coming from everyone owing to it being a religious holiday here...
I also witnessed a traffic accident – two people came off a scooter. They were fine though.
Also, an international phone call only costs about 5p per minute from a local SIM – expect a phone call soon!
Oh, and I had an interesting conversation with a beggar...
'Money!'
'I'm a holy man!'
'Oh...'"

January 9 2016 – Hotel Shivam Plaza, Kathmandu

If you take the finest parts of my past memories, fantasia and general madness, that's Kathmandu in a nutshell. Fact.

Nepal's Answer to the Cheese Shop

A boon of travelling to Nepal with Restless Development was the fact that they paid for just about all of our expenses, including at least two substantial meals a day when we were on the ground. On the ninth of January, we found ourselves walking down Battisputali Road; I had travelled down this road the previous day in the company of Ksenija – one of the team leaders – and a few of my cohorts searching for an operational cash machine. We eventually found one that belonged to the Siddhartha Bank, and later we witnessed a motorcycle accident occur right in front of us.

Today though, all of us had come over all peckish, esurient even – we were all 'ungry-like! – and were looking for an establishment that could seat and feed over twenty hungry Westerners. As we meandered down the street past informal marketplaces, the amiable entrepreneurs calling out "Hello, hello! Welcome to Nepal!" in our wake, we found a banquet hall that looked vaguely appetising, and were presented with great menus promising the finest in Nepali, Indian and Western cuisine. Soon, the waiters came to take our order, and we began to negotiate the vending of some fine Nepali comestibles.

"Do you have any mutton?" I asked.

"No. No mutton."

"Any chips?"

"No, sir."

This went on and on as I mentally ticked off the non-existent items on the menu. I was beginning to wonder if they actually had anything in; through delirium brought on by the onset of hunger, I started having visions of the waiter telling me that they was nothing in and that he was deliberately wasting my time, causing me to produce a revolver and shoot him at point-blank range. In the end, it turned out that they had two things in – chow mein and *daal bhaat*. I ended up having the *daal bhaat* and immediately regretted it – the chow mein that most of the other twenty white devils and the team leaders were devouring looked much more appetising.

Soon it was time to settle the bill. There were two other genuine items on the menu – the ten-percent service charge and the fourteen-percent tax. They couldn't include it in the price of the food of course. An hour, two calculators and many major headaches later, we retreated to the Hotel Shivam Plaza for the afternoon.

'Insert Relevant Colonel Mustard and the Dijon Five Song Here'

A rather common misconception of Nepal is that it is not as great a religious monkey house as India – a number of travellers I have met on the road over the years still believe that the predominant religion of Nepal is Buddhism on the basis that the Buddha was born in northern India. Both of those facts are about as truthful as a British political analyst.

Despite the fact that the Buddha was born in Nepal, Hinduism is practiced by over eighty percent of the local population, and was the state religion until a new constitution secularised the government in 2015. Though many Hindus, such as my good friend Bibek, practice Buddhism at the same time also; some even believe that the Buddha was an avatar of Lord Vishnu.

The Hotel Shivam Plaza was located close to the Pashupatinath Temple – the holiest Hindu temple in Nepal and a UNESCO World Heritage Site. Obviously, we had to visit it on the day after we arrived. Now, between us and the temple lay the insanity of the Kathmandu Ring Road, upon which lay a significant lack of pedestrian crossings, nor any strict obligation to follow the local traffic regulations, and absolutely no hope whatsoever for a sizeable group of white devils to cross the road. It was getting dark as well, and the public buses which made up most of the traffic were presumably navigating by echolocation, having no working headlights. Or power steering. Or licenced drivers, for that matter. Their horns would make up for their inadequacies. My cohorts – especially the womenfolk – started backing away from the First Circle of Hell slowly.

Except me. I started crossing the road.

I knew what I was doing. I walked across slowly, arms out, not varying my pace or direction in order for the vehicles to pass around me. My cohorts closed their eyes and shat themselves, mentally preparing for my funeral. Ten seconds later, I was across the road and happily waving at my cohorts.

"Well, come on then!" I shouted over the five-tone air horns and belching diesel engines.

They crossed gingerly. Very gingerly.

As we approached the temple, we were greeted by our first wild monkeys. And for me, there was only one thing I could do, and that was to summon my best Johnny Vegas impression.

I gurned at a random primate who had just crossed my path.

"Ee, monkeh! You got any P.G. Tips, lad?"

A fellow white devil named George, who in just under two weeks would join me on my placement in Khalte, collapsed in a fit of laughter.

January 9 2016 – Hotel Shivam Plaza, Kathmandu

My, my, what an afternoon. We went to the Pashupatinath Temple – the holiest Hindu temple in Nepal – where we saw wild monkeys, bodies burning on the riverside ghats and full-blown Hindu worship.
And all I have to say is wow. That's all I'm saying.

(This particular form of Hindu worship was *aarti* – in which fire from wicks soaked in *ghee* or camphor is offered to one or more deities. Considering the location (the Pashupatinath Temple), these particular offerings would be to Lord Shiva in his incarnation of Pashupati – lord of the animals.)

Nagarkot Nights, Ratnagiri Days (and Days, and Days…)

"…as we were climbing up from Kadu, I thought to myself: 'this place is about to overtake Yorkshire as God's Own Country! If only there was a sign…' – then we passed a sign for the 'White Rose English School'…"

- A message I sent to Hamish Finlay when I was at Nagarkot

The roof of the world…

I was glad to be out of the Hotel Shivam Plaza. My roommate Tom and I had plugged up the toilet in our en-suite shortly after we arrived, and I found out the hard way that 'Nepali Time' has a much looser feel than the seemingly-liberal 'Island Time' that I was used to thanks to growing up on Arran. In Nepal, if somebody elicits the phrase "It will be done after some time/half an hour/immediately", it inevitably means that whatever needs to be done will not be done at all. With a brand-new civilisation awakening from the contents of the crapper, I wrote a letter and left it in the general vicinity of the Most Glorious Republic of Cackistan (a *de facto* theocracy ruled by the Len Til dynasty) for the people in charge of the subsequent genocide:
"THANK YOU FOR CLEANING THE TOILET WHEN I ASKED YOU TO.
SINCERELY, MERLIN MAHADEVA."

On the tenth of January 2016, my cohorts and I packed out a bus that was marginally more road-legal than the common Nepali standard (having a massive sign on the front reading 'TOURIST' and working lights) and made our way to the Ratnagiri Resort at Nagarkot to undertake over a week of pre-placement training, meet our Nepali counterparts and become organised as teams. With any luck, we would become fully prepared for our new lives in our placement communities.

After the bus nearly collided with a motorcycle which was heading on the wrong side of the road outside the Ministry for Transport, we headed east out of the city. We were surprised by the number of vehicles on the road considering that there was a humanitarian crisis at the time; specifically, the fuel blockade at the Indian border. Nepal was accusing India of the blockade; the Indians were in turn accusing Nepal. Many put it down to local Madhesi protestors campaigning for social justice. Either way, most official petrol stations had been closed, the Nepali Army had taken over the few that remained open, and taxi drivers were queuing up overnight in order to obtain five litres of strictly-rationed petrol. In Khalte, I would notice that the local electronics outlet was selling litre-bottles of petrol under-the-counter at prices higher than Snoop Dogg in a ganja field.

We competed for space on the road with everything: pedestrians, motorcycles, three-wheeled electric-powered *tempos* carrying fifteen people, taxis, bullock carts and overloaded public buses. Psychedelic Tata, Ashok-Leyland, Mahindra and BharatBenz goods carriers with five-tone air horns and hand-painted slogans reading 'PUBLIC CARRIER', 'HORN OK PLEASE', 'SPEED 40K', 'GOD IS WATCHING', 'OM' and 'USE DIPPER AT NIGHT' passed us with fury; the drivers presumably drunk or stoned, destination unknown. We even saw the occasional private car on the road. I imagined what would happen if we collided with another vehicle and the process of reporting said collision with the traffic police – the local number plates are almost exclusively written in the Devanagari script, which of course none of us ignorant foreigners knew…

The vast sprawl of Kathmandu gave way to small towns, then villages, then hillside peasant farms together with the occasional ashram. After a few incidents where we nearly went backwards off cliffs thanks to the bus having only a few gears, a driver lacking in the cerebral department and a spotter who spent much of his time on the roof either dicking about or re-securing bungee cords whilst the bus was still in motion, we pulled into the resort compound and were met by our beaming Nepali counterparts.

"*Namaste. Mero naam Scott ho.*" (The god within me salutes the god within you. My name is Scott.)

I was blown back by the crowd of twenty-one speaking my name out loud in an attempt to memorise it.

Our training went well, despite the fact that we found out that David Bowie and Alan Rickman had both changed their cosmic addresses. I was sorted into a team with my Nepali counterpart – Bibek, in addition to George, another white devil named Olivia, and two other Nepalis named Ram and Aashika. By the end of the trip, our team would gain the moniker 'Unnati A' (Progress A) and would subsequently give that name to a library we would set up at Shree Dirgha Pradip Higher Secondary School in Khalte. But we didn't know that yet…

Now, a few days previous at the Pashupatinath Temple, my cohorts had taken photos and videos of the bodies burning on the riverside ghats. I never mentioned it at the time, but I took serious offence to it. I mean, my grandmother had just died, and if a bunch of tourists had shown up and started randomly taken photos at her funeral at the church in Lochranza, I would have taken much pleasure in kicking their arses. So, at Nagarkot, rather than eating my meals with the rest of the white devils, I often ate with the Nepalis.

As I was chowing down on my *daal bhaat* one lunchtime, a beaming Nepali lass named Sharmila quizzed me about what life in Scotland was like. I rambled on about how the mountains met the sea in Pirnmill, and how I used to commute for eight hours a day to get to and from college in Kilwinning. I described in vivid detail the sickening pleasures of being on a CalMac ferry on the open sea during a storm, of what a haggis was and how they taste amazing when they are deep-fried in batter and served with chips (and subsequently finding out that there's a deep-fried Snickers tradition out there). I also told them what a 'Berneray Week' was, complete with an explanation of what the effect of downing a half-bottle of Whyte & Mackay in one go at a cèilidh is like. The little things, you know. And when I looked up from my plate of *daal bhaat*, I was surrounded by girls.

Try our shampoo/deodorant/aftershave and this will happen! (Yeah, right…)

The training itself consisted chiefly of games, dancing, language lessons, being ill from eating the Western food that the serving staff had little idea how to prepare, and being bored off our arses during the bits that didn't matter – such as a well-natured but pointless lecture delivered by a senior figure from Nepal's Ministry of Youth and Sports.

At one point, we were forced to speed-date, which is an even more surreal experience when many of the Nepali girls were less than five feet tall. The fact that I was sort-of seeing a girl back in Scotland at the time – the first time in my life I was in any form of a relationship – further added fuel to the surreal fire. We also had to speed-date with those of the same gender, for which I had a plan.

"Well, hello darling!" I flounced in the style of Kenneth Williams at my-then-roommate Sushil. "I hear that Nepal has some A-MA-ZIIING laws regarding the legality of homosexuality! Ooh, they're so nice, aren't they!"

Sushil struggled to control his piss flow as I moved on to the next person. At one point, I was paired with yet another Nepali girl who couldn't have been more than four-and-a-half feet tall, and a team leader called out another question for us to discuss.

"Would you rather live by the mountains or by the sea?"

I pulled out my phone and showed the girl a picture of my house in Pirnmill – where the mountains met the sea.

"I'm thankful that I don't have to make that decision!" I smiled, much to her astonishment.

At one point, I was unexpectedly drafted into starting my volunteering earlier than most. You see, much of our training took place on the second floor of the Ratnagiri's main building. As I was going up the stairs one afternoon, a member of the serving staff caught my attention.

"Ho, dai!" he exclaimed. (Brother!)

I turned to look at him.

"Yes?"

"Help?"

He was carrying a hot urn containing approximately ten litres of our afternoon *chiya*, and was struggling because one of his two lackeys had spontaneously disappeared. Along with the remaining lackey, we helped him carry the urn up the two flights of stairs to my restless, thirsty cohorts. One of the team leaders seemed vaguely amused that I had taken up the post of assistant tea boy.

"Ah, I see you've started your volunteering early!" she exclaimed. "You know you're not supposed to start for a few days, don't you?"

"Meh," I replied. "These guys genuinely needed help. I provided it. Haven't you ever heard of socialism?"

One day, a few of us finally got the chance to practice our teaching skills. We were paired off into teams of two – I was paired with Sharmila, who by that time of the day was cuddling me and mildly humming with ecstasy – and was told that 'you may be asked to do anything to your partner...' ("You mean like convert Sharmila here to Pastafarianism?" I asked). Turns out a select few of us were to teach a mock class to a small group of our peers, with ten minutes preparation-time. Sharmila and I would be the first up.

After scribbling some notes, I was ready to go. However, one of the Nepalis had accidentally taken my notebook inside, but then I discovered something; I was one of those jammy bastards who could naturally teach. I leant back and watched the other pair in the group mess up, and looked over at the other group messing up, and I thought to myself; 'God help the nation of Nepal.'

One night, towards the end of our training, I became pretty ill owing to my consumption of badly-prepared Western cuisine and greasy papadums. After a brief spell of dry-wrenching in the en-suite toilet, my then-roommates Tom and Sushil summoned Udit – the program officer for our placement.

"Have you drunk any warm water yet?" he asked me.

"Um, no..."

I drank a glass of warm water, and a few minutes later I was vomiting up a treat outside. Well, I was vomiting up the eggs I had for breakfast at least. Unfortunately for Udit, the sight of me vomiting had an adverse effect on him. He proceeded to crawl under Sushil's duvet, dashing to the toilet to vomit a few minutes later.

'That's it,' I thought as I vomited for the third time. 'I'm going vegan for a bit!'

Other than making some safe purchases in the Thamel district once we got back to Kathmandu, my dedication to veganism lasted until a week and a bit into my placement, by which time I was consuming up to a litre of dairy products a day.

On the night of the sixteenth of January, we were all in for a treat. We had a 'cross-cultural showcase' that night – both the Nepalis and the Europeans had practiced their sections in secret all week, and now was the time to show each other what made our cultures so great.

The Nepalis put on a display of traditional music and dance, and now it was the turn of the white devils. We put on an *X-Factor*-esqe show that included, amongst other things, an accurate portrayal of stereotypically British behaviours and a display of what many people consider to be music but is quite the opposite. You know, like the Spice Girls and One Direction.

Then, it was time for the *pièce de résistance* – my part in the British showcase. I had been training the white devils all week how to dance the Orcadian Strip the Willow – a dance I knew well thanks to mandatory social dancing at Arran High School – and most of them had now assembled in their lines.

I smiled, and opened one of the DJ apps on my phone, which was plugged in to the sound system. I loaded 'Shedmau5' by Sketch – the band that was playing the first time I attended the Isle of Eigg Anniversary Cèilidh.

And I pressed play.

I turned the already-epic Celtic techno fusion piece into a live eight-minute long stonker – four minutes is just simply not long enough for a Strip the Willow. By the end, everyone was spinning like whirling dervishes. The only white devil who wasn't dancing at the start was Hannah; instead, she enticed the Nepalis to join us on the dancefloor, solidifying the legitimacy of the cross-cultural showcase. As the traditionally-dressed Nepalis danced with the white devils to the sound of violins. squeezeboxes and Maeve Mackinnon's Gàidhlig vocals mated with the raw arpeggios and kicks of Iain Copeland's electronic wizardry, I deemed my first live DJ performance a complete and total success.

"Tapadh leibh, mo charaidean," I announced at the end. *"Oidhche mhath!"* (Thank you, my friends. Good night!)

As someone commandeered the sound system to play the latest Western mating noises at ear-splitting volume, I snuck outside to get some fresh air. I was soon joined by the manager of the hotel, who was present at the showcase.

"Can I ask you something, *dai?*" he asked.

"Sure."

"At the start of your showcase, when you were all introducing yourselves, you said something about the Lama Yeshe Losal Rinpoche."

"Yeah – he lives on a small island just off the coast of mine. It's called the Holy Isle."

"Please, tell me about him," he begged, eyes sparkling with curiosity. "I'm a Kagyu Buddhist."

So, I told him about how the lama had fled Tibet with the Dalai Lama during the Chinese invasion, and how he eventually ended up on a tiny island in Scotland. The manager clung onto every word I was saying.

"So how did he end up there?" he eventually asked.

"The previous owners of the island were devout Christians. Apparently, they saw an apparition of the Virgin Mary, and she told them to sell the island to him so he could start a spiritual retreat. Thus, there is a link between Christianity and Buddhism here."

His eyes widened at this last remark.

"I must say, he's a humble man. I was once over on the Holy Island on a school trip with my philosophy class, and the lama met us saying 'Welcome, welcome!', then he looks over at one of my friends and says 'Oh, hey Lewis! How are you?'"

He burst out laughing.

"Is your friend a Buddhist?"

"No – he's a Judeo-Buddhist. He informally practices Judaism and Buddhism at the same time – means he believes in giving up all your possessions but keeping the receipts."

We didn't talk for much longer – the showcase had tired us out. Also, we had to get up early the next morning for a special treat…

The next day was the day we left Nagarkot. We woke up early to witness something amazing; a sunrise view from Nagarkot Tower. Following the road through an alpine forest, we climbed to an altitude of around 2100 metres above sea level – an icy walk in January – and immediately climbed the prayer-flag-decorated tower in time for sunrise. And what a view we were treated to! We were overawed by one of the broadest views of the Himalayas – the great ranges of Annapurna, Manaslu, Ganesh Himal, Langtang, Jugal, Rolwaling, Mahalangur and Numbur seemed to entomb us as if we couldn't leave Nepal, even if we had wanted to at this point. But of course, we didn't; not now we had witnessed the majesty of this view.

The hotel manager had accompanied us to the Nagarkot Tower, and as the white devils took photos of the prayer flags fluttering in the icy wind, he pointed out the mountains to me.

"See that one there? That's Annapurna. And that one there's Manaslu."

"Forgive me for being a stupid Western idiot, but which one's Everest?"

"Ah. It's at the point where the sun rises itself. You can see it at the bottom of the sun as it rises."

I made my way back down to the road and had a cup of tea with Binju – one of the Nepali team leaders who had regularly flirted with me at the Ratnagiri Resort – in the presence of a group of locals as we gathered around a burning oil drum for warmth. As the rest of the group slowly made their way down, we started walking back down the road, where I had a chat with a group of park volunteers who maintained the tower and its surroundings. They deduced that I was a Western celebrity, but couldn't decide which one; I was reminded of the time when I was mistaken for Jack Black when I was going through a passport check in London a few years previous, but that's another story…

After breakfast, we boarded our bus back to Kathmandu once it had managed to negotiate its way back up the mountainside – we had correctly deduced it was ours after we watched it stop and go backwards on numerous occasions from our vantage point at the resort. Eventually, we made our way back down into Kathmandu, and were deposited near an establishment called the Hotel Pacific.

January 18 2016 – Hotel Pacific, Kathmandu

Hello. I'm still alive. This is not a test.
Sorry for the lack of chat – my phone couldn't connect to the WiFi properly at Nagarkot. I have now returned to Kathmandu for a few days, and I have some exciting news…

I've found out where I'm going to be spending the next few months! Turns out it's a chicken farm in a place called Khalte, which is somewhere near Sindhuli[2]. With my fantastic Nepali counterpart Bibek – whom you'll hear about a lot more in the coming months I'm sure – we're going to change some lives for the better in the local community :)

In other news, this morning I watched the sun rise over Mount Everest from a viewpoint in the hills whilst listening to the Sigur Rós track 'Hafssól' with the volume at 11. Your argument is invalid.

Oh, and I did my first cèilidh up there in the hills using my iPhone DJ decks and the Sketch song 'Shedmau5'! For my fellow volunteers, you guys can do an awesome Orcadian Strip the Willow :D

This will probably be my last post for a fair while – I cannot confirm or deny that there will be internet where I'm going. There isn't even electricity for 16 hours of the day[3]...

Unless you get word otherwise, assume I'm alive.

Peace.

A Random Online Conversation with Hamish

"I'm back in Kadu for a bit now – my hotel room's straight out of 1991! I want to listen to a lot of acid house now... And yes, George is on the same volunteering team as me. As for my Nepali counterpart whom I'm sharing a room with – Bibek – he's a fucking Zappa nut! Also, it's 0540 here and I've just had about 10 hours sleep."

"That's a lot. You're living the high life – no 3-way pun intended! Did you see Everest?"

"Sort of."

---

[2] Specifically, Khalte is around 44km from Kamalamai Sindhulimadhi by road.
[3] Not in Kathmandu anyway. In Khalte, being close to a hydro-electric station, power was almost continuous. Nevertheless, if your beloved electronic devices are permanently attached to your consciousness, I'd recommend a small travel solar panel for use in Nepal.

"Hmm. Looks like the Holy Isle…"

"Sigh!"

"…crossed with the Brodick Castle Grounds."

"Technically, you can see China from where I was standing. Not to be confused with *Chaina* – the Nepali for 'No'!"

"Do you have enough Internet for FaceTime? I'll get to the loo first…"

"No – roommate sleeping next to me."

"I bet *chaina* is no coincidence… Wait, roommate?"

"Yeah. I'm having to share a room with my big-eyed bean from Venus. Again. Speaking of the bedroom, the girls keep banging on my bedroom door for assorted reasons. The Nepalis want to flirt with me or take selfies with me, and the Europeans just want to use my working WiFi. And curl up with me and Tom in the process."

"What?"

"Yeah – things are a bit promiscuous out here. Hence the photos of me with a lot of girls on my arms."

"You're terrible!"

"It's fucking strange for me man… Mind you, I found out where I was going the other night when Bibek – my Nepali counterpart – burst through my door shouting 'Scott, where we're going, there's over 100 cocks!' And I was like 'Ooh, where are we going? Canal Street? Greenwich Village? Miami?'"

"Ha! So why isn't it you could move to a place without sleepers and with some WiFi? Then FaceTime?"

"I'd have to go outside and it's literally fucking freezing…You also wouldn't be able to hear me for the noise of the many vehicles. Speaking of which, there are buses fitted with air horns that sound suspiciously like the Magic Band…"

"It's 0c here too… Oh, like the opening to 'Mirror Man'?"

"A lot weirder. More like 'Flash Gordon's Ape'…"

"Ha! I could easily sing that song to Everest tourists with passion…"

"There was this one bus that went past the resort at Nagarkot that sounded like it anyway, and I was like 'Fucking Zoot Horn Rollo again…' That was when George was like 'OMFG YOU'RE INTO CAPTAIN BEEFHEART!'"

"How much is he into it?"

"A fair bit… Oh yeah, and weed grows wild by the roadside in Nepal, but the few plants I found were dead."

"And dried out enough to smoke?"

"No."

"Aw! Also, that Sigur Dos song you picked sounds so perfect for Everest."

"Sigur Dos? Is that a cover band? Lol!"

"Yeah, except they're homeless!"

"Ahahaha!"

"One of the guitarists on the Hitchhikers theme died, by the way."

"Oh yeah, Glenn Fry – I just noticed…"

"How many more people have got to die, man? I'M NOT DONE YET, said Pratchett's Death…"

"Heh. I still can't believe that Ozzy Osbourne and Iggy Pop are still alive…"

"NOT FOR LONG"

"Who do you think's the next to go? David Attenborough?"

"FUCK"

"Dave Brock?"

"The 3 remaining members of Led Zep?"

"Mick Jagger?"

"Keith Richards took more drugs..."

"Drumbo?"

"Good one..."

"Actually, I think it could be Gilli Smyth from Gong – she was in a bad way when I knew her."

"One of the old Doctors? But not Tom, dear God not Tom! Maybe Colin…"

A Random Online Conversation with Calum Paterson from Berneray

"May the soundtrack of Tangerine Dream follow you through your journeys in Nepal! All the best, Scott!"

"Thanks man! Although it's been mostly Captain Beefheart up to this point..."

"Just as good in my opinion!"

To Khalte: Down Through the Mahabharat

"...I take the trail from Kathmandu
With a different kind of trip in view..."
- Hawkwind – *Kadu Flyer*

Local transport in Banepa...

That day, after becoming acquainted with the 90s-esque décor of our rooms at the Hotel Pacific, and wondering what the heck that fenced-off pond with the temple in the middle was around the corner (it was the *Ranipokhari* – the Queen's Pond), we ambled along towards the beating heart of Thamel. For the uninitiated, Thamel is the touristy area of Kathmandu where one can obtain Western food that doesn't make you shit yourself, and also the cheapest and purest charas in the world (let's call it twenty pounds an ounce at January 2016 prices, assuming that you don't get ripped off, but I didn't tell you that...). A group of local men heard me talking with Eilidh – one of our team leaders who hailed from South Australia – and tried to join in.

"You Aussie? Good-day mate!"

I turned around and grinned.

"*Ngali garima wala jugun. Yahweh!*[4] I'm no Aussie mate, I'm Bundjalung!"

They backed away. Slowly. Then another man came up to me as we were walking away.

"Hello, from?"

"*Poblachd na h-Alba.*" (The Republic of Scotland.)

"Ah yes, very good country!"

"Ha! *A ghlaoic!*" (You fool!)

He backed away slightly quicker than the loitering mob. No-one was going to sell me expensive taxi rides or fake gemstones that day.

"You sound like my grandfather, mate!" Eilidh commented.

"Why, because I was speaking Gàidhlig just there?"

"Yeah."

"Ah. That explains why you have a British passport then…"

Making our final turn into the Thamel district proper, a pigeon took the opportunity to disrupt the local power supply by cooking itself on an exposed transformer above our heads, much to our surprise. Composing ourselves, many of my cohorts went off to buy thick woollen psychedelic jackets worn equally by genuine activists at raves and phony hippies at Glastonbollocks. I, on the other hand, bought a very good pair of baggy green parachute pants, a rucksack made of woven hemp and a pair of shades. If it was twenty degrees in January at the same altitude as Ben Nevis, who knows what it would be like in March in the lower altitudes? The English teacher at the Khalte school would later inform me during my placement that the temperature regularly hit forty degrees during the summer… (I picked up a woollen jacket en route home instead.)

I later found out that my cohorts had brought polar gear from home because they thought they were going up the mountains. I, on the other hand, was fully prepared for the temperature thanks to my experiences in Australia. Over the next few months, George and Olivia would complain bitterly about the heat and I would either be almost indifferent, or start singing 'Ice Cream for Crow' by Captain Beefheart and The Magic Band every time someone said "It's so hot!"

After another night at the Hotel Pacific, we had one last Western feast at the Northfield Café – we were correctly assuming that we would be subjected to months of *daal bhaat*, momos and chow mein whilst out on our placements. Although, to be honest, the momos weren't much of a problem – they were more of a treat…

On the twentieth of January, we made our way to a nearby commercial vehicle park, which was occupied by two buses, a small dumper truck missing its muffler and, rather unusually, a campervan with Italian number plates advertising a strange species of globetrotting circus – the 'General Pico Zircaos' or something along those lines. We correctly assumed that the buses would be for us, and boarded them according to our placement locations, filling up both the roof rack and the aisle of the bus with suitcases. If we had all had brought a single medium-sized rucksack like I did, life would have been so much easier for us all.

---

[4] 'We love this here country. It's the way of the spirit.' Apologies to my Bundjalung brothers and sisters if I buggered up the spelling and/or the meaning…

"The emergency exits are located, erm, nowhere," I intoned half-jokingly. "In the event of an emergency, put your heads in between your legs and kiss your arses goodbye!"

Soon, we were squashed into our seats, each of which was designed to support nothing larger than a small, legless dog, and had fewer belts than a British Leyland car plant, and we took off towards the Araniko Highway. My basic rights as a *homo sapien* significantly diminished for the next number of hours, I stuck a Rob Zombie mix on my Walkman and made the best of things. As we headed out of the city, we passed Nepal's Ministry of Silly Walks – this being a military parade ground where men, horses and the occasional wild monkey and pye-dog all minced around like John Cleese for the obvious realistic benefit of no-one. My anti-military sentiment rising to five percent, I leant out of the window and chanted "STOP THE WAR!" "STOP THE WAR!" for shits and giggles.

Changing my Walkman selection from Rob Zombie to Hawkwind, we slowly made our way to the town of Banepa, stopping at numerous police check posts – mandatory for locally-registered commercial vehicles in this part of the world. In Banepa, as one of our group was sent to purchase a number of basic water purifiers to be placed in our host homes, hawkers with hawkish gazes selling what appeared to be Bombay Mix flocked to us as if we were, well, white devils on a bus going nowhere fast.

"*Dai, khana?*" (Brother, food?)

"*Chaina.*" (One of a great many ways of saying no in the Nepali tongue.)

"*Didi, khana* for you?" (Didi – sister)

"Chaina."

"Khana?"

"FUCK OFF! *BHOK LAGYO CHAINA!*" (I'M NOT HUNGRY!)

To be perfectly honest, the Bombay Mix that Ram had bought and handed to me wasn't too bad – at least I didn't need to take a shit for the rest of the day. Or for the next week, for that matter…

In a town called Dhulikhel, we turned off the Araniko Highway and onto the newly-completed B.P. Highway – named after the former leader Bishweshwar Prasad Koirala and not the morons responsible for the *Deepwater Horizon* spill. The road twisted and descended like an aircraft in a holding pattern for many miles – so much so that we could hear the tyres catch the side of the bus as the suspension slowly failed. Or at least we could have if the speaker system on the bus wasn't blasting out a mashup of Eminem and something else that passes off as music to Westerners[5] on repeat, and I wasn't playing Kyuss through my in-ear buds with the volume at eleven to minimise the effects of my personal Second Circle of Hell.

After nearly colliding with numerous local buses (complete with passengers, goats and the occasional motorcycle riding on the roof), the occasional military convoy and a few smart 2015-model pickup trucks owned by non-profit 'every little penny can help these poor bastards' NGOs, we stopped in the one-street town of Bhakunde Besi for lunch. Now, as my route from the back of the bus to the door was blocked by a considerable number of suitcases, there was only one way I could get off the bus.

I nodded as I realised what needed to be done, and removed my sunglasses.

---

[5] Let's call this act 'Smarties'. Gettit? Eminem? Smart… aw, never mind, just read on!

"Hold my specs…" I said to a bemused-looking Ryan.

Following the Nepali standard, I proceeded to exit the bus head-first through the window – accompanied by the encouragement and delightful squeals of my fellow white devils and the concerns of the team leaders – and went for lunch. Many of the Nepalis opted for the *daal bhaat*, but many of the white devils, including myself, and Bibek opted for the chow mein. This would become a favourite staple of mine in the cafes of Khalte, but I didn't know this yet. I was still about two or three hours away from Khalte, after all…

Later, as some of us were queueing politely to use the squatter, a local raisin materialised. She looked like she had seen at least ninety summers and lost all sense of sanity halfway through the eighth one; as such, she nonchalantly skipped the queue and opened the door as one of the girls was in there…

"*AAMA! ROKNUS! CHAINA!*" (Auntie! Please stop! No!)

The Sun-Maid seemed unphased upon hearing the screams of the person inside, and remained equally unphased when one of our group grasped her by the shoulders and led her away.

We descended through valleys that reminded me of a sub-tropical Glen Coe, the sounds of Gong and Pink Floyd coming from my Walkman providing the soundtrack to the backdrop. Now, we had hired a driver who promised to behave whilst he was driving – no dangerous stunts like overtaking a bus on a blind mountain road with no safety rails at a slow speed relative to the bus in front. It took a bit of shouting from the team leaders to remind the most trustful man in Nepal of this fact, by which time we had nearly overtaken the bus in front and were about to crash into an oncoming car.

Soon, we crossed into the Sindhuli District, cheering when Binju informed us that we had crossed the district line. Jettisoning various teams in villages by the side of the road, we soon reached my destination – the great metropolis of Khalte. My team and I exited from the bus into a great welcoming crowd, and we were introduced to our host families.

Alas, there was a significant complication. The chicken farm where Bibek and I were to reside were now unwilling to accept two strange men into their domicile owing to the fact that there was a distinct lack of their own menfolk on the premises for the duration of our stay. We traded accommodations with Aashika and Olivia, and we made our way to our new homes for the next few months. Aashika and Olivia made their way to what would become known as the Chicken Farm, just two doors down from what Bibek and I would call the Animal Farm. George and Ram would have a much longer walk to what would be dubbed the Crow's Nest, being about a mile further east along the highway and up a series of switchbacks.

An hour later, Bibek and I were sitting on the floor of a cookhouse eating *daal bhaat*, the eyes and smiles of my extended host family, two dogs, several chickens and a goat fixed upon the sight of the strange, relatively pale yeti from beyond the mountains, silently questioning how this strange being would take to their hospitality. Not so much for the Newari in the Team Russia tracksuit.

"There's waiting for you to start," Bibek was explaining.

"Really? I thought Nepal was one of those societies where the elders eat first, or some religious thing happens before we eat."

"No, no. The guest always eats first, the head of the house always eats last."

"That explains that old Sanskrit phrase – *Atithi Devo Bhava* (Guest is a God)."

"Where have I heard that before?"

"The Indian Ministry of Tourism?"

"Ah."

I took a spoonful of *daal bhaat* – to the amusement of the others in and around the cookhouse, who were using their right hands like all good Nepalis do – and chewed on it for a few seconds. My extended host family, the two dogs, the several chickens and the goat all leant in expectantly, wondering what the yeti's response would be to their home-cooked Nepali national dish. I nodded.

"Mitho cha," I said honestly. (It's delicious shit.)

The family breathed a collective sigh of relief. Dipak Rijal, our host father, gazed over Bibek and I with his patriarchal eye as we ate. He soon spotted something unusual about the yeti.

"Yo ke ho?" he asked pointing at the strange lump on my left foot. (What is that?)

"Oh, *yo mero* tumour *ho*," I shrugged. (Oh, that's just my tumour.)

A nervous expression came over his face.

"Tumour?!" He glanced at Sunita, his wife.

"It's not cancerous," I continued in English. "It was larger, painful and, yes, growing until I had an operation a few years ago, but's it's fine now." Bibek translated this information for Dipak as the rest of the family gazed upon the sight of this, their first tumour.

I found out the hard way that, traditionally, *daal bhaat* is served in portions that make a Texan 72oz steak challenge seem insignificant – your plate is customarily refilled with lentils and rice without you asking, or even noticing in many cases such as my first home-cooked Nepali meal. After causing minor offence when I refused a second kilogram of *daal bhaat* ("It's polite to refuse food in my country!"), I settled in for bed, ready to take on the world the next day.

The Rise of the King of Khalte and His League of Pathetic Gentlemen
(And Lovely Ladies)

"If you're chasing angels or fleeing demons, go to the mountains."
— Jeffrey Rasley, *Bringing Progress to Paradise: What I Got from Giving to a Mountain Village in Nepal*

Khalte from the Crow's Nest. The school is to the centre-right of the picture.

February 10 2016 – Khalte

Yes folks, I'm still alive. And eating pizza.

February 23 2016 – Hotel Mahabharat, Kamalamai Sindhulimadhi

Greetings to you, astral travellers. Let it be known that my existence continues. Just. What I'm about to write is but an abridged account of what I've been up to over these past weeks...

In late January, I took an interesting bus trip to the Sindhuli district of Nepal, and got deposited in Khalte; a fair-sized village in a valley that looks like a cross between The Good, the Bad and the Ugly and Glen Coe on crack. Due to local complications, I ended up not on the chicken farm, but on the property a few doors down. It's an interesting place, owned by the mostly lovely Rijal family, who appear to number around seven, with a plethora of free-roaming buffalo, cows, goats and chickens.
Of these animals, the one of note is the family fleabag. Rakesh, for that is his name, is an incredibly dim and slightly paranoid Alsatian cross that blunders into me whenever I take

him for walkies and attacks anything and everything at night. He's cool, though. Maybe he has cataracts or something.

Needless to say, I've been ill a few times from the food, but I'll live. The food provided by my host family is mostly basic and monotonous, but delicious. It is, of course, daal bhaat. The cafes in Khalte do good food too – the chow mein and momos are to die for!

The community is very accepting – especially when you go hiking in their traditional dress and looking like a dreadlocked Jesus like I did on day 2 in Glen Coe-on-Crack. Later that day, my group and I met with the principal of the local school to negotiate our teaching arrangements. Despite the fact that he hates my dreads, he decided to let us teach at his fine educational establishment. Further down are details of what happened next...

Oh, I also slept through an aftershock measuring 4.6 on the Richter scale, despite sleeping on a wooden pallet that's hard as nails. Your argument is invalid.

Before we started school, my group and I also visited the local temple at Beni Ghat, which is located at the confluence of two major rivers. Needless to say, I went for a wee bathe...

After sleeping through another aftershock, I taught my first lesson on self-awareness at Shree Dirgha Pradip Higher Secondary School on the 24th of January. It went down well a lot better than I expected...
Later that evening, I played some volleyball with the local guys, and spent the evening playing 'Cheat' and drinking masala coffee with my partners as two of my host children watched Nepali nursery rhyme cartoons (Meow Meow Birallo – not one of George's top ten all-time hits…) on the card table. I don't think David Lynch could have directed that scene...
That night, an English teacher named Rosio, who was cycling from Japan back to her native Spain, stayed at my place, much to my bemusement. She departed early the next morning after my host mother provided me with what looked and tasted like Weetabix – again, much to my bemusement.

And now, for an interlude. For those who care, Captain Beefheart and The Magic Band are still alive and well up in the mountains! Except the Magic Band is a bus (the multi-tone horn sounds like them anyway...) and the Captain is the guy hanging out of the side door. Or at least, it's a Nepali guy that looks suspiciously like him...

Returning to reality, once we solidified our position in the school by personally meeting the rest of the students and faculty, we planned a lesson concerning the differences and links between dreams, aspirations and goals. After delivering said lesson, we retired to the canteen for yet another delicious anda chuira – which is some kind of muesli/rice dish mixed with egg and chilli and fried in oil. It tastes amazing, trust me!

Despite the fact that I didn't end up living on the chicken farm, I spent a lot of time there due to the central location between my group's three host families and comparatively-large open space. We spent our days at the chicken farm planning events, eating biscuits and meeting the animals on the farm, which also included a number of goats. I christened the billy as 'Shitty Bill' owing mostly to his scruffiness and partially after his namesake – a minor character on the Canadian mockumentary Trailer Park Boys...

The one thing that surprised me about the school was not the fact that the main building had been levelled by the 2015 earthquake, nor the presence of goats on the premises, but the fact *that the children actually WANT to learn – a seemingly comparative rarity in the so-called West. Well, at least at the many schools I attended anyway. I personally think that Nepal has something to teach us regarding the attitude towards learning. I mean, when a Nepali child studies a textbook, they also study the jargon that we somehow subconsciously know means little in our own pursuit of knowledge. For me at least, it's pretty inspiring, and gives me hope for the future of the Federal Democratic Republic of Nepal.*

I also found out in my third class that some of the children are about as politically-minded as a Scottish teenager. That is, one child informed me (in Nepali, of course) that the local political leaders weren't acting upon their promises. ("Just like the UK!" I smiled back...)

I also found out how much of a corrupting sod I actually am. Let's put it this way; I taught Dipesh – one of my host kids – to play blackjack and poker, and how to deal both. Seriously, if the Lisboa Casino in Macau's looking for employees, they should hire Dipesh... After yet another relatively successful lesson, we gathered at the chicken farm to plan for the school's anniversary – which was coming up at the weekend – as a rave started in the valley below. At dinner that night, my host father invited me to hunt wild birds in the forest, which I accepted (as of writing, it has not yet come to fruition[6])...

And thus concludes week 1 in Khalte.

The first day of the second week in Khalte started badly – I felt a nail going into my skull as I used the toilet at the chicken farm. Thankfully, it didn't go into the bone, and my compatriots and I delivered a lesson to classes 6 and 7 that day as we had planned. Later, after a plate of anda chuira and two doughnuts, I went for a walk down to the river, and discovered an unparalleled river beach, with fantastic views up and down the valley. I didn't go in this time: the current was too strong. The hydro-electricity plant up the river was discharging at the time, so that didn't help. Also, I wasn't wearing my trunks.

I also found out that day that some of the kids are so dedicated to their secondary education, they walk for nearly three hours down from their homes on the mountains to get to school in Khalte. I'll just let that sink in. THREE HOURS. And that's going down. Now imagine those kiddies going up the mountains, of which the altitude difference is roughly equivalent to that of Ben Nevis. In other words, these kiddies are descending over a thousand metres down a mountain to get to school, and climbing it again in the evening. Now imagine doing that six days a week – occasionally seven. I'll say no more.

We later learned that there was no school the next day due to anniversary preparations, so instead we prepared for a 'stakeholders meeting'.

The next day, we ambled down to the village hall – a Portakabin-based structure left by the Japanese after they finished constructing the road in 2015 – and booked our meeting for the next Tuesday. Subsequently, we returned to the chicken farm to properly prepare a 'wall magazine' showing who we were and what we stood for.

Later that day, three of us pounded the streets in an attempt to entice the local business owners to attend our meeting. After inviting ten people, and realising that the local population like to take a siesta (or run their farms outside of peak trading hours), we returned to the chicken farm to complete the wall magazine.

After a trip into town for some chow mein, I was presented with some strange, but tasty food by Aashika – one of my teammates. The food was some sort of 'churro' (a long horseshoe-shaped thing that tastes like a really good doughnut), something that tasted like vegetarian biltong and spicy peas – all served on a banana leaf. Aashika explained that it was a special

---

[6] It never did.

meal eaten on the anniversary of a death in order to remind the diner of the deceased. ("So that's where the term 'soul food' comes from," I mused...)

For the second time on the trip, the first being at the resort at Nagarkot, I ate a plate of food so good it subsequently, to use the local term, opened my third eye. The food was daal bhaat *and* saag *(spinach), of course, but I didn't expect the omelette. Or the pure protein that came in the form of curd[7] for the second time that day. The girls at the chicken farm were eating chips that night, but after the meal I had, I couldn't care if they were eating the same steak recipe that I had perfected in Australia. All I could think about was love, understanding and how a new indigenous religion was forming around the hypothetical dinner table, and that the congregation consisted of the diners united as one, one common aim in mind, and how the server could be considered as the presiding priest or priestess. The world was good that evening as I sat listening to a Swedish band named Goat in the darkness of my room. As I laid on my pallet, I remembered the words of a very good friend of mine in Nimbin - 'Food is a drug.' You're not wrong, Gina. Not wrong at all.*
With those words in my head, I floated off into a kaleidoscope that looked like it had been created using Deep Dream, and watched deities resembling myself, Dipesh, Bibek and Olivia playing cards. As my music selection changed to Klaus Schulze's 'Mindphaser', I meandered by into a world of blue skeletal butterflies studded with white diamonds – or, as I was interpreting it at the time, nature in its raw form – as the song peaked. It was a good night.

The next day was the anniversary of the establishment of the school – as guests of honour, we meandered along to the festivities. Or, from what it felt, total boredom thanks to long speeches in Nepali and a faulty soundsystem that made the few festive parts look like something out of This is Spinäl Tap. *Bored off our arses, my Nepali partners and I sauntered off to the cafeteria for food, where an older teacher espied my presence.*
"Brother!" he grinned, motioning with his eyes towards a bowl in front of him. "You eat puri takaari!*"*
'Erm, OK...' I replied.
And almost before I could sit down, my host mother served me with four deep-fried puris *– which resemble pitta breads but taste so much better – and the best bowl of vegetable curry I'd ever tasted. This was followed by 'beaten rice' – if you mix some Rice Krispies, an uncooked pack of your favourite noodles, some pre-cooked peas, cabbage and a few chillies together, you can imagine what it tastes like – served with sweet tea and biscuits. Or as many biscuits as possible mixed in with the tea and eaten with a spoon. It tastes better than it sounds...*
I returned to the boredom a very content man. One thing that that alleviated the boredom somewhat, however, was the fact that Dipesh won three awards – one of which was for least absence from school. Well, when both of his parents work in the cafeteria, what do you expect?

We spent much of the evening and the next morning planning a lesson on personal skills. After delivering said lesson – and making faces at the other classes – we went for a communal shower at a random spring in a dried-up river bed, also washing out clothes in the process. Subsequently, the girls, Bibek and myself returned to the chicken farm to telephone the local stakeholders. Okay – so that day was relatively boring, but still a lot of fun...

---

[7] Well, it was a form of curd locally known as *muoy*. The fat is completely separated to make *ghee* (butter that tastes a little like Scottish tablet), and the result is a drink that solely consists of protein and calcium. Hollywood or Byron Bay-esqe types would most likely pay through the fake nose for a shot glass of it – I ended up making the stuff daily and drinking it in vast quantities for virtually nothing…

The first of February dawned with Dipesh bringing Bibek and I our morning tea. As per standard procedure, we later delivered another lesson on personal skills (with girls from the higher years attempting to flirt with me, of course...), before we ventured off to the canteen for chow mein. Well, I had to vary my anda chuira diet at some point...
When Bibek and I returned to our host home, Dipesh presented us with some sort of deep-fried French toast, which was amazing! Especially the chip shop-eque batter...

The next morning, I was woken by a series of raves happening up and down the valley. After breakfast, I dressed up in my Nepali formal clothes, and presented myself at the chicken farm, ambling past the recently-decapitated corpse of Shitty Bill in the process. We then wandered to the local village hall for the meeting, and were formally invited to a wedding by a local shopkeeper en route...
After a relatively successful meeting, we went to the school canteen for some special chicken chuira, and returned to my place to watch Ant Man. As I ate dinner that night, the rave started up again, which turned out to be part of some big wedding celebration. At this point, I wondered what the wedding I was invited to would be like...

The next morning, I was woken for a special job – make the day's curd and butter. The house cows had already been milked, and it was my job to operate the churn. It was no churn like I'd seen before – it was operated like a rowing machine. Thankfully, with my experience in the Arran High School gym, I could operate the churn without making a complete arse of myself – much to the surprise of the surrounding Nepalis. Afterwards, I was rewarded with an excellent milk tea that tasted suspiciously like Weetabix with too much sugar added, a bowl of 'Weetabix' with fresh milk and, best of all, a large bowl of my own creation. Heading to the chicken farm after rice, some sort of vegetable creation that tasted like an outdoor pursuits shop and a second bowl of Scarwood's Home-Made Curd (Just Like Auntie Used To Make), I was presented with three bowls of Shitty Bill's curried innards, which tasted disturbingly amazing.
We met up with the rest of our cluster in downtown Khalte, and had our meeting in the local medical hub – I took the opportunity to weigh myself, and found that my weight had dropped below 100kg for the first time in years! During the meeting, it transpired that the wedding party was for a child marriage. I felt so glad that I didn't gatecrash it...
After the meeting, I joined the Nepalis in the cluster for beaten rice and pani puri – some sort of hollowed-out pastry ball filled with mixed vegetables and spicy water – before bidding the Ghumaune Chainpur half of the cluster farewell and returning to my place to plan our next lesson on livelihoods. The second week in Khalte subsequently ended with daal bhaat, another bowl of my infamous curd and mokai – better known to you and me as popcorn.
("Not popcorn, mokai," my host-cousin told me.
"Mokai? OCH AYE!" I enthusiastically responded.)

Day one of week three dawned with the announcement that my host father was preparing to go to Kathmandu with his youngest son so that he could have an operation on his ballsack, and he was going to bring us back a fresh supply of Oreos and Dairy Milk – much to my delight. Bibek and I then made our way to the temple at the two rivers, returning in time for breakfast. Heading to the chicken farm, we resumed our lesson planning. After delivering our lessons that day, we subsequently went for chow mein, and ate dinner less than an hour later.

The next day started well. It was Dipesh's birthday, so everyone ate sweets that morning[8]. After scaring my host family with my guang ho attitude towards cooking and chopping wood

[8] In Nepal, birthday person give sweets to you! Vot a country!

(they still loved me afterwards...), a chicken decided to trample through the best daal bhaat *yet as I was eating it. Abandoning my meal for a different reason, I went to school for our Friday homework club. We subsequently returned to the chicken farm, where I finally managed to plan a lesson without my mind wandering.*

After delivering a rather fun lesson, we went and ate another chow mein before returning to my place to watch Walk of Shame *and play cards to end yet another action-packed day.*

After sleeping through an earthquake measuring 5.5 on the Richter scale[9], I prepared the day's curd and went to wash some clothes with my team. Afterwards, we went for a picnic at the river beach, where we ate, played games and got chased by a buffalo.

Later that day, my host father returned early – apparently, another child got very ill, so the youngest couldn't have his operation. There was one benefit – he brought back Dairy Milk *and* Oreos...

After a delectable feast of Shitty Bill's *innards, rice and another pan of my own creation, I went to bed a very content man.*

The next day dawned with the fact that I had spent exactly one month in Nepal. After making the curd and eating my daal bhaat *– and defending it successfully from the same chicken from a few days ago ("One-all, bitch!" I growled as I picked it up by the neck and threw it out through the cookhouse door to the laughter and applause of my host family) – Bibek and I went to the school to teach the children some new games. As per standard procedure, school assembly happened at 10am, and I hung around to witness it. At assembly, the kids did basic exercise and sung* Sayaun Thunga Phool Ka *– the national anthem of Nepal – before marching off to class to the sound of two drums being played by two kids in the style of Drumbo from* The Magic Band. *Well, the nation underwent a successful communist revolution in 2008, so what do you expect?*

Our lesson that day concerned an interesting topic: sustainable livelihood. It was an interesting lesson indeed – thanks in part due to my ever-increasing skill at delivering the fun parts of the lesson! After going for yet another chow mein and accruing 500 rupees in phone credit, I phoned a few people back in the UK to let them know I was still alive, ate some daal bhaat and went to bed.

The next morning, I was awoken by the sound of rain for the first time in nearly three weeks. My group and I went to school early that day for our new homework club – as it was still raining, we decided to talk about the weather.

That night, the girls, Bibek and I went to see the grandmother of one of our students – a lonely old soul who was reduced to tears owing to the fact that a group of people had decided to her. She gave each of us a bowl of fresh buffalo milk – which tasted amazing – and Bibek and I subsequently returned home.

The next day was Losar *– a public holiday – so there was no school that day. I was woken that day with two pieces of news – one was that the previous prime minister of Nepal[10] had died, the other being that the infamous fuel blockade along the Indian border had been lifted, much to my amazement.*

---

[9] Every time I slept through an earthquake, I would have one of two lucid dreams – either I would be running around on a space station or I would be on a CalMac ferry on the open sea somewhere off the west coast of Scotland.

[10] Sushil Koirala – who ruled from 11 February 2014 to 10 October 2015 as part of the then-ruling centre-left Nepali Congress Party.

We had a successful meeting with the local out-of-school youth, and retired to a local cafe for tea.

Later that evening, we all returned to the grandmothers' house for a chat, much to her delight!

The next morning, Bibek and I rose early and took Rakesh for a good long walk. Walking up the road towards Ghumaune Chainpur, we came upon a small settlement with a shop that sold tea for only five rupees a cup (although that may be because we bought a pack of biscuits as well). Even more surprisingly, this settlement overlooked a small village on the opposite side of the river – the only methods of getting in and out being either a long cross-country walk or a short trip across the Sun Kosi on personal inner tubes that one would more associate with the Barnsley Metrodome than bona fide essential transportation.

That morning, I found out how incredibly dim Rakesh was – he couldn't catch biscuits in his mouth and didn't know what to do with a stick when it was thrown. He just looked at me with an expression that said 'So? What do you want me to do with it?' Poor creature – I suppose you can't teach an old dog new tricks.

We had another meeting with the out-of-school youth that day, and went to wash afterwards. Later, I prepared the vegetables for my family, and then we all went out for pizza. Yes. Pizza. When I got back, I phoned another friend in Scotland[11] and had dinner. Dinner that night was half-unexpected: in addition to my daal bhaat *and curd, I was served a mountain of pork, complete with crackling and a few chips. I went to bed that night very, very content indeed!*

And thus concludes week 3 in Khalte.

After sleeping through Earthquake No. 4, I watched part of the state funeral of the dead prime minister before having a meeting with the local Red Cross regarding future collaboration, which was successful.

Later that day was the wedding. It occurred to me that if I wore my white man-dress, I would be mistaken for the priest. Turns out I was – by a group of obese women, who were in all likelihood the mothers and aunties of the bride and groom.

"Babu! Aanus!" ("Priest! Please come here!") they exclaimed as they pushed me towards the bride and groom.

"Look, I'm A qualified priest, but I'm not THE priest! He's that bugger in the tracksuit!" (he was better known to us as George and Ram's host father…)

We later taught games to the kids instead of our program – there was a survey in the school and the people doing it had picked our regular classes. The girls, Bibek and I then returned to the chicken farm to watch the fantastic documentary Saving Face.

The next morning, after making curd, we went to the school for homework club before retiring to our host homes for breakfast. Much of the rest of the day consisted of meeting with both in-school and out-of-school youth, before retiring for chow mein. The girls, Bibek and I then returned to my place, and spent the remainder of the day making bins for the cleaning campaign the next day.

---

[11] It was Jade – the girl I was sort-of seeing at the time back in Scotland. I was surrounded by lust-filled maidens on all sides during this trip – an extreme rarity for the likes of the Virgin Sex God…

The cleaning campaign the next day was an immense success, with a huge turnout of local youth eager to clean up the village. After the cleanup, we went for a communal wash and a picnic before returning to my place to watch Inside Out. *Just another day really.*

Valentine's Day dawned with the first anniversary of myself being admitted to hospital in Australia and the fact that Bibek had turned our room into what looked like a love nest, presumably to impress Olivia – one of the girls on our team. It being Valentine's Day, my Nokia brick phone I had bought in Kathmandu loved me so much it decided to commit suicide, much to my displeasure.[12]
The rest of the day was good – more so than usual. I spoke more than usual when doing my lessons, and was involved more than usual in planning said lessons. I went to bed that night feeling pretty good, until I heard the mosquitoes hatching anyway.

The next morning, I made the curd, went to homework club and dived into an intense planning session with my teammates before co-hosting a lesson with the out-of-school youth. After a visit to the river temple – where we were blessed by a local priest – we were to dine at the grandmother's house. It was the anniversary of a death in her life, so we were served a huge plate of soul food each, and copious amounts of sweetened curd for those who wanted it. It was a lovely experience, to say the least.

The next day was one of those days where everything seems to go wrong. It was a hot day and tempers were beginning to fray: when I was teaching a lesson that day, a fight broke out in the room next door and one of the kids was bloodied. And before you ask: no, I didn't get involved. It wasn't the best of days, so let's move on.

The next day marked exactly one month in placement, in addition to my halfway point in Nepal itself. And that day, my team was expected to materialise in the neighbouring village of Ghumaune Chainpur for another cluster meeting. In the morning, we boarded a tubercular species of bus that was less roadworthy than the non-running van I used to live in during my Nimbin days; it was held together with gaffer tape and prayers directed towards Jagannatha, and yet advertised (non-existent) free WiFi on board. And what the hell is an 'LED Coach' anyway?
We stumbled our way towards the back of the bus over numerous boxes, barrels and various species of poultry, and forked out the equivalent of 6 pennies each for the 10-minute bus ride each way. Over those ten minutes, the ear-piercing sounds of Nepali love ballads and other such muzak blared from the industrial-strength sound-system in the roof which, in all likelihood, was worth much more than the actual bus itself.
As we disembarked next to the school in Ghumaune Chainpur, we noticed a large group of our students standing in the road, all of whom were wondering why on earth their teachers had just materialised off a public bus. It turned out that the school in Ghumaune Chainpur was only so large, and the older students had to travel to Khalte for their education. They were standing in the road because, as students in uniform, they were entitled to free bus travel as per the law of the land. As such, many public buses would refuse to stop for them unless they blocked the road – the buses wouldn't be making money from them, you see…

---

[12] It had cost me the equivalent of six quid in a phone shop around the corner from the Hotel Shivam Plaza in Kathmandu. Before you ask, yes I had a smartphone as well – I just needed a brick to make and receive local calls since Nepali SIMs aren't readily compatible with foreign smartphones, and at the time foreign SIMs just did not work in Nepal full-stop. Take heed – if undertaking one of these adventures, buy a brick phone BEFORE you go. See – I do dispense practical advice from time to time, albeit in miniscule amounts!

The cluster meeting was a success, although it turned more into a 'getting the gripes out of your system' session towards the end, but even that was worth it. Hannah – one of the Ghumaune Chainpur team – also taught many of us the concept of laughter yoga as a team building exercise, which we all loved! Afterwards, we waited for an hour and a half for a bus to Khalte to materialise, and as we decided to walk home, one finally showed up! Well, The Alchemist – a brilliant book that Aashika lent to me – implies that what you're seeking reveals itself at the moment you give up looking for it…

That evening, Bibek and I bought a pizza for our host family as a thank-you for their generous hospitality so far, and I presented it to our host mother in front of most of the family. "Dhanyabad!" she smiled. (Thank you!)

"Swagartom!" I replied (You're welcome!)

The thing is, none of the family actually knew what a pizza was, so Bibek had to explain the concept of a pizza to them. They thoroughly enjoyed it, though, even if they did offer half of the pizza back to me as a sign of generosity and I had to rebuff them – "The ladies shall eat first!"

The next day was interesting: we took classes 6, 7 and 8 on a field trip to the river temple and a local reforestation/permaculture project to teach them about environmentally-friendly livelihoods – a topic which I had more knowledge than some, thank you Gina, Djanbung Gardens and every other person in Nimbin! It was a lovely but stressful day – I see why teachers don't take students on field trips more often. Then again, I do admire the devotions of the students, skipping away from the crocodile to offer prayers at the temple…

After returning to the school, we delivered a session to the out-of-school youth before retiring to a local cafe for food. When we got back, my host mother presented me with the best bananas I'd eaten since Nimbin and a few of those churro things before dinner and bed. Again, another interesting day.

The next day was a holy day, but a group of our students still showed up at the school to help us dig a garden, teaching about livelihood options related to planting flowers and trees in the process. It was a long, sweltering day, but it was worthwhile. It was a bit humorous for our child labour force when I sat down in the mud in order to plant some aloe vera…

The next day, Bibek and I went to water the plants that we had put in before retiring for breakfast. That day, I decided to take my compatriots to a river beach that we had not yet walked on, where we played 'quonzebored' (a game my dad and his mates invented when they were at school decades ago) and frisbee, amongst other things. It was a great time! Afterwards, we went for momos and pizza and retired to our host homes.

The next day was the hottest and most humid day yet. We spent much of the day lounging, and taught our classes during the hottest part of the day when the air felt like melting butter. I don't know how I made it through that one, but I did, and after accruing 2800 rupees each in allowance, we did some planning at the chicken farm and ambled home.

The next day, we planned for something special: what we were to present as a team at our upcoming midway training in the great city of Sindhulimadhi itself. We planned all day – except when we were teaching and eating, of course – and planned for much of the evening also.

Which brings us to today - what we either know as 23/02/2016 or 11/10/2072, depending on your nationality. I travelled on a specially-chartered bus for two hours, over hill

*and down dale, to the Hotel Mahabharat in Sindhulimadhi for our midway training, where I
have published this – the first part of an epic status.
Part two will be written by the end of March.
In other words, OMG AM HAVING A FANTASTIC TIME LOL!!! :D*

February 24 2016 – Hotel Mahabharat, Kamalamai Sindhulimadhi

*Oh my, oh my. For those who missed it, I gave what is possibly my best ever free poetry
recital/rant ever at my midway training here in Sindhulimadhi. We had an 'open clinic',
where we could just rant about the shortcomings of the Restless Development team – which
chiefly consisted of a distinct lack of communication between the staff and volunteers. Everyone
else made posters: I just spoke from the heart. No mercy, no practice, just pure soul, love for
my team and too much caffeine (thank you, team leader Jemma Stern for giving me the tea she
didn't want!). And it wasn't even my grudge – it was everyone else's. Well, mostly.
The time was right, the place was right, everything felt right as I drove the points home in my
own unique style (and probably offended a few people, for which I am sorry, but it had to be
done for the benefit of the placement…). I only wish someone had filmed the spectacle.
I don't know where in the universe Daevid Allen is, but out there somewhere, he's smiling
upon my revolutionary actions.
Fact.*

(I found out later that Hannah filmed my rant (or at least part of it…
unfortunately it's not available online. At least not to my knowledge…)

A Random Online Conversation with Hamish

"I have Internet for two days…"

"FaceTime?"

"Shittiest Internet on the planet. It's worse than Pirnmill! Also, read my new
post."

"Where are you?"

"Sindhulimadhi, I think."

"Holy shit that's a long post! Why don't you phone me?"

"I haven't got a working phone right now…"

"Ah, but you still have your iPhone? No SIM?"

"It's in Bibek's dual-SIM phone. You would know this if you read my post."

"Did you lose your iPhone or something?"

"No – my cheap-ass Nokia brick died on Valentine's Day."

"By the way, I'm now learning Gàidhlig. Have you ever listened to BBC
Radio nan Gàidheal?"

"Yeah – they were playing some space-rock when I was driving home from
work once…"

The conversation moved to FaceTime Audio for a few minutes.

"Connection crapped out. Just in time too, they're calling us to dinner!"

"I'll leave you to eat now."

Observations from Around Khalte

At the beginning of the last chapter, I mentioned that it was to be an abridged version of my first month in Khalte, and I didn't exactly want to edit my social media postings too much for reasons of authenticity.

So here, in this chapter, I'm going to describe a few things that happened that I didn't mention in the last chapter.

The English Teacher

We first met the English teacher on our second day in Khalte. He introduced himself in my native language, claiming to be from the east of Nepal, and later told us about his obsession of Russian literature (especially Tolstoy).

He took a particular shine to George, inviting him for a walk up to a temple early into our stay in Khalte, and later invited him over to his house to discuss literature over a cup of tea or something stronger. George declined – he, along with the rest of us, was beginning to assume that the teacher would rather get into a sari than get into the traditional wearer of a sari. He became increasingly alienated from us after this, which only bolstered our suspicion of his intentions…

One day, outside the main café in Khalte, the English teacher had stopped his motorcycle next to the hole in the wall to order some goods.

"I wonder what would happen if he fell off…" George mused.

"Well, let's put it this way," I responded. "He would break his leg, but the pain would be masked by his ejaculation when he sees you standing in front of him."

George couldn't even stand for his laughter.

The BBC Reporter

Early into our stay, a female BBC reporter (who didn't speak any English) suddenly materialised at the Chicken Farm, interviewed Bibek and left.

To this day, I have no idea why.

The *Rangichangi* Guy

At the wedding where I was mistaken for the priest, an old drunk decided to talk to me.

"<I don't have any English except for the numbers,> one, two, three, <you know. I only speak Nepali!>"

Good for him. He really needed to cut down on the *rakshi*.

The Germans

"Let me give you a good example of a faux-hippie," I was saying to Hannah.

Hannah, along with the rest of the Ghumaune Chainpur team, had come to visit Khalte for a cluster meeting. At the time, we were chowing down on a *jeri* each – these were deep-fried, pretzel-shaped yellow-orange loops dipped in saffron syrup, purchased from a local shop in Khalte for the ridiculously low price of ten rupees each.

"The other day, I saw a Volkswagen campervan with German number plates speeding through Khalte. There were two dreadlocked guys in the front – from the look of their faces, they were having the time of their lives."

"Okay."

"Here's the thing though. Those guys would have to fork out about six thousand Euros for the campervan, and I don't know about you, but I've never had that much money in my life. Then there's the sundries – insurance for the van once they get beyond Bulgaria, the fuel cost of getting from Germany to Nepal, visas, food, van repairs…"

"I'm beginning to believe you!"

"It gets better. They have to apply for a *carnet de passage*, too."

"What's that?"

"It's a document that tells the customs authorities at each border that you are definitely going to export the vehicle at the end of your trip, hence you don't pay the local import tax. Also, Pakistan and India simply won't let European vehicles in without one. But here's the catch. You have to deposit three times the value of your vehicle with the authorities where the vehicle is registered."

"You mean…"

"Aye. Those guys would have had to deposit about eighteen thousand Euros before turning a wheel. Shared between the two, that's nine thousand euros each they would have to source before they even started driving!"

"Well, that's shit!"

"Yeah. I mean, it's not as bad as having to cough up a carnet deposit for a Land Rover or a Unimog like many overlanders drive, but it's still a fortune."

"I know! You could get the train or the bus, and it would work out so much cheaper! Plus, you get to talk to people beyond the local words for 'Petrol, please!' or whatever!"

"True that – that's real travel right there! You know what's just as good?"

"What?"

"Not having to pay for anything except souvenirs, like us! Also, these *jeris* – they are delicious!"

We laughed, and ordered some more *jeris*.

The Out-of-School Youth Girls

These girls were pretty much my biggest occupational hazard in Khalte. They were roughly between the ages of twenty-one and twenty-five, worked behind sewing machines to earn a meagre income, and many already had children. One could pretty much assume that their menfolk were absent in their lives, presumably working in India or the Gulf, judging by how the girls were behaving in class.

During our lessons, instead of focusing on what was on the whiteboard, the girls would look at me, whisper and giggle – I didn't need to speak Nepali to understand what was happening here. Although, there was another possibility here. During my training at Nagarkot, one of the Nepali girls kept following me around because she thought I was an incarnation of Shiva based upon my dreads and body. That being said, Nepali girls marry young – in 2016, just under forty percent of girls in Nepal were married before they turn eighteen. Ten percent were married by the time they were fifteen. And these figures apply to a country where the legal age of marriage is twenty.

Of course, there was no way on earth that I could get involved with any of these girls, partially because I was their educator and had duty-of-care, partially because they probably had men in their lives already (judging by the kids they would bring with them to our lessons), and especially because my visa was running out. Oh, and none of them spoke much English. I would pretend not to notice their fantasia for a few minutes, then suddenly turn to look at them and say, "What are you looking at?" Red-faced, they would turn to face the front, concealing their embarrassment.

During a brief period where I was feeling down because I felt that I wasn't contributing enough to the placement, Bibek would inform me that that I was pretty much the only reason why these girls would show up at our classes, for which I felt slightly better about myself. George would later echo this statement, giving me the moniker 'The King of Khalte' in the process.

One of the few times the girls were facing forwards in class…

On Beating the Shit Out of Kiddies

About a week before we set off for our midway training, an unfortunate incident occurred. In Nepal, the concept of personal possessions is taken much less seriously than in the West – people have a penchant for borrowing things, then returning them much later. Whether Dipesh would do this when it transpired that he took the equivalent of five pounds from Bibek was doubtful; after his parents found out about this, they took a stick to him.

Bibek and I were in the next room, passing notes as not to arouse suspicion. Eventually, he passed me one note that had particularly got me: 'HE'S DENYING IT – THAT'S WHY HE'S BEING BEATEN.' I immediately passed him a note saying 'STOP THEM. NOW.', and thankfully he obliged. It was an upsetting and demeaning situation, and not just for Dipesh. As Dipesh and his parents entered my room to talk it out with Bibek, I stayed silent – partially to avoid fuelling the fire, partially because I didn't understand what was being said. It transpired that our host family were informed that Westerners didn't agree with the concept of beating kiddies with a stick, and they promised to just send their kids to Bibek and I in the event that something like this ever happened again. Eventually, Dipesh offered something that was unmistakably an apology and returned the money, and quickly became his usual self, or so it looked like from the outside.

That night, Bibek and I went out for our nightly walk to a quiet spot where we would discuss the events of the day and cultural comparisons. We sat down.

"Do you want to talk about earlier?" Bibek asked.

`I nodded slowly.

"I'm going to tell you a story," I said.

"Okay."

"Once upon a time, on a council estate in my country, two parents decided to punish their child by beating him with a stick. The neighbours heard everything, reported them to the police, and they were soon arrested. Thing is, the neighbours decided to sell the story to the right-wing tabloid newspapers and glam magazines in exchange for a fair-sized lump sum, and soon the support of the masses turned against the parents. After their conviction, these masses started baying for their anal rape in a Serco-operated private prison in a fucked-up demand for karmatic justice."

Bibek looked at me. I continued.

"Would you like to know when that story took place?"

"Okay."

"Well, it seems to take place every other week – it's a common story. I mean, we used to beat our children, I'm not denying this, but now we've realised that all it does is cause permanent psychological damage. Today, Western society regards people who abuse children as the lowest of the low. I've seen people high on crystal meth taking it out on their children – I hope you never see anything like that, crystal meth really fucks you over – and I immediately reported them to the police. Now, I have no idea whether or not beating the living shit out of kiddies is legal in this country, but it's fundamentally wrong by default."

"I see. But can you not tell anyone else that you saw this?"

I stared blankly at him.

"What?"

"Well, they're scared that, in the future, Restless Development won't consider them for a host family, and they'll miss out on the stipends that Restless currently pay them for hosting us!"

I remained silent; Bibek thinking that there was a tacit understanding between us. By the next day, everyone in the team knew about the incident (and knew not to discuss it), and by the midway training, as did the team leaders. After my rant at the midway training though, everything that I had bottled up had evaporated, and I was back to my usual cheery self. Nevertheless, Dipesh had betrayed my trust – I didn't let him (or any of the other kids, for that matter) in my room unless Bibek was there for the remainder of our stay.

The Dead Dog

On my way from my host home to school, I had to walk a short way down a hill, then up another after a short flat section. As I made my way onto the flat one day, I was surprised by the presence of a dead mongrel. Shady, short and stocky, it laid in the recovery position with its mouth formed in a surreal grin; its tongue lolling out, almost as if it was giving a surreal fuck-you to the world it had recently departed.

In Nepal, dogs are much less doted upon than in the West, as evidenced by the sight of a man breaking a dog's leg with a stone in front of me one day. For one week a year, though, the canine community is commemorated in the Hindu festival of Tihar, which takes place sometime in late October or early November. The rest of the year, they are treated as – there's no other way to put this – the scum of the Earth. At least the feral ones are anyway. Even Kālī and Rakesh – my two semi-adopted mongrels – were mistreated and abused by their genuine owner, though not as much as the ferals. She would often come over to where Rakesh was lounging outside my room, grab him by the scruff of the neck, chain him up in the sun and not feed or water him properly. Nevertheless, he would still come to my place later in the day, as would Kālī, wait patiently outside the cookhouse for my surplus *daal baat* and sleep outside my room in the relatively-cool shade, but still. At least the kids liked the dogs – Rakesh would sometimes follow me to school. One day, George popped by my class when I was teaching the English homework club before school started.

"Why is Rakesh there?"

"Because he wanted to learn English!"

"So why is he asleep under your desk?"

"He got bored!"

"Ah."

Rakesh (left) and Kālī (right) at the school.

Admittedly, though, the feral dogs are hated for a reason – they almost outnumber the human population of Khalte and have a penchant for attacking people. They are rated so low in the local psyche, they are not even buried after death. After a few days in the heat, the dead dog started to smell, so somebody unceremoniously booted it into a nearby gulley filled with cacti and aloe vera. A few more days later and the stench had ceased, indicating that the dog had been eaten by something deadly.

Now, I know what some of you may be thinking at this point – how dare these people attack these poor, innocent creatures! Or something along those lines, anyway. But when was the last time you saw a feral dog? Or a great mass of feral creatures? And if you were living on less than a few dollars a day like many people, would you have the finances, time or effort to put into a genuinely friendly furball?

Okay, I admit that animal cruelty is very, very wrong, and what I witnessed in Khalte and other parts of Nepal was a significant culture clash for me, but I suppose people's attitudes out there stem from witnessing localised dog attacks from an early age. Of course, most of us in the West can't visualise this, instead doting much more on our pooches (and having sympathies for the plight of their global kin) than on, say, humans in genuine need.

I'll say one more thing on the subject. It happens, has happened, and will happen for the foreseeable future. Deal with it.

On Communism in Nepal

The avid reader will remember that we went to the local school on our second day in Khalte in order to negotiate our teaching arrangements. As the principal began to insist that we teach the full curriculum, and our team leaders quickly rebuffing him in the process, I noticed some interesting framed pictures on the wall of the staffroom. The most notable of these pictures, reflecting the ideology of the local government, were of Marx, Lenin, Engels and Mao.

In 2008, after many years of unrest, political instability (including total suspension of the democratically-elected government at times) and thousands of deaths, Nepal voted to oust the American-backed monarchy, and formed a republic. Since then, Nepal has been ruled by a number of parties, including various factions of Maoists and Marxist-Leninists, and also the socialist Congress Party. One can also find much small numbers of Madhesi nationalists and right-wing Hindu nationalists in the parliament, which was a unicameral (single-chamber) establishment until 2017.

A new constitution was implemented in 2015, just a few months before I arrived which, among other things, federalised the nation, secularised the government, banned discrimination against the nation's women and sexual and ethnic minorities, banned proselytization, and enshrined a wide range of human rights. In other words, they implemented genuine communism. I witnessed this daily in the form of the national anthem – which celebrates the diversity of race, language, religion and culture in Nepal – being sung at school every morning, in the local co-operatives in the area, and also in the hammer and sickle being painted onto many walls.

With all that said, I know absolutely nothing about the political system of Nepal, except that certain aspects of it can be deemed by some to better than much of the equivalent in the West. So now, I'm going to stop commenting about political affairs, and resume this book's intentional course.

Further Adventures of the King of Khalte

"In Nepal, the quality of conversation is much more important than accuracy of the content. Maybe we get overexcited about information in England?"
-     Jane Wilson-Howarth, *A Glimpse of Eternal Snows: A Journey of Love and Loss in the Himalayas*

A typical class…

March 20 2016 – Khurkot Hospital

Guess what? I've been admitted to hospital in Khurkot with a suspected parasite in my stomach – the second time in my life that water has made me ill, the first being after I accidentally drank a rare tadpole from an old water tank on Mount Nardi and projectile-vomited Irish potato pie and sarsaparilla everywhere at the Oasis Café in Nimbin. They were not exactly happy…
Since there's WiFi here, and I've completed nearly everything I have to do in Khalte, here's part two of my epic status...

I returned from Sindhulimadhi to Khalte a happy man. After my epic rant and playing games with the entire Sindhuli placement, whatever anger and frustration I had had completely evaporated. After getting a henna tattoo from George that resembled a double-edged Trishula (Shiva's trident), I returned home for daal bhaat and bed.

The next morning, I taught the kids at school how to play quonzebored before returning to the farm for daal bhaat and, much to my delight, bread!
That afternoon, we held a relatively successful gender equality rally with the two year-9 classes before pitting them against each other in a gender-neutral football match by the riverside. It was a lot of fun!
After chow mein and momos, we retired to our host homes for the night.

The next day was nice and relaxing. After washing at a standpipe on the otherwise-dry Niguli Khola, we watched a film at my place before heading for the pizza place for fried momos. I also got another henna tattoo on my hand from Aashika. Now, considering the fact that in the Hindu religion, henna is traditionally associated with good marriage, and by this stage in the trip Aashika would frequently join me on my bed, contort herself into a suggestive pose (notably on Valentine's Day) and playfully call me "Scott-husband", I have come to the conclusion that these signs probably mean nothing.

The next day, we reached our quota of forty in-school lessons, much to our delight! We celebrated with anda chuira before relaxing for much of the afternoon.

The next few days brought more of the usual: lessons, planning and girls wanting to check out my henna tattoos. No big change.

The third of March saw something different: after my breakfast feast of goat innards, potato wedges and a cup of Scarwood's Oh Shit – I Accidentally Made Cheese Again cheese, we took our out-of-school youth group to the metropolis of Khurkot via the public bus ("Erm, sixteen to Khurkot, please!"). After a bus ride where I dangled precariously within the vicinity of an open door many metres above the Sun Kosi river – one hand clinging on for dear life, the other recording the journey on my phone – we visited a noodle factory and learned about the process of making said culinary delight. We spent the remainder of the afternoon in a cafe with WiFi, chatting with the Khurkot team and some older Germanic tourists looking for samosas – during which time I had a live text conversation with my mother and a FaceTime audio conversation with one of my friends back home. Oh, and the out-of-school girls were chatting me up. Yet again. I even got a marriage proposal from one of them...
As we boarded the bus back home, a lone white dreadlocked cyclist ambled by. Later that evening, as I was passing the main cafe in Khalte, the proprietor introduced me to him. His name was Dario, and he had cycled from his native Switzerland to Oman, put his bike on a plane to Mumbai and was now touring the subcontinent. For those who are interested, his exploits can be found at http://darioeberli.wordpress.com/.

The next day, we held a series of events in and around the local school, including a quiz, a drama and a game of kabaddi – the latter of which was spectated by almost the entirety of Khalte's populace. It was also the day that we officially opened the Unnati A Library at the school – the principal cut a ribbon and the room was immediately flooded with students eager to read and learn. An interesting day was had by all...
That night, I had a house guest in the form of a cheery Madhesi chartered surveyor who spoke fluent English ("I'm a vegetarian, you know," he was saying to me as I chowed down on chicken. "No meat, no eggs, none of that for me!"). For those who haven't being paying attention to the news, the Madhesi people of Nepal were the folks behind the infamous blockade. I found out that night that the Madhesi were, in Bibek's words, 'the blacks of Nepal' – i.e. they have always been treated like how we used to, and some of us still do, treat black people in the West. When the new constitution was implemented in 2015, it fully empowered all the minorities of Nepal. Except the Madhesi felt that they were still marginalised – hence the blockade. So imagine, if you will, a rural Brahmin family sitting on the floor of their cookhouse, eating a substance (meat) which is banned in their religion, but especially in their caste, with a Madhesi, a Newari (Bibek) and, horror of horrors, an outcast white man. Such a scene is quite possibly unthinkable in Nepal. Humbling, eh?

The next day was Saturday – a day where we do nothing and have a lie-in. Except for the fact that the kids woke us up by screaming at half-past five in the morning, prompting some swearing in English from Bibek and resulting in the fact that we couldn't get back to sleep. After washing in the river, we witnessed another wedding (which we weren't invited to)[13], and as dark fell, we sat round a fire at the chicken farm eating pizza, momos and noodles and exchanging stories and secrets. A fine day was had by all...

The next day almost dawned really badly. A few weeks ago, my host parents beat the shit out of Dipesh with a stick because he stole the equivalent of five quid – a substantial sum of money in these parts – from Bibek, until we intervened and requested that he, along with Dipshika and Dishab (his younger sister and brother) be sent directly to us if such a thing happened again. I'm not going to forget that incident in a hurry.

Anyway, that morning, Dipshika decided to take a knife Bibek had borrowed. Fortunately, she wasn't beaten – just subjected to a few harsh words and tears. But still, it could have gone very badly indeed...

It was the first day of a week-long exam leave at the school, so our only planned activity was with the out-of-school youth – which, like a CalMac ferry in a light breeze, had to be cancelled due to the weather. After breakfast, we meandered round to the chicken farm and spent much of the day watching films, eating potatoes and looking forward to the next day – Maha Shivaratri. Or Weed Day, as a number of young Nepalis eagerly refer to it.

At dawn on the Great Night of Lord Shiva, we could be found at our local temple with the Khurkot team, much to our delight! It was an interesting sight: the number of people, the joss sticks burning, people offering fruit and other prasad to Shiva and pouring liquid over his sacred image in the ritual of abhishek – all very mesmerising. Later, after being joined by the team from Ghumaune Chainpur, we retired for pizza and momos and spend much of the remaining day at the beach.

And thus concludes three days of doing almost nothing.

The next day was International Women's Day, and as such, we hosted a very successful gender equality rally and street drama at a local cafe. Four armed cops showed up... but only so that they could support the cause and take some photos!

We then had some speeches and music at the local Women's Cooperative and, as one of the organisers, I was expected to dance. Well dancing is an integral part of Nepali culture, so how could I not? Needless to say, as a by-product of mandatory social dancing at Arran High School, I adopted the local dance tradition within seconds and danced beautifully, much to the surprise of the onlookers...

The next day was interesting, to say the least. Our plan that day was to elaborately plan everything we had to do before we left Khalte, but we decided to inform the village of food and poison information that Bibek had procured from the Nepali government. Many listened – the shop owners, the Green Club, the out-of-school youth, the women's co-operative – the list goes on. It was a successful day.

The next day, we taught life skills lessons with both the out-of-school youth and a few members of the Green Club, which went rather well despite the fact that I had to shorten my

---

[13] Funnily enough, one of the people getting married was a girl we used to teach – she had just left school in March and had gone straight into married life. Even funnier, the wedding took place next door to Olivia and Aashika's host home…

lesson due to time constraints. Technically, we delivered 12 sessions that day, much to our delight!

The next day, we were supposed to travel to Ghumaune Chainpur in order to do a volleyball tournament – Khalte's volleyball pitch having rather annoyingly been turned into a construction site. However, Ghumaune Chainpur's headmaster was stingy about the idea, so we merely established a new volleyball pitch at our school for our purpose. It went well – everyone had a good time playing volleyball and drinking fruit juice!
In the afternoon, we did separate things. The girls and I made our way home as the boys went to play football. As I was washing a few of my shirts at home, I was being watched over by the Washing Wehrmacht of the family, i.e. all of them...
"<Wash this shirt again!>" my host cousin scolded.
"Ja, Frau Goebbels..."
I mean, not to offend my host family, but if I want to pro-actively leave a bit of dirt or ochre in my clothes, that's MY decision. It wasn't like I was going to try and get into Berghein any time soon! Besides, I easily wiped all the crap off as soon as they were dry...
After the family realised I wasn't going to submit to authoritarian cleanliness, I meandered down to the river to bathe myself in relative privacy. I found a magnificent bathing spot in a rocky alcove – just big enough for one person to entirely submerge himself safely, and just private enough for nudity. The feeling of slowly sinking naked into the cool of the Sun Kosi was BLISS – it was one of the few times I was truly alone in Nepal. With the relative coolness of the river, it was just what I needed. That, and three hours in a locked room playing GTA San Andreas on my phone afterwards...

The next day was a lot of fun. There was a cluster meeting in Khalte, and it was the birthdays of both Ksenija (one of the team leaders) and Salina (one of the Ghumaune Chainpur team). As such, we celebrated with cake and momos...

The next day – the first anniversary of the deaths of Daevid Allen and Terry Pratchett – was a bit poor. I woke up with a raging ear infection – presumably from the Sun Kosi – and a rotty botty, so I decided to stay home that day. Or rather, the team decided for me. I spent my day watching films and composing music whilst my cohorts played snakes and ladders with the school kids. It was so energetic I could hear it from my room...
The team later came around to my room to plan, and also brought me cream buns – which I am still very much thankful for! And later that night, I was glad to learn that we were having buffalo for dinner...

The next day – Monday the 14th of March – dawned with an interesting fact: we were due to leave Khalte next week! After our homework club and breakfast, we went to the chicken farm to finish planning our sessions that day – we had combined three into one for each class. Everything went well that day, despite the fact that Bibek and Olivia had to travel to Khurkot to do some things for the next day's session. Oh, and we learned that a man from Ghumaune Chainpur had drowned in the river.

The next morning – after being surprised by the corpse of one of Shitty Bill's kids, who had succumbed to the effects of dysentery – we spent much of the day delivering sessions to both the school children and the out-of-school youth before retiring for momos. A relatively boring day.

The theme of death continued the next morning with the news that two of our neighbours had been killed in a motorcycle accident. With that in mind, we went to George and Ram's house to plan – something we had done only once before – before delivering our final in-school lesson.

141

Afterwards, we subjected the Green Club and out-of-school youth to first-aid training with the Red Cross, which was a lot of fun!

*The next day was Ram's birthday, so we dressed up in our Nepali finery before delivering a session on safe migration (if there is such a thing for the poorly-educated denizens of Nepal) to the Green Club and out-of-school youth, many of the latter actually having menfolk working long-term in the Gulf (which may be a contributing factor for them taking a fancy to me..).
Many other Nepalis I met during my travels (including Bibek) would tell negative tales of friends and family working in the Gulf.
After a farewell party for Year 10 and, to a lesser extent, ourselves, we meandered along to the VDC hall for a meeting – the subject of which was the establishment of a risk assessment committee in association with the local Red Cross.
That night, we were all invited to dine on* daal bhaat *and goat innards at the chicken farm, much to my surprise. To my delight, I returned home early to discover that the power was back on for the first time in two days, so I celebrated by playing 'Electricity' by Captain Beefheart and The Magic Band and singing along to it – I could hear my host kids crying with anguish in the cookhouse...*

I woke up the next morning to the sight of milk tea and – much to my delight – roti! *On the flip side, I was presented with the information that the people from Restless Development I had ranted at in Sindhulimadhi were due to visit Khalte, and were expecting a presentation from us. They arrived two hours late and stayed half an hour, if that. However, it was memorable when one old gent who had studied in Edinburgh looked at us with tears in his eyes and said, "You have done a great service for my country, my friends" ...
I spent the rest of the day and much of the next one sitting it out with a bad stomach as my cohorts planned and undertook a street drama.*

Which brings us to today – the 20th of March 2016, exactly two calendar months into the placement – and I'm laid up feeling like Neo from The Matrix *after he's been 'bugged'. It isn't pleasant, but I'll live. I've still got a lot to look forward to over the next six days, including the festival of Holi! Then, it's off to somewhere near Kathmandu for our debrief and a few days off. Then – brace yourself – I'm flying back to the UK...
See you all in a week and a bit!*

March 27 2016 – Hotel Mona Lisa, Sauraha, Chitwan National Park

Well guys, I didn't expect it either, but here's part three of my epic status...

I returned from hospital in the front seat of a sumo, having been diagnosed with gastritis rather than a parasite. When I got back to the farm, it transpired that Bibek and Ram had stolen my idea to go and surreptitiously visit another placement – as such, I had a room to myself for the first time in around two months. I ended up staying up half the night watching films on Bibek's laptop.

The next day, we delivered our last session to the out-of-school youth and spent the remainder of the day looking forward to the next day – Holi.

The Festival of Colour dawned with the fact that the family had slaughtered a goat for the occasion. At our training in York, they had tried to prepare us for such an event – I was cool with it, but wondered what the numerous vegetarians and vegans in the entire placement would think…

My team was summoned to the Animal Farm for a delicious meal of goat innard chuira, which was almost immediately followed by subsequent meal of daal bhaat, *goat (I ate the heart…) and curd. George didn't have the goat, though – as a vegetarian, he had an omelette). After breakfast, we embarked on the greatest event so far in the entirety of our lives: taking part in the Holi celebrations at the school! We were bombarded on all sides by colours and water by children (and children at heart) cheering 'Happy Holi!' – I was grinning so much, even my teeth went* rangichangi! *Eventually, someone acquired the school's battery-powered PA system and started playing the subcontinent's finest electronic dance music through it – I taught the kids how to say 'Taps aff!' and 'Here we, here we, here we fucking go!' and turned them all into good little ravers… It was such that it will remain one of my all-time best memories. Fact.*

After washing at the river, we went for momos and chow mein before retiring to our homes for dinner – in my case, more goat. No complaints from me!

The next morning, we meandered to the main café in town to plan, where we were subjected to the sounds of the proprietor's kids watching porn and playing it through the speaker system. The Ghumaune Chainpur team showed up, so we spent much of the day planning for the next day – our debrief with the local stakeholders.

The next day, the Ghumaune Chainpur team showed up again, and we held a successful joint debrief before retiring for c-momos (deep-fried chilli momos). Owing to the distinct lack of buses and sumos heading towards Kathmandu in the afternoon, we found them a lift on the back of a big, blue Mahindra lorry, much to their delight!

The next morning, Bibek and I were surprised by the fact that the women's co-operative had decided to hold a meeting literally outside our room. The women's co-operative were just as equally surprised that Bibek and I lived there…

After breakfast, we lazily started the day by preparing wall magazines and other posters. That afternoon, we congregated at the school for what turned out to be a surprise send-off. We were presented with tika, flowers, a garland each and, much to our great delight, high-quality pictures of us! It was a beautiful day, especially the point where the headmaster stated in English that he would remember me every time he watched the WWE 'wrestling' on TV (a strangely popular timepass activity in Nepal)…

After one final meal of anda chuira at the school cafeteria, we meandered down to the river to bathe and wash our clothes, madly celebrating the fact that we had finished everything that needed to be done in Khalte! We went for momos and chips – yes, chips, with cocktail sticks in each chip (most drole, what?) – before retiring to our host homes for the night.

The next day was, to our collective dismay, our last day in Khalte. That morning, George, Bibek and I went to the school to do some things with the new library as Rakesh played on the slide outside. That afternoon, we established a new 'resource centre' in the Red Cross building and spent some time playing games (and popping copious amounts of bubble wrap) before visiting the friendly grandmother one last time. Afterwards, George and Ram's host father met us in a cafe and bought us anda chuira *and fizzy drinks each, which was very nice! Subsequently, we returned home for one final night.*

The next morning was leaving day. Bibek and I went to George and Ram's house to collect their stuff and take it to town, only to get a call that the bus was coming early! Early! In a country where everything happens 'after some time!' Well, they had to wait – we had to get tika, flowers, garlands, food, good-luck money etc from all of our remaining host families[14] and collect our own stuff before we could head for the bus. And when we got to where the bus was standing minus many of our cohorts – many of them were helping us with our bags – the school kids which I had taught until recently turned out to give us more multicoloured tika! I boarded the bus looking very, very rangichangi *indeed...*

I spent the next twelve hours travelling by bus through the southern regions of Nepal. We descended through the Himalayas to the low-lying subtropical plains of the Terai, the smell of many species of vegetation (legitimate or otherwise), curries and road dust breezing through my face, and the cornucopia of psytrance, jungle music and Underworld pulsing through my in-ear buds. I attracted the attention of a number of locals every time we had a piss break...
"Holi was a week ago, man!"
"Don't blame me – blame the kids I used to teach at their school!"
"Ah. Well, do you want to buy some weed?"
"Sorry – our team leaders are travelling with us…"
It was one good day.
So now I'm at my debrief at a lodge in Chitwan National Park! Shame I'm only here for three nights...

A Random Online Conversation with Hamish

"Hamish, I'm about to go and bathe some elephants. I'm going to bathe some fucking elephants! Oh, and last night, I looked out of my window into the resort next door, and saw a white guy having a violent wank..."

"Well I'm lying in the shadow of Goat Fell and it was hailing today. Also, awesome! And EEEW, what the fuck?"

"I thought you meant awesome as in the wank..."

"Ha!"

"Also, I'm sharing a queen-sized bed with a distant cousin of mine..."

---

[14] The garland presented to me by George and Ram's host family didn't fit over my bulbous head, so off I went wearing the garland that was, until two minutes previous, hanging above their door. That's how I ended up travelling through Nepal wearing the décor from a Hindu priest's house. Your argument is invalid.

"Who? One of the limited supply? Are you down to the dozens...And why?"

"He's called Tom. He's from the village of Great Harwood, where my grandfather came from..."

"Ah, you told me of him."

"Oh, and I got woken up by an oriole singing like an orange, his breast full of worms... They're one of the most common bird species in this park."

"I think this is the best batch yet..."

"So yeah, I'm going to have breakfast, bathe some elephants, and then on with the debrief. Should be fun! I'd best go and have a shower before the others wake up..."

"Good, I should sleep now. Night. Or *madainn mhath* for you!"

The Pissed-Off Pachyderms and Pot Plants of Chitwan National Park

It was the twenty-eighth of March 2016. I woke up that day at the Hotel Mona Lisa, and I was excited, for I was supposed to be bathing elephants. Here's what happened that day…

We boarded a literal shell of a bus, green in colour, which took us to the local elephant breeding centre within Chitwan National Park itself. Disembarking from the bus, we made our way over a bridge, passing several stalls selling, amongst other things, 'elefant souveneeras' and 'elephants hunny' at prices that made the Libor rigging scandal pale by comparison.

Before seeing the elephants, though, I decided to visit the on-site museum. The museum seemed like one would expect about elephants (multi-lingual information boards, fossils, a random tusk or two etc.), but there was one exhibit I didn't expect. The museum demonstrated, via the use of information boards, how they trained the elephants. What they do, is take an elephant calf away from its mother, expose it to fire, severely ration the poor little bastard's food and water, and keep it shackled to ensure maximum conformity ("It's painless, and only lasts a month!" said the board cheerfully).

I got a second opinion from Eilidh.

"Eilidh – you would regard this as animal cruelty, wouldn't you?"

She studied the board, adopting a sombre attitude.

"Yeah, sure mate."

After visiting the museum, I decided to see the elephants in the flesh. And there they were, chained up like a prison gang in the humid air, screaming, begging for goodness-knows-what. It could have been food, death, freedom… I don't speak Elephant, but those poor pachyderms deserved something better. I may not be a radical environmentalist, but if I was there by myself, I would have procured some bolt cutters and set them free.

The only elephants that weren't chained up were the babies – in a desperate bid for freedom, one charged my group. Thankfully, no one was injured.

After witnessing the crap that was going on, we re-boarded the bus and pootled off to another local museum. En route, I smelt the pungent smell of what was unmistakably Shiva's favourite food – cannabis. Then I saw it – field after field of the largest ganja plants I'd seen outside Amsterdam. For all I know, I could have been on the set of a Cheech and Chong film...

When we got to the museum, we were told that only a few of us could go in at a time. I elected to stay outside; marvelling instead at a large clutch of cannabis plants growing on the museum premises. I spied Hannah emerging from the museum building, so I plucked a leaf off one of the plants and went up to her.

"I've got a present for you!"

She shied away from my enclosed hand.

"It's not a bug, is it?"

"Why the fuck would I give you a bug? No, I think you'll enjoy it..."

I dropped the leaf onto her hand, and grinned at the mixed expression of disbelief and delight on her face.

"Oh. My. God." She began to tremble with excitement.

"You want to come and pick some flowers with me?"

She did. Sadly, they were all male plants – the ones which don't flower. Nevertheless, it was a much better experience looking for pot plants rather than looking at pissed-off pachyderms...

Reboarding the Flintstonemobile, we finally went off to bathe some elephants in a nearby river. Or, at least, some of us did.

When we arrived, I looked at the elephants. I looked at the sad looks in their eyes. I looked at the chains and hooks pressing deep into their skin. I looked at the mahouts and their whips. I looked at the misinformed Caucasians meandering by. I subsequently decided to play no part in the perpetuation of animal cruelty for the benefit of some mindless white bastards. Neither did Hannah or Eilidh for that matter.

Hannah and I sat on the river-beach together musing about the human condition, being passed by white five-year-olds screaming *"Mutter! Ich bin eine kleine scheiße!"* or something to that effect, and faux-hippies with hypocritical Buddha tattoos on their necks, having paid for their marks of the deity opposed to consumerism. In the end, we left the cruelty behind and found ourselves in yet another field of cannabis plants.

High times!

So, here's my advice: unless you're dim-witted enough to bring your young children on a foreign adventure that they won't remember and/or appreciate, you're a hypocrite on a few weeks holiday from your crappy office job, or you're a strain-hunter from the Greenhouse or whatever, I recommend that you avoid Chitwan. At least, thanks to Restless Development, I didn't have to pay to witness the animal cruelty that was going on.

Also, don't eat the Western food in the resorts. It will give you dysentery. That's what happened to me...

March 29 – Hotel Mona Lisa, Sauraha, Chitwan

So tomorrow, I'm heading back to Kathmandu and am having to say goodbye to all the fantastic Nepali volunteers who have supported and inspired me over these past months. It's going to be a hard transition.

The Seemingly-Endless Indo-Nepali Car Karma Dharma Jam and The Four Israelis

It was the thirtieth of March 2016. The previous day, I had emerged from the shitter for the tenth time to been told to congregate by the buses for a prompt five-am departure for Kathmandu. By six-am, we were all ready to go. The Nepalis got onto one bus (a few would be getting off at their homes along the highway to Kathmandu), the white devils on another. It was goodbye-time – we had got to know and love our Nepali friends well over the past few months. But, like everything, it had to end.

We headed north from Sauraha and headed further west along the East-West Highway, the smell of cannabis plants coming from all around, including from within a military barracks of all places! Well, I suppose that they would come in useful for treating post-traumatic stress disorder should the soldiers ever be involved in a war…

In the city of Bharatpur, we stopped briefly for a monastic breakfast of sandwiches consisting of vegetable shavings before joining the Narayanghat-Mugling Highway. The road followed the eastern bank of the Trishuli River, passing small villages and isolated settlements where it looked like one could easily grow ganja without being harassed. Many of the villages were located on the west bank of the river, and linked to the other side by cable cars designed for hauling goods. I would later find out that local children would cross the river by hand, holding onto the cable and fearing for their life just to get to school. Descending a thousand metres to get to school like some of my students did six days a week would probably seem easy for them…

As I listened to a dub and ambient techno mix on my phone, the breeze blowing in through the open window, the traffic slowed significantly. Essential repairs to the road were being done before the wet season, and it took half an hour before we started making significant progress again. I wasn't complaining

– the valley was a spectacular place to be and there was plenty to look at. Well, at least when there weren't any people pissing by the side of the road anyway.

Eventually, we reached the town of Mugling, where much of the heavy traffic from India and the Terai meets the heavy traffic from Pokhara. We turned right onto the Prithvi Highway, and I soon saw a sight uncommon outside the Alps. This was the Manakamana Cable Car – an Austrian-built gondola lift which shuttled pilgrims from the village of Kurintar to the eponymous temple a further thousand metres above sea level in the Gorkha district. I would later find out that the Manakamana Temple is a sacred place of the Hindu goddess Bhagwati, an incarnation of Parvati, and it is said that that the goddess grants the wishes of all those who undertake the pilgrimage to her shrine to worship her.

I wanted the bus to stop so I could go up and have a gander, my excitement peaking like a diabetic squirrel being presented with a Nepali deep-fried Snickers bar. Unfortunately, we didn't have the time or the ten pictures of George Washington's head (the white devil fee) per person to stop.

When we finally stopped, it was at a relatively hygienic roadside restaurant with excellent chow mein and, to my mild amusement, flushing squatters. And here, we had to say one final goodbye to our Nepali friends. Well, officially anyway. I would later meet up with Bibek in Thamel the next day, and see a few more of our Nepali friends at the airport, but this random eatery along the highway was where it officially ended. Aashika used the opportunity to hand me an envelope.

"Open this on your birthday!" she smiled.

I lost the envelope after I got home, and found it again a year later. I read what was in it. I cried.

I stuck The Doors on as our buses departed our separate ways – The End really worked under the circumstances. An hour or two later, after the Prithvi Highway merged with the Tribhuvan Highway at Naubise and I had changed my music selection from Frank Zappa to Tom Waits to Beardyman, we were stuck in a jam more epic than ever before. The traffic – mostly lorries and buses, some bearing the registration plates of the Indian state of Tamil Nadu many thousands of kilometres to the south – stretched out in front of us as far as the eye could see along the narrow two-lane highway. Leaning out of the window, I must have been hallucinating from all the fumes coming from the badly-maintained diesel engines, because four grinning white devils materialised in front of me.

"Hey man, you wanna spliff?"

It turned out they were from Israel, having just finished their Defence Force conscription, and they had clearly blown their faculties with some of India's finest. They were on the bus in front of us – a luxury contraption operating an overnight-running public service from the Indian holy city of Varanasi to Kathmandu.

"Yah, it's really boring. There's only a few other people on board, and they're old. And they don't speak much English, let alone Hebrew. Not our scene, you know?"

"Yeah."

"So, what are you guys doing here? Where are you from?"

I told them of Restless Development and how we had volunteered in Sindhuli for several months.

They nodded. They were too high to respond. Either that, or they secretly looked down on us, having just dedicated a longer time in the military. In any case, I would bump into them in Thamel the next day, and they wouldn't even recognise me.

After we finally set off – leaving a few of our cohorts behind who were pissing behind a stone edifice and had to run a mile up the hill until we stopped again – we finally noticed the two things that were causing the holdup. One was a broken-down car, the other being yet another bloody commercial vehicle checkpoint. Despite being assured by the team leaders that we would be back in by lunchtime, the day was just about over by the time we got into the Kathmandu Valley. As we descended back into the sprawling metropolis, the traffic flowed freer than the highway we were just on, and we soon arrived at a familiar establishment.

March 30 – Hotel Pacific, Kathmandu

Back at the Hotel Pacific for a few nights... :D

Time We Left Nepal Today (Weather Permitting)

"Don't fly into clouds – there are rocks in them."
-    Nepali proverb

Spot the monkey…

A Random Online Conversation with Hamish

"I'm about to head off back… I bought a shit ton of psychedelic clothes here in Kadu! Also, if you substitute the words 'San Francisco' with 'Kathmandu' in Frank Zappa's 'Who Needs the Peace Corps?', it makes a lot of sense…"

"Because of all the 21st century phony hippy schizoid men?"

"Yeah. Also, some dickhead tried robbing me yesterday… He went for my bag of food (?), so I looked at him, made myself ugly and shouted *'RACH THUSA!!!'* in his face. He fucked off!"

"What exactly does it translate to, I know it's a curse…"

"It means 'FUCK OFF!' The literal translation's a bit different – it's something like 'get moving quickly'. Wee Pete from Berneray taught me that one. The other Gàidhlig insults I know are worse because they reference religion – you know, it's like the French language in Quebec."

"'*Na meanabh-chulligan ort!*' is my favourite, as it's so utterly hateful and depraved said right."

"What does it translate as?"

"'May the midges get you!' I mean, it's not necessarily swearing but it's about the worst thing I think you could wish someone."

"Damn right!"

Typical. My flight to Delhi was scheduled for 0950, now it's departing at 1205 due to the weather. Which means that we're probably going to miss our connection to Heathrow. Buggeration.

Homeward. Again. (Part 1)

"I'm sorry – did you understand what he just said?" asked the elderly German lady sitting next to me.

"Yes. He said that the Jet Airways flight to Delhi was delayed until 1205, but they were going to try to hold a few international connections in Delhi. Hopefully."

"Ach – I'm connecting to Kerala." She looked disappointed.

"It's like my friend Thorsten once said – 'Shit Happens – Assholes Cause It.'"

"*Ja*, that's true," she smiled.

Boredom came quickly in the airport. Some of us slept. Others made frequent trips to the one airside shop; this was an affair which sold bottles of Highland Spring water imported from Scotland at 'only' four-hundred rupees for a half-litre bottle. They also sold litre-bottles of local water run through reverse-osmosis purification at fifty rupees, but finding these would be as difficult as looking on the other side of the fridge in the unpopular knick-knacks section.

The lady at the checkout looked like she had been fleeced by a rugged mountain man.

"Any Jet Airways passengers connecting to London or Bangkok in Delhi?" asked the representative to the bored looking crowd in International Departures.

My ears pricked up.

"Yeah – a group of twenty-one of us!" I shouted back.

"Okay, one minute."

He chatted into his phone.

"*Dai*, where is your group going?"

"London."

He briefly spoke into his phone. A short pause followed before a smile beamed across his face.

"The plane to London is being held for you in Delhi, my friend!" he smiled.

"*Dhanyabad!*"

It looked like I was going to make my bus connection in London after all. Between Kathmandu and Hamish's flat in Glasgow, though, it was going to be literally non-stop for me…

We had already been through two different security checks before we reached the departure lounge. Most of the gents in our team were wearing the full traditional Nepali dress, and at the last security check, the guards had laughingly demonstrated to George the proper way to wear his *topi*. Just before midday, when we were ready to make our way to the plane, we were subjected to two more checks. The second took a little longer when the guy pretending to manually search my woven-hemp rucksack for narcotics…

"What's in the bag?"

"Books, clothes and a bag of crisps. Mostly books."

"OK, *dai,* I believe you!"

…answered his phone and left us hanging for a few minutes whilst he discussed the intricacies of the English Premier League with one of his mates. Just under two hours later, our bellies filled with *daal bhaat* and complementary beer, we were back in Delhi and I was ready to face my fear of Indian airport security. There was a few small problems; there was no queue and the guards appeared to be happy!

"Good afternoon!" I beamed at the guard checking my passport and tickets.

"Good afternoon, *sahib.* How are you today?" he replied.

He directed me through where the gents' queue should have been, and after a thorough pat-down where the guard was treated to my cheery humming, I raced through the airport to get on the next plane to London. Regrettably, I didn't have enough time to pick up a bottle of Indian liquor, but it wasn't necessary – the plane to London had more than I could drink. And it was 'Sci-Fi Season'…

When we boarded the plane, we encountered something we didn't expect. A group of older English women had occupied our seats.

"Um, you're in my seat…" I said to one of them.

"Oh, sorry!" she apologised with a Northern lilt. "We've all been stuck on t'plane for over two hour, and we didn't know what were going on, so we thought it were safe to just spread around t'cabin!"

"Meh, I can't blame you. I would have done the same thing if I was in your position."

"So do you know why t'plane's delayed? We've been kept in t'dark!"

"Well, me and my twenty cohorts have just transferred from a delayed flight from Kathmandu – they decided to hold the London plane for us. Probably works out cheaper and less bureaucratic than putting us up in a hotel in Delhi."

"Fair enough. So what were you lot doing in Nepal anyway?"

"Volunteering. We're teachers."

"Really? So are we!"

I chatted with her for a while before sticking the new *Star Wars* film on and, once again, getting drunk on the supply of whisky. In fact, we all got sozzled to the point that my group and I had pretty much drunk the plane dry. Or at least, the point where the serving staff just could not be arsed to serve us anymore. Nine hours of films, banter and excitement later, we were descending on London.

April 1 2016 – London Heathrow

I'm back, baby :D

Homeward. Again. (Part 2)

Because the plane was so late, I didn't have much time to socialise beyond comforting a crying Hannah and having a chat with George's parents.

"He really loves you, you know," I said to George's mum when he was out of earshot. "Every day, he would us tales about you. Take good care of him – you've got a good lad there."

Leaving a second person in tears, I boarded a Tube train into central London, where a group of drunken lads took it in turns to open the emergency exit so that they could take a piss on the tracks. After changing en route at South Kensington, I made it back to Victoria, where my bus to Glasgow was already loading. I grabbed the last remaining seat with a power socket, swallowed a sleeping pill and made my way north.

Unfortunately, I didn't meet up with Jade the next morning, or in the days to come, despite having a long phone conversation with her whilst I was waiting for the sleeping pill to kick in on the bus. I did, however, meet up with Hamish, and when I woke up on his sofa the morning after I arrived, I found Lewis passed out on the floor for no apparent reason. Such is Lewis.

April 3 2016 - Pirnmill

Well guys, once again I've returned to the north-west of the peanut that is called the Isle of Arran.
It's been an interesting journey, and I have a great many to thank. You know who you all are.

April 5 2016 – Pirnmill

So I've been thinking a lot. Every time I go on social media or go outside, I notice things. I see people advancing with their conventional lives. I see friends getting engaged or married. Sometimes, they bypass it completely and have kids of their own. Many get jobs, follow the latest fashion trends and believe the lies on television.
Then there's me. I'm about as far from normal as Tristan da Cunha is from the African mainland. I live on a peanut-shaped rock in the middle of the sea. The three peers of my age whom I regularly contact live around sixty miles away from me. One of them is a very beautiful and intelligent young woman who said yes when I asked her out, but I still haven't been on any dates since 2011. So I'm a pretty lonely bugger.
Nevertheless, I have lived more in the last two years than most will live in their entire lives. In Australia, I became renowned as a poet. In Nepal, I changed the lives of a community I had no idea about with five individuals whom I consider some of the finest that humanity has to offer. And I also became renowned as a poet after that rant in Sindhulimadhi. And every night, I can transport myself to different universes through on-command lucid dreaming thanks to my screwed-up pineal gland.
Closer to home, some clusters of society recognise me as a hero, or the re-incarnation of Merlin or someone similar. Some know me as the Virgin Sex God. Some know me as Chewbacca. Some in the Outer Hebrides even know me as Hurley. But you know what? I'm just a weirdo.
A weirdo with a computer full of what can actually be considered music, and a new collection of vintage happy hardcore, gabber and club bangers that nobody remembers!
I'm lonely. I'm weird. But I'm really bloody happy.
(No drugs were consumed during the creation of this rant. Not even caffeine.)

When my cohorts and I gathered at Heathrow, the thoughts of the extreme majority were of excitement coupled with just a little anxiety – such as one would expect for an undertaking of such magnitude. I appeared to be the exception – for me, it was a return to the normality I had become accustomed to in Australia. My perception of normality being travel of a bare-bones and avant-garde nature, of course. I didn't even feel so much as a flutter of anxiety that day.

Nevertheless, even for a seasoned traveller such as myself, I encountered many unexpected things on this particular voyage. In Nepal, I was blown away by many things, especially the dedication to education shown by the children of Nepal. I mean, if you lived at the top of a mountain and had to descend over a thousand metres to get to school, would you? And when you got there, would you gladly suffer your education in a shell of a building with no doors or walls, chairs and desks so rotten they collapse to the slightest touch, scant educational resources written in a language you cannot understand – the accuracy of which is at best questionable – and mild corporal punishment? Of course you wouldn't. Unless you're a Nepali child attending a government school in a rural area, of course.

So, the question I pose now is: what are we going to do? Do we throw money at Nepal? Do we encourage we encourage 'voluntourism', where you volunteer for a week and go trekking for two? I don't think so. In his novel *Dark Star Safari*, the writer Paul Theroux suggests that, because of the work of aid agencies, there are now 'two different Kenyas – the one controlled by the ineffective government, and the one controlled by the aid agencies.' Something like that anyway. Of course, such a statement could be applied to many underdeveloped countries. In the case of Nepal though, in order to help it thrive, what I did can definitely be regarded as a viable option.

That is, go there. Stay out of Kathmandu and Pokhara, or at least stay out of the tourist districts of those cities, as much as possible, and definitely stay out of Chitwan National Park.

Be a local, not a tourist. And definitely don't be a 'voluntourist' – excuse my Esperanto, but that is fucked up right there.

Educate your fellow locals on sustainable development for both themselves and the community. Ask the kiddies what they want to be when they grow up because few, if any, people ask them. Man, they were surprised when we got on the scene and asked them!

Dig gardens.

Stay in a local home.

Eat daal bhaat.

Be yourself.

Oh, and learn some of the local language because, unless you're fortunate to meet a kid who has learnt English from playing *Candy Crush* on his phone like I did, you're going to be stuck up shit creek otherwise.

In summary, if you ask me, volunteering out in Nepal is one of my top-ten all time gigs, and definitely the most productive!

POSTSCRIPT

April 24 2016 – Glasgow

My, my, it's been an interesting few days.
I went down to York for my Action at Home training and met and caught up with most of the folk who went to Nepal with me, which was amazing.
When I got to Glasgow last night, I went clubbing in Nice and Sleazy's where they were playing Can upstairs, and The KLF, The Prodigy and Rob Zombie downstairs. That night, I met people from various stages of my travels, which was fun.
Oh, and two women came up to me and started speaking Gàidhlig. So I responded correctly because I knew how (and I was also drunk enough to know how), and ended up making out with one of them. And they say Gàidhlig doesn't get you girls... HA! Amadain!
So yeah, it's been a good few days. And I'm still not home yet...

A FEW MUSINGS FROM CLOSER TO HOME

"Man is free at the moment he wishes to be"
- Voltaire

May 11 2016 – Pirnmill

So we have a sizeable parking area for a few cars at my place, which we need full access to on the basis that we all work split-shifts at the Co-op, and also one of us is a first responder. Unfortunately, a significant number of tourists use it on the basis that they can do what they like because they're on holiday. Something like that.
Now most of these cars are registered in England and driven by older people. So imagine my surprise when five faux-bohemian French girls emerged from the latest English-registered Astra and went down to the beach. You know the kind – the ones that think they're alternative because it's cool and they can afford to go to Glastonbollocks and/ or Coachella and realistically know f-all what it means to be alternative...
So when I – a dreadlocked member of the Green Party, a veteran of anti-CSG, pro-migrant and cannabis law reform protests, ex-support poet for Daevid Allen and former Restless Development volunteer in Nepal – emerged from my room to take down my erected tent which was airing for the Eigg Anniversary Cèilidh next month, the girls took one look at me, ran back to their car screaming 'MERDE ALORS!', and immediately reversed into the path of an oncoming car, forcing it to perform an emergency stop before they all pootled off north towards Lochranza.
Their loss I suppose.

May 15 2016 – Pirnmill

Ah, Pirnmill. That centre of peace on the west coast of Arran where old folks move to die and nothing ever happens.
Except the coppers have been going past the house up to three times a day, and yet another one has just gone past with the blues and twos going.
Whoever dropped their tenner in da sea, and reported it to the popo, yoos turnin' my hood all ghetto yo! WESSIDE!

May 30 2016 – Pirnmill

Disclaimer: the following insight into the universe was written on two substances which are now technically illegal to sell under the Psychoactive Substances Act 2016 – tea and bananas.

Tonight, all I have been able to think about is sheep. And not just the furry kind I see eating, eating, eating and occasional playing – if they are young, that is. As soon as I turned on channel 2 of the Biased Brainwashing Conglomerate to give the new so-called 'Top Gear' a chance, all I could see were sheep. The guys presenting were artificial, the crowd were artificial, everything was wrong. The liars, cheats and frauds that we somehow have elected as our so-called legitimate government appear to have more control of the BBC than I thought.
I mean, take the news. Has the BBC mentioned anything about the Tory election fraud and the latest expenses scandal? Have they looked back on when a few weeks ago the MP Dennis Skinner shouted 'HANDS OFF THE BBC!' during the opening of Parliament? Did they at all mention the convoy of nuclear weapons that passed through the centre of Glasgow about a week ago? No.

How much media coverage did Boris Johnston get when he was Mayor of London? How much is Sadiq Khan getting?

Okay, you get the picture, or at least I hope you do. Now, for part 2.

So I'm driving to work, and like every night I see an assortment motorhomes wild-camping on the shore. Now I really should respect that considering the many voyages I have undertaken in recent years, but let's look at the bigger picture here.

Let's say you grew up obeying the system, and become a wage-slave. You believe the lies. You follow fashion. You watch the methadone-metronome known as television. One day, you have had enough. You finally decide to do something about your pathetic little droney life, so you splash out somewhere between £20,000 and £100,000 for a brand-new – or relatively new – custom-made box that you have absolutely no idea how to drive. It looks like every other custom-made box, but hey, it's yours, you like it, it's all good. You decide to only use it for a few weekends a year. One weekend, you pop over to a giant peanut-shaped island in the Firth of Clyde. You take everything with you – food, fuel, electricity, the kitchen sink – and decide to wild-camp for one night on the basis that you're doing something 'different'. The next day, you pootle off to a peninsula that you have only heard about because of that one song cranked out by Wings. The thing is, at least 20 people are doing the same thing at that very same point in time. So in actuality, despite your attempt to break free from the system, you're still following some of it. The only sign that you're trying to break free is that you don't provide anything for the local economy – you merely clog the ferries with your behemoths and prevent the locals from getting their vehicles off the island – a necessity for shopping, visiting family and, for some, going to the hospital.

Okay, I know that what I just wrote isn't the case sometimes, but much of the time it is. I respect those with tents – if I didn't, I'd be a hypocrite. I respect those who live in their beasts full-time – I used to live in one after all. As for the rest of them, I don't want them dead, or let them come to harm. I want them to wake up.

The same goes to everyone out there. Remember school? It's a system that makes you conform; churning out bureaucrats on a day-to-day basis. They may make you feel individual, but they somehow prepare you for the drudgery of wage-slavery whilst at the same time teach you virtually nothing about the various practicalities associated with it. You know, like paying your unfair taxes. And for those who don't live in Scotland, you have to pay for the pleasure of taking your education to a more advanced level, making you substantially more employable in the eyes of the corporate machine.

Of course, many who go through further education are tempted to try some random mind-bending substance on the sole basis that it's illegal. Not on the basis that it will make you see the truth, or give you immense pleasure, just that it's tempting on the basis of its prohibition. Now I'm going to say this once – there is no reason whatsoever why psychedelics should be illegal. There are two reasons why they currently are: one is that hemp is a very, very versatile plant, and the many backers of various industries – timber in particular – are very wealthy, influential and backward-minded individuals that would lose out if hemp were to go mainstream again. The other is the fact that subconsciously – or even consciously in some cases - many officials in the government don't want people to question the fact that nearly everything that the proletariats know is wrong. That their lives are lies. That they have been brought up by wage-slaves in order to become wage-slaves.

Now I'm not saying that you need to take psychedelics to convince yourself to break free. Your brain produces enough cannabinoids and DMT for that - most of the population is just subdued too much in order to use them. On that basis, think before you come out with stuff *like 'DRUGS ARE FOR MUGS!' – your body is a drug factory. As is your local supermarket, for that matter.*

Now here's a little extra about waking up. I realise that many people don't actually want to question authority, as it takes them out of their comfort zone. And naturally, they don't want to do that. But here's the thing – I've found that once you leave your comfort zone, you have a blast. For example, I once hitchhiked halfway across New South Wales wearing a kilt, caught a bus the rest of the way and ended up witnessing my first orgy (I didn't participate...). You can do amazing things and the universe seems to conspire to help you – all you have to do is stop being a sheep.

So here's a wakeup call. There is no such thing as normality – just a loose collection of ideals. People lie. The government lies. School lies. The media lies. Fashion is ugly and unrealistic. Popularity is a stupid and demeaning concept for the insecure. Much of the shit you see on TV is deliberately stupid to appeal to the masses. The stock markets make up numbers and have no realistic meaning whatsoever. And much of the truth that is told is distorted. Much of everything you know is wrong.

The truth is out there – you just have to wake up and look for it.

July 25 2016 – Lochmaddy Ferry Terminal, after a trip to the island of Berneray

It's been a strange old sort of Berneray Week. The ghosts of my Nepal trip came back to haunt me – I saw many Nepali flags by the roadside on my way up and found myself listening to 'Selfie Hanulah' whilst killing time on North Uist. Also, there was a girl called Jaishree Maharjan staying at the Berneray hostel... unfortunately she left before I could talk to her.
Many times over the course of the trip, I questioned why I still travel to Berneray annually after seven years. I've seen and done so much across the world, it's got to the point that when I woke up to the sight of a naked 20-something Portuguese girl in my dorm early into my stay, I was totally indifferent. Therefore, it looks like I'm going to put my travelling on hiatus for a bit – at least until my sense of excitement comes back anyway.
It's not been all bad though – far from it. Yes, I missed a few events and I didn't come first in the quiz, but the numerous cèilidhs and BBQs were as good as ever...
And now it's time for me to roll on home, shut myself off from most of the outside world and earn some cash...

August 4 2016 – on the CalMac ferry *MV Isle of Arran*

So right now I'm on the outer deck of a ship. My fellow passengers are dark-skinned, and the womenfolk are dressed in burkas and hijabs. The men are yelling at their womenfolk when they aren't praying towards Mecca. Their children have no regards towards my personal space or my bag – except when I quietly spoke to them in an Indo-European language native to the subcontinent. I could be on the slow boat to Jeddah for all I know.
But here's the thing. A skimpily-clad faux-bohemian and her boyfriend are sitting to my right. And Arran's only a few miles away.

In other words, that's me on my way back from an appointment at Crosshouse Hospital, appreciating Scotland's multiculturalism and keeping an eye out for self-centred bigots who think that all Muslims are terrorists and can't handle a little culture-clash. Thankfully, there are none.
Life is good.

September 18 2016 – Pirnmill

Sometimes, I think I'm too weird to go out in the daylight.
There have been a lot of older English tourists in Pirnmill recently, and as I was walking up the road, two did something very unusual. They said hello and asked me how I was.
So I raised my head, smiled and replied "Aye, I'm fine. How are you?"
Then they saw I was wearing a T-shirt with what looked like a pentagram on it (it was actually the instructions to play Rock Paper Scissors Lizard Spock), looked at me with fearful appal and picked up their pace without responding to me.
Point proven I think...

October 16 2016 – Nice n Sleazy's, Glasgow

Success. How do you define it?
Well, since you asked, here's my most recent take.
Success is downing a bottle of Buckie and a few cans of lager at a random house party at your mate's place.
Success is convincing the bouncer on the door at Sleazy's that your red eyes are caused by your mate's dog (which they actually were), and that you're one of the Bundjalung Nation (yahweh, brother!)
Success is finding that the DJ upstairs is playing William Orbit, and the DJ downstairs is playing the best of funk and disco, and that it feels like the working men's club in Flockton circa 1976 wherever you look. Except that the clientele is a lot younger...
Success for me ends there. I'm a humble sort of fellow...

November 27, 2016 – Pirnmill

I have no idea whether the past twenty-four hours or so was a dream or reality.
I went to Glasgow, and the first thing I did was to buy some momos from a Nepali takeaway in Partick ("Dai – patho momo portion dinus!"[15]). Each bite took me further through my memories of Nepal...
A few hours later, I went to my first St Andrews Day torchlit parade in Hillhead, which was pretty enjoyable.
Then I went to see – and later met – the current line-up of Gong at Audio. There are no original members in the band anymore, but they can still rock – I'm almost willing to say that they're just as weird, if not weirder, than the late, great Daevid Allen himself...
Then one of my friends from Pirnmill showed up.
"I didn't know you liked Gong!" I said.

---

[15] "Brother, please give me a portion of lamb momos."

"Who are Gong?"

"Erm, those cool dudes on the stage..."

"Well, I'm just here to set up the soundsystem who's on after these guys..."

So half an hour later, I was joined by folk I vaguely knew from the Scottish psytrance scene and Yellow Movement associates ("Hey, didn't I see you at Deoch an Dorus?" "Probably. I was that idiot doing the raffle in the bar tent..."), dancing to jungle remixes of Kraftwerk, Gorillaz and Black Sabbath with a can of Red Stripe in each hand and watching random people toasting over the top of the music...

So, in conclusion, the line between dreams and reality is blurring. Again.

THE INSANITY TRIP

"It is sometimes an appropriate response to reality to go insane."
- Philip K. Dick

In February 2017, I embarked on a little adventure I like to call the Insanity Trip. Why? Because it was completely and utterly insane, and pushed the boundaries of my understanding of the human consciousness, which is unbelievably difficult to put into words. I laughed, I cried, and unintentionally pissed off a lot of people in the process. But hey, it was four of the best days of my life.

I should also mention that for the first three days of the trip, I was going through a health scare. I was displaying a few symptoms associated with brain tumours, and I wouldn't find out my results until I was on my way home (I had a clean bill of health!). So, I was living this trip like it could be my last – well, it would probably be my last trip in the possession of the many freedoms of the European Union provided to British passport holders, anyway.

So, join me as I travel to Amsterdam overland for the fifth time…

February 21 2017 – DAY 1

In October 2015, I embarked on a very, very strange voyage. I travelled to London on a night bus to attend an interview with Restless Development (I would later get sent to Nepal, but that's a different story). Instead of going home like a good little boy, I took another night bus to Amsterdam that had more action and drama than a Nollywood film (which was especially true when I had to direct the bus out of a housing estate in Breda. Actually, on second thoughts, just about everything has more action and drama than a Nollywood film…), spent the day there and spent another twenty-four hours coming home on the bus again. It was, in my view, a complete and utter success.

So I'm going to do it again.

Except I'm not.

I mean, why the hell would I pay for a €55 bus ticket from London to Amsterdam when I can pay for a €25 ticket to Rotterdam?

So now, my lovelies. Here I stand, decked out in my Nepali rangichangi jacket and parachute pants, looking like I spend my life pimping ladies who are more of the free-love and carbon-neutral persuasion. But I'm not the Hippie Pimp – I'm the Virgin Sex God, and I have embarked on a twenty-first century ascetic wandering to the Low Countries, carrying little more than a small woven hemp bag and some writing apparatus in the manner of an Indian sannyasi.

Funnily enough, unlike many of my wanderings, this one actually has some limited intent:

- *Buy momos in Glasgow. There's a Nepali takeaway in Partick which, I found out a few months ago, is amazing…*

- See Brussels. Technically, I've visited Belgium eight times, but I've never actually stepped foot on Belgian soil. Apparently, the district of Molenbeek's got a different vibe since I last passed through in 2014… Either way, I've two hours to kill in Brussels before my bus to Rotterdam, so let's see how that goes!
- Procure an OV-Chipkaart. I should have bought one of those little bastards a long time ago considering I've been to the Netherlands so many times…
- Get a train to Venlo (yes, it's a real place – I never heard of it until yesterday…).
- Walk to the German border.
- Cross the German border, marking my first time in Germany since 1996…
- Go home.

So. Here we go on what is my fifth overland trip to the Low Countries, and it looks like you're in for the ride, amigo…

STILL DAY 1

Well, well, my dears. I haven't even left Scotland, but I'm already having an interesting experience.

I left home, and whilst waiting at the bus stop something very unusual happened. A party of tourists showed up, whom I later discovered owned the holiday home two doors down from me after they mistook the Kintyre Peninsula for the Mull of Kintyre. I realised at that point I was going to have to get used to actual people, considering I was setting off on this trip…

After the bus finally came, I put on a podcast – specifically Late Night Live with Phillip Adams – and waited for my good friend Hamish and his dog Bòidheach to board the bus at Corrie. A short while later, we had placed our collective arses in the pet area on board the MV Caledonian Isles, our attention focused between the husky barking its head off behind us, the people's opium of daytime television and the military bomber flying low over Brodick ("Ach, it's not like anyone would give a toss if Brodick was bombed…")

As we were waiting to disembark at Ardrossan, Bòidheach turned into the doggy avatar of Donald Trump as he grabbed a random woman by the pussy. Well, he attempted to bury his snout up the you-know-where. But here's the thing – Bòidheach's gay. As we were walking up Sauchiehall Street about an hour later, he mounted a ten-month-old malamute the same gender as himself…
It was about this point where I started feeling sane for the first time in, well, ever. I looked around and saw people on their phones, busy with business, Tinder or Tinder business; destined to be plugged in forever, never being free. And there I was, surveying the scene, feeling sane, feeling free of the system, trying to ignore the fact that Bòidheach was engaging in gay sex in the middle of Sauchiehall Street. I smiled beatifically.

We stopped by Chinatown for some drinks and a fish floss roll before we got to Hamish's flat in Hillhead. Our friends Lewis and Liam – also Arran folk – at we dispatched Hamish to buy a shitload of momos from the CEQWA takeaway in Partick. When he finally got back, we feasted out arses off whilst listening to Nepali folk music. I would subsequently tell this to a few friends who went with me to Nepal, making them very, very jealous…
We spent much of the evening playing Cards Against Humanity before we retired for the evening. Lewis and Liam made their way to their Glasgow flats, and I passed out on the most comfortable bed I had encountered that day. After all, I had been up since 3am…

So here I am, once again back on the cold concourse of Glasgow's Buchanan Bus Station, waiting for the 0820 Megabus to London.

Let the insanity truly begin…

DAY 2 – BRING FORTH THE INSANITY

We resume the story on the cold concourse of Glasgow's Buchanan Bus Station on day two of the Insanity Trip. I had just boarded a brand-spanking new Megabus to London, upon which I correctly predicted that the power sockets would fail and the WiFi wouldn't work after leaving the bus station. It was a relatively boring journey to London, the mind-numbing voyage punctuated by a hitch-hiker in central Glasgow (?!), a lorry advertising the 'Van Vliet Flower Group' (presumably, it was carrying a cargo of sweet, sweet bulbs) and a random dumper truck being hauled down the M6 just outside Penrith.

Now, when I entered London, I realised why so many tourists who visit Arran drive like complete and utter fuckwits; because they do so on their home turf. At one point, a car reversed out of a side street, reversed away from the bus on our side of the road, then drove at us in a strange game of chicken. On Baker Street, I witnessed three lanes of traffic turn into five, blocking pedestrian crossings and running red lights. As it was getting dark, they all had their lights on – except for the one sedentary police car, of course.

I had four hours to kill in this land where every other person thought they were the dark side of Jeremy Clarkson, so I visited one of many homes of a world-famous family of benefits-scroungers before I returned to Victoria Coach Station to get the next bus to Brussels. I waited for several hours on the concourse in the presence of a child with Asperger's Syndrome, who commented loudly about my *rangichangi* jacket to the surrounding passengers before he went off to play in the toilets when his bus was called.

"Excuuse me?"
I glanced up from reading Timothy Leary's *The Politics of Ecstasy* to a creature almost as strange as I.
"Hajur?" I asked.
"Have you feeneshed with your London Underground teeket for the day?"
"Chan eil Beurla agam."
Successfully conveying the illusion that I wasn't a tourist, and that I only spoke Nepali and Gàidhlig, he buggered off.

I had no further disturbances before the ME4 to Cologne via Gent and Brussels was finally called. And that's where the fun began. In front of me in the queue for the bus was a man who had decided to empty half the contents of his flat and take them with him to Cologne; specifically, a table, a mirror and a large bag of frozen food – all of which could not be taken on a bus.
"You can't take that on my bus!" the driver exclaimed.
Flat Man placed his stuff in the hold anyway.
"You know I'm just going to take them out, right?"
"But the guy at the desk said I could bring them on!"
"And I'm saying you can't! That's glass you've got there! And frozen food!"

"You're being very rude!"

An epic shouting match started, complete with more gesticulating than Manchester's Canal Street on Pride Day, which ended up delaying the bus by around half an hour. Finally, Flat Man was allowed to board – God knows why – and soon we were balling down the M20 towards Folkestone. Having booked my tickets through Flixbus, my carbon emissions for this portion of the trip had apparently been offset by the fact I had paid an extra euro, which was to be donated to 'internationally certified climate projects'. I wondered if any of the other passengers on the bus were as pious as myself…

The bus was diverted to the Channel Tunnel owing to the imminent impact of Storm Doris; this was despite the fact that the ferries were still running and the bus in front of us – the ME5 from London to Barcelona via Paris – had gone on the ferry. We disembarked from the bus at the Folkestone terminal to pass through what would be the quickest passport control I had ever encountered; there was one Eurotunnel employee checking passports, scanning them into a computer and sending the details to the British and French authorities. And it worked! I can't see why more authorities do this if they're not prepared to open the borders…

We were instructed to return to the bus by midnight, the driver having locked the bus so he could go through passport control, use the loo, get a coffee, check the passenger manifest etc. Anyway, when he returned, a group of Africans who had boarded the bus in London were banging at the door after he boarded through the driver's door. Another shouting match ensured.

"Why are you banging at my door?"

"Because we're cold and you're not letting us on! The other buses are letting their passengers on, why aren't you! You threatened to drive off without us if we weren't back before midnight! You're not very nice! We're all cold! It's cold!"

(I wasn't cold. Not really. The weather was decent by Scottish standards…)

The argument went on for ten minutes (which the driver won) before we were all allowed back on the bus, upon which I found out that my in-ear buds had died.

Bugger.

DAY 3

"Okay, ladies and gentlemen, we are now arriving at Brussels Gare du Nord," the new driver was announcing over the PA system, the other driver having been relieved in more ways than one at Gent. "Unfortunately, there has been a spate of luggage theft here, so I would like to ask all Brussels passengers to disembark from the bus before I open the hold – that way the thieves will be less likely to steal your stuff."

I didn't have any hold luggage, so I was immune to the non-existent luggage thieves. Stepping into Belgium for the first time (having passed through on the bus many times without getting off for as so much as a piss), I went straight to a nearby café.

"*Bonjour monsieur, puis-je vous aider?*"

I was so jet-lagged by this point, I could speak and understand French pretty much fluently.

"*Oui, un espresso normal, s'il vous plait.*"

"D'accord. Autre chose?"

"Á oui. Un croissant avec jambon et fromage, s'il vous plait."

"Jambon normal ou Serrano?"

"Ooh! Serrano, s'il vous plait!"

I paid up, grabbed my exotic crescent-shaped cheese and ham sarnie and coffee, and plonked myself down on a convenient bench on the station concourse, reading *The Politics of Ecstasy* and glancing up at the occasional Belgian Army contingent patrolling the station. It hadn't been a year since the Brussels attacks, after all…

After an hour or so, I made my way back outside to the bus stop to catch a Belgian-registered Flixbus to Rotterdam. I found myself sitting at the front pretty much opposite the driver, an old Jewish fellow who had most likely survived the Shoah sitting next to me. He was travelling to meet his nephew in Rotterdam, and had picked up a Dutch-language copy of the *Metro* in a bid to improve his Dutch. He asked me to translate a phrase from Dutch to French, being only fluent in French and Hebrew.

"Je regrette, je ne parle pas Néerlandais. Je suis Écossais."

The driver, listening in, chuckled at the fact that I was from Scotland. Then again, I suspect that not many Scottish people catch the bus from Brussels to Rotterdam. By this time, around thirty drunk Legia Warszawa fans had boarded the bus chanting "PO-LISH! PO-LISH! WE'RE PO-LISH! WOOO!", en route to see their team play Ajax in a UEFA Cup match in Amsterdam. Over the next hour or so, they would chant the Legia Warszawa chants at full volume and become so steaming they wouldn't be able to find the power sockets.

As the bus pulled out of Brussels, the traffic heading out of the city was forced to pull over so that the Prime Minister, Charles Michel, could pass the traffic on our side of the road. Finally, we drove towards Antwerp, the old Jewish guy quietly singing an old Hebrew song. I realised at that point that I could have been missing so much if my in-ear buds hadn't died. Sometimes, the best sound in life is the song of an old man mated with the creaks and drones of a Euro VI-rated engine, especially when you're on the verge of passing out from fatigue. Well, the sound was beautiful until a truck nearly ploughed into the bus, causing the old Jewish guy to break from his song to give the tablet-reading truckie the finger and swear at him in Hebrew.

Soon, we had crossed the Dutch border. A car belonging to the *Koninklijke Marechaussee (KMar)* – the Royal Military Constabulary – immediately pulled in front of the bus and turned on its 'POLICE – FOLLOW' lights. I felt a pang of anxiety, but I knew I was in no trouble. The car directed us into a service station just outside the town of Bergen-op-Zoom, where two armed *KMar* officers boarded the bus.

"Ladies and gentlemen, we are the Royal Military Constabulary of the Netherlands," intoned the first officer in English. "We are looking for illegal migrants. Please have your passports or National Identity Cards ready."

The second officer smiled at me.

"Hello, may I see your passport, please?"

"Now, how did you know I speak English?" I said, handing over my passport.

"We Dutch can tell!" he chuckled.

He looked through my visa pages.

"Heh. You've been to Nepal!"

"I sure have!"

"Good country?"

"Yep!"

He handed my passport back and moved on to the old Jewish guy.

"*Identiteitskaart?*"

He seemed confused.

"*Avez-vous une carte d'identité ou passeport?*" I asked him.

He understood, handed over his Belgian ID card and the *KMar* officers moved up the bus. The old Jewish guy sighed.

"*Oy, vey. La police!*"

"*C'est immigration. 'Le problème des migrants.' Problème, bof!*"

"*Ah.*"

Presently, a member of the Polish contingent made his way up to the driver.

"Excuse me driver, may we get off and have a smoke?"

"Yes, but be quick. You have two minutes – we have to go soon!"

I had been talking to the driver in French until now and I found out his English was decent. I felt like a muppet as I watched all but two of the Poles got off the bus for a cigarette.

"Come on, we have to go!" shouted the driver.

The Poles threw a map of the Netherlands onto the ground and did a little quasi-ritualistic dance on it, lit another cigarette each and moved behind a lorry to get out of the wind.

I leant over to the driver.

"I have an idea. Why don't you close the door and move forward five metres? That will make them run!"

The driver smiled.

He closed the door.

He waited a few seconds.

He moved forward five metres.

He moved forward ten metres.

He moved forward fifty metres.

He merged onto the *autosnelweg*.

"Are they running yet?" I asked.

He checked his mirrors.

"No," he replied, gunning the bus up to a hundred kilometres an hour, safe in the knowledge that if he was in danger, a Scotsman built like a brick shithouse could maintain the peace.

I exchanged glances with the old Jewish guy.

"*C'est la vie,*" I shrugged.

"*Oui, c'est ça,*" he replied.

We burst out laughing.

The two Poles remaining on the bus, feeling humbled, remained expressionless all the way to Rotterdam. Evidently, dancing on a map of the Netherlands had angered a Dutch god or six.

As the bus prepared to pull off the *autosnelweg* into the outskirts of Rotterdam, I began to doze off. I was so tired that I began to hear hidden messages in the local radio station, a siren's voice tempting me in English, "Now how about you sleep for fifteen hours a night for the next six-and-a-half days, just like you used to in Australia?"

I couldn't exactly follow her advice, as I was about to disembark at the Zuidplein metro station in Rotterdam.

"*Shalom Aleichem, mon ami,*" I said to the old Jewish guy.

"*Aleichem Shalom,*" he smiled.

I purchased a disposable *OV-Chipkaart*, loaded €60 onto it and made my way to the nearest electronics shop to purchase a new pair of in-ear buds. Now, my initial plan was to get a train to the German border, walk across and go home, but I decided I didn't have enough time for that after wasting an hour looking for something more vital, so I caught an express train to Amsterdam instead. I spent an hour on the train, and I would have probably slept if not for the listening to the worst pronunciation of the English and French languages coming from the conductress. Still, they weren't her native languages, so I shouldn't judge.

I visited a few old haunts before I caught a local train back to Rotterdam (as opposed to the express I came in on) a few hours later; setting off earlier than I planned owing to the football match that day and Storm Doris cancelling half the trains. I was falling asleep on the train to the amusement of a gaggle of teenage girls sitting next to me; they were laughing every time I dropped off, singing Dutch lullabies, wondering if I was tripping. In a semi-dream state, I opened my eyes, bloodshot from lack of sleep. The girls immediately shut up and went red in the face.

"WOE BETIDE THOU WHO SPEAK OF ME!" I intoned uncontrollably, grinning like Beelzebub himself, eyes darting from side-to-side.

Their facial expressions resembled molten lead hardening, or at least I thought they did. In a state of fear, they moved to another bay of seats, watching my every move. They were in no danger; I had somehow put a Niteworks album on and subsequently fell asleep, waking up long after they had disembarked.

The train arrived into Rotterdam Centraal an hour later. I left a copy of *The National* I had picked up on the Caledonian Isles on the train for shits and giggles, and made my way to a nearby coffeeshop. I spent a few hours there eating some food I had bought downstairs, socialising with Turkish fellow named Arda who grew up in Rotterdam and a pair of Georgian tourists seeing Europe on a Schengen visa. I helped Arda with his colloquial English, having nearly qualified for my TEFL certificate, and told the Georgians about my shenanigans around the world. I was about rate this place as the best establishment in Rotterdam, and leave in order to get the bus back to Brussels, when a skinny speccy bastard materialised seemingly out of nowhere. He had the personality of Bernard from *Black Books* and claimed to work at the coffeeshop.

"Have you bought a drink?"

"Eh?"

"Have you bought a drink?"

"I bought some food..."

"You've been up here three hours, you haven't bought a drink, and all you've done is moved from that seat to this one!"

"So? I gave up that other seat so that couple there could have an intimate date. Who the fuck cares where I sit?"

"Why haven't you bought a drink?"

"Because I'm not thirsty, so I bought some food instead."

"Buy a drink, or GET OUT!"

By this time, half the coffeeshop was looking at me – they had been listening in to this strange storyteller and his wacky adventures in Australia and Nepal with awe. With my bus due in an hour, I picked up my stuff and made my way to the top of the stairs. I turned my head and grinned.

"LAY AFF THE SKUNK, YA FACIST JAKEY BASTART!" I shouted.

Before Speccy Bernard could react, I was down the stairs and out the door, having wished the doorman a pleasant evening. I ran to the nearest metro station, laughing at the fact that the local weirdos didn't want me. In those days of strife, brother-on-brother violence was the last thing I needed. Nevertheless, my dark side was peaking that day, and for some reason I was loving it…

I caught the metro back to Zuidplein, grinning at the fact that despite my views on the subject, I had checked off the stereotypical Brits Abroad checklist (piss off the locals, get barred from local establishments) in a most spectacular way. Soon, I was back at the bus stop, waiting with a Rotterdam local of African descent for the bus to Brussels.

"Hello, my friend."

I looked up at a Senegalese man whom, like Speccy Bernard, had the capability of materialising out of nowhere. I knew what was coming; he was dressed well, he was going to try and make friends with us in perfect English, and claim to be homeless and have no papers so he could scrounge some money off us. In other words, he was what the people of the Gambia like to call a *bumster*.

Now I don't believe in giving money, I believe in giving advice. I could have told him that his English was so good he could qualify as an TEFL teacher and earn more money in Senegal than he would in the Netherlands. I could have told him about Restless Development. I could have told him that the world was looking towards Africa for the next great idea, how Senegal had a better culture than most of Europe. But sadly, I didn't, because I was so knackered.

"I don't have any Euros."

"But I'm homeless!"

"I don't have any Euros!"

"But they're going to deport me!"

"I. DON'T HAVE. ANY. EUROS. ON. ME. BECAUSE. I SPENT. THEM. ALL." I code-switched to broken Gàidhlig. "THA MI LUCHD-TURAIS." ('I'm just a tourist…' Well, I wasn't, but what the hell.)

The Gàidhlig language saving my skin (or was it currency?) once again, he moved on to the Dutchman sat next to me, who gave much of the advice I would have given and so much more, so I didn't feel so bad afterwards.

The Flixbus to Brussels came along shortly afterwards, the driver route-learning with his colleague, and we meandered onto the *autosnelweg*. Then, as I was falling asleep for the *nth* time, Storm Doris scared the living shit out of me by blowing the emergency exits on the roof open, prompting a guy sitting behind me to close one of them again. The bus continued its journey at a hundred kilometres an hour, the drivers unphased that there were no vehicles on the road and that the bus started dancing every time the emergency exits blew open, which was every few seconds.

"Scottish weather…" I commented to the guy standing up.

He looked at me with a serious Germanic expression.

"*Sprechen sie Deutsch?*"

"*Nein – Englisch?*"

"*Nein – Français?*"

"Oui, un peu."

He launched a conversation at me in rapid, but accentless and perfectly understandable, French. I thought for a second about what he said, and felt my face going a bit pale.

"Je comprends ça," I replied, nodding slowly.

A young Eastern European lady leant across the aisle towards me.

"Excuse me, do you speak English?"

"Yes – what's up?"

"Do you understand what that man's saying? He's been talking like that since The Hague."

"Yes. He's concerned that because the wind's blowing so hard it's blowing open the emergency exits and making the bus swerve across the road, and that the road's so wet, he thinks that the bus will hit the point of no return and blow over, possibly into that dyke currently passing to our right."

"Oh."

"In short, he's convinced that we're all going to die tonight."

The colour drained from her face. I turned towards the front.

"Conducteur," I shouted at the driver, *"ralentissez à soixante, s'il vous plait!"*

It transpired that the two drivers only spoke Dutch and German, so the German guy – who by now was literally holding the bus together along with another guy at the back of the bus – translated my plea. The drivers finally got the message, and slowed down to sixty kilometres an hour.

I figured if I was going to die, I was going to do it in style, so I leant back and stuck Frank Zappa's *Freak Out!* on. By the time we got to Antwerp, though, we were heading inland and the wind had died off, leaving the passengers holding the bus together to sit back down again.

DAY 4

An hour later, we were in Brussels and I was chatting with the Dutch guy who had boarded the Flixbus with me in Rotterdam – it transpired that he was on his way to England for the first time and was wondering what to see. Needless to say, I told him to go straight to Scotland, or failing that, Oxford.

Presently, the bus to London materialised, complete with the same driver who had taken me from London to Gent. He did a double-take.

"Oh, hello! It's you again!"

"Yeah – I'm an apparition that appears when you're having a bad period and you need cheering up."

"So, did you enjoy Brussels then?"

"Yeah – it's a lot less boring than I thought! I saw the Prime Minister…"

I boarded the bus and drifted off as we were passing through the outskirts of Brussels. It felt like a second had passed, when suddenly the lights came on. Once again, the drivers had changed at Gent.

"Ladies and gentlemen, we are now arriving at the Eurotunnel terminal in Calais. Please have your passports ready for inspection. You may also need to take your bags off the bus for inspection by the French authorities – we'll see."

In front of us was a Megabus from Amsterdam – the passengers had been forced to take their bags off to put through the scanner. Our driver soon got back on the P.A.

"The French have just told me that it will be just an ID check for us. You can leave your bags on the bus." Presumably, there were no drugs or Dutch people on the ME4 from Cologne to London via Brussels and Gent…

After passing through the British passport check, where a beaming lady who had obviously drunk too much coffee checked my passport and wished me well, the bus boarded the train whereupon I immediately went for a massive shit. A French lady constantly pulled at the door (and obviously didn't hear me shouting *'occupé'!*), and by the time I finished, a crew member was about to put a staff key in the lock.

"You all right, mate?"

"I am now…"

I returned to the bus and slept until London. Walking with the Dutchman to Victoria railway station ("London's suburbs are shit!" he was musing aloud. "I thought that they would have the romance of Amsterdam, but no!"), I boarded a Tube train to Euston and paid over the odds for a train ticket for the 0930 Virgin service to Glasgow Central. Thing is, Storm Doris had cancelled all the trains the previous day, and the trains to Manchester were still cancelled, so the train was packed to what Mumbaikars refer to as 'super dense crush load'. The aisles and vestibules were packed with standing bodies, even in first class. I had nowhere to sit until Warrington, and had nothing to grab on to, so I had to adopt a surfing stance for the first two hours as the train was travelling at two-hundred kilometres an hour.

The faulty toilet door didn't help matters either, especially after a French kid went for a shit and didn't flush it down. Eventually, the conductor came on the PA and, mumbling more than an actor in a BBC drama, casually mentioned that there were twenty free seats at the front of the train. Unfortunately, there were at least fifty people in between me and those seats. I contemplated my late grandfather's advice – try to get a seat in first class, and if the ticket fascist comes round, just hand over your address and say 'Sue me!' – and immediately dismissed it. There were just too many people on the train to pull off a stunt like that.

The conductor would later announce that the refreshment trolley was coming round, and ask that any standing passengers would make way for the trolley. Now, these people had paid through the nose for a ticket, and Virgin Trains were attempting to squeeze them for every other penny they had and run them over in the process. Needless to say, the trolley never materialised.

When I finally got a seat, I slept until Lockerbie, and realised that the ticket fascist had given up all attempt to beat his or her way through the train. Either that, or they didn't want to wake me up for fear of the resulting destruction of their mortality. I felt like I had flushed ninety pounds down the toilet that read 'Please don't flush nappies, sanitary towels, paper towels, gum, old phones, unpaid bills, junk mail, your ex's sweater, hopes, dreams or goldfish down this toilet' – maybe I should have done a 'Hannah' and hid there like when she came up to Scotland to see me. At least I would have had somewhere to sit…

The fun ended there. I caught a train back to Ardrossan, a ferry to Brodick and the bus home – an uneventful journey. I was knackered; my consciousness had been altered & expanded, I was several hundred quid worse off and I still hadn't been to Germany since 1996. But it was one of the greatest experiences of my life. It was just like an LSD trip, except I actually lived it and it cost a lot more. Needless to say, I slept for the next twenty hours, and vowed not to travel until the Isle of Eigg Anniversary Cèilidh in June. The fun would re-start then…

STORIES FROM SUMMER 2017

"We look to Scotland for all our ideas of civilisation."
— Voltaire

Actually, the fun didn't restart on Eigg. It restarted a week earlier than expected.

In the days not too far back, before my rampant pan-global hedonistic voyages, I used to extensively travel around the Hebrides of Scotland. I still do to some extent, but there has always been one island that has alluded me.

Well, until June 2017 anyway.

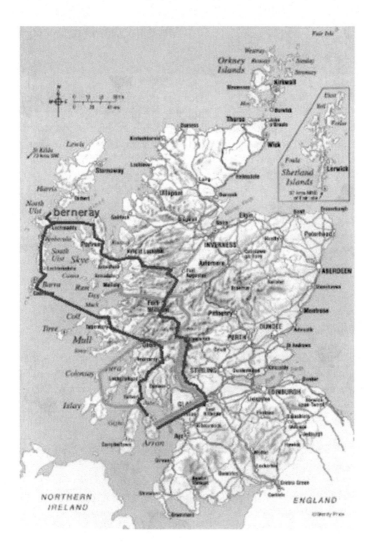

Colonsay

Colonsay, a wee island in the Inner Hebrides measuring eight by three miles, had always been an island that had alluded me. I first tried getting to Colonsay in the summer of 2010, but alas, the MV Clansman had suffered a disastrous engine failure. That summer, I visited Islay and Jura instead, returning to Arran for a few days before I travelled directly to the Outer Hebrides via Skye and accidentally discovered the Berneray Week in the process.

Fast forward to June 2017, and I was granted a week off work with only four hours' notice – I had worked beyond my sixteen-hour contract, you see. At the time, I was in Glasgow, having attended a great big Scottish independence rally with my friend Hamish, drinking bubble tea in our spare time. Hastily, I returned to Arran to pick up my other bag – which had already been packed for my trip later in the month to Eigg – and ended up kissing a girl at a freakout session in my village. But that's another story. My original plan was to go to the north end of Jura, but since I had already been there, I decided to go to Colonsay as I was falling asleep that night.

I caught the bus to Brodick the next morning, and a quad bike caught my eye. Well, it looked like any other quad bike, but it had a Thule box on the back and German number plates. Much more noticeable, though, were the large amount of police and mountain rescue volunteers at the ferry terminal. A local man with dementia was still missing, after all. Plus, there was the security situation – there was no left luggage at the ferry terminal as a result (but leaving luggage in the racks on the ferry was perfectly OK…). Not that anything concerned me, though.

I arrived into Glasgow Central at 1022, and walked to Queen Street to get a train onwards to the port of Oban, where I would get the CalMac ferry to Colonsay. My original plan was to get the early afternoon train to Oban, then I discovered that there was a 1037 train departing in just a few minutes! In front of me at the ticket machine, however, were a pair of slow-moving backpackers using the German language function on the machine. They looked at me fidgeting.

"Sorry," one of them mumbled.

"*RAUS! SCHNELL!*" I shouted at them.

As they picked up their bags and ran off at the sight of me, I punched in Oban as my destination, procured a one-way ticket and leapt aboard the train just a few seconds before the doors closed. I knew I was in no danger finding a seat; I had found out the previous year, thanks be to Hamish, that there was at least one carriage on the train that mostly comprised of unreserved seats and was half-empty. This train was no exception – as I went through to the toilet, I found out that the next carriage was occupied by old farts from Loud America. I truly felt like the Yoda of the West Highland Line.

I broke off a piece of sausage and put some Sula Bassana on, looking over towards Ferguson's Yard where the MV Glen Sannox (the new ferry for Arran) was being built as the train sped past the Clyde. After the train waited for an up train to clear the West Highland Line at Craigendoran, we started moving north up what Wanderlust once voted at the most scenic railway line in the world. I looked forward to travelling up past the Horseshoe Curve at Auch, but then I realised that I was on the train to Oban as opposed to the good one to Mallaig. That journey would have to wait for another week.

The train motored north past the Faslane nuclear submarine base, and soon we passed a small cabin by the side of the track. Back in 2011, I had accidentally spilled a cup of boiling tea down my crotch whilst trying to photograph this cabin, and the memory has remained with me ever since. I was in no danger this time – the train didn't have a refreshment trolley.

As the train got to Tarbet, I was treated to my first view of Loch Lomond that year – the view from the train overrated thanks to the prolific growth of wayside vegetation. In the days of yore, flying sparks from the steam locomotives used to keep the vegetation at bay. Alas, a diesel-powered Class 156 unit is incapable of this feat. I almost expected the next carriage to break into song ("By yon bonnie banks and yon bonnie braes…") – they probably did, but I was listening to Small Faces with the volume at eleven and was more fascinated with the antics of Happiness Stan, or rather the tremedifold wordy-speechy-most of Stanlonius Unwin the Great – oh my!

After passing a southbound tanker train at Ardlui, the train motored into Crianlarich, where it would join the line to Oban. Now, I had travelled from Oban to Glasgow on the train before, but never to. Technically, I was entering virgin territory at this point, so unlike my extensive trips to Mallaig I was fascinated by every little bit of scenery, including the sight of an Airstream caravan at Taynuilt, and the Pass of Brander signals.

Eventually, the train pulled into Oban – a major west coast port where the local Wetherspoons had Gàidhlig signs. I had a few hours to kill before the MV Clansman (yep – that ferry that failed seven years previous) departed for Colonsay, so I obtained some fish and chips from a place recommended by Rick Stein, chatting briefly with the Nepali man behind the counter. After a delicious lunch, I walked back to the terminal, passing French families, Loud Americans, Gàidhlig-speaking grannies and, of all people, one of my neighbours from Arran who was heading to Mull. At the terminal, I smiled with a sense of *schadenfreude* at the number of people who wanted tickets to Lochboisdale on South Uist, not realising that the ferries from Oban had ceased over a year previous. Finally, I was allowed to board the ferry to Colonsay, surprised that there were only thirty or so passengers on board a ship designed for six hundred. Then again, Colonsay only has a population of around a hundred, and they needed a large vessel due to the swell around the

Corryvreckan Whirlpool. I went to the bar and bought myself a bottle of Colonsay 80/-…

"That will be £26!" the barman joked.

"*Chan eil mi neach-turais, tha mi à Arainn!*" (I'm not a tourist – I'm from Arran!)

"Okay, £3.30!"

…and settled in for the two-plus-hour journey to Colonsay.

After I reached Colonsay, I managed to get a lift to the bunkhouse with a local couple and an American girl I met on the ferry before realising I had to check in at the pub in Scalasaig – two miles back down the road. After checking in and downing a much-needed pint of Colonsay IPA, I somehow managed to get a lift back to the bunkhouse with two blokes from Yorkshire who had a holiday cottage on the island.

For the next two nights, I had a room to myself – in fact, for the first night I had the entire bunkhouse to myself! I had a shower and watched a beautiful sunset as a number of corncrakes rasped nearby.

I rose early the next morning and started hiking anti-clockwise round the island, passing such sights as the local primary school (the local high school kids boarded in Oban), friendly sheep, Dharma Cottage and an old WWII pillbox. After visiting the latter, I was picked up by a pair of old German ladies in a hire car, who took me past the airport to the end of the track leading to the tidal island of Oronsay.

I visited Oronsay for five minutes, my brief stay coinciding with the mean low tide. An hour later, I found myself in the pub in Scalasaig chatting with a couple named John and Barbara, who coincidentally owned a holiday cottage on Arran. Another IPA and a trip to the shop later, I walked back to the bunkhouse, where I had some strange dreams that evening.

DREAM 1

The two stereotypical 1940s American politicians – fast-talking, trousers pulled up high – were talking to each other in Twin Peaks country:

"You know why you lost the election? Because your policies don't work, see!"

Eventually, one of them gave me a lift. Unfortunately, he gave me a lift in a Ford Edsel – the worst car ever made. In time, the brakes failed – we ended up hitting a man by the side of the road and didn't stop until we reached British Columbia.

DREAM 2

I was walking down through a mountain pass, when I noticed a sign: 'WELCOME TO INDIA. PLEASE PRESENT YOURSELF AT IMMIGRATION.'

So, I did what the sign told me, and presented myself to an officer who looked like an Indian Jack Black. Unfortunately, my smartphone (which had all of my visa information on it) died, so he refused my entry into India. Needless to say, I was pissed off. Then, I had an idea. I turned around to the gathering crowd behind me.

"OH MY GOD!" I shouted. "IT'S JACK BLACK ON IMMIGRATION!"

The crowd rushed forward to take photos, and I ran off in the mayhem.

The bunkhouse was a decent place in the end, but the beds creaked, the rooms were freezing and there could be a little more room in the toilets. But hey, I paid twenty-one pounds per night and had the entire place to myself until two guys from Lancashire showed up, so I shouldn't complain.

Later that morning, another English couple showed up, preparing to move into my room, which was named *Dùn Ghallan* (the sapling fortress). I taught the English how to aspirate in the vocative, but alas, the cleaners responded using the English pronunciation. After watching a few episodes of *Sheep in the Big City* (the most underrated animated show on television), I started walking back to the ferry terminal.

On my way back to the ferry terminal, I amused myself by shouting 'ALLEZ!' at a small group of posh English cyclists slowly climbing a hill. Instead of heading straight for the ferry terminal, I called in at the shop to buy three bottles of Colonsay 80/- before heading to the Pantry for a much-needed cheeseburger and Malteser tiffin slice.

I eventually returned to the ferry terminal and settled in for a long wait for the ferry to Islay. I produced a copy of Timothy Leary's *The Politics of Ecstasy* (a book I hadn't read since I was in Belgium earlier in the year), and plonked myself down outside the ferry terminal.

I was disturbed a few times over the course of the next four hours. An Englishman off a pleasure craft asked me where the Pantry was. An Irishman who was based in Cape Cod discussed *The Politics of Ecstasy* with me. An old English couple noticed a sign next to me:

"Ooh, look Henry! That sign's in a foreign language!"

I looked over.

"You're right – it's in English!"

Eventually, I spent the last hour talking with an old Scottish couple, who were visiting from Islay for the day with a coach tour. Finally, I boarded the MV Hebridean Isles – I once spent seven hours on this vessel when I was sixteen, travelling from the island of Barra to Oban on a special overnight run. I still remember sitting on the outer deck in my underwear at four in the morning with a pack of Hobnobs in one hand and a can of McEwan's Export in the other, the settlements of Lochaline and Fishnish passing by in the night. Alas, I was only going to be on this ferry for about an hour this time. But there was somebody I knew on board – the onboard services manager. I had previously met him on the Caledonian Isles and the Hebrides, and I knew exactly what he was going to say once he came on the tannoy system. To the amusement of all the other passengers other than myself, this Gael's vocal capabilities were a stilted cross between a five-year-old and William Shatner:

"AAAVE YOUR ATTENTION PLEASE, PASSENGERS PLEASE NOTE. THE CAFETERIA IS NOW O-PEN. SERVING HOT MEEEALS, LIGHT SNAAACKS, TEAS, AND COFFEEEES. THAAAT'S HOT MEEEALS. LIGHT SNAAACKS. TEAS AND COFFEEEES. ARE NOW BEING SERRRRVED, INTCAFETERIA."

I attempted to tune him out by listening to Led Zeppelin with the volume at eleven, focusing more on the beautiful scenery as we approached the sound of Jura. The peaks of Jura, on the left, stood out in particular.

"AAAVE YOUR ATTENTION PLEASE, THIS IS THE FINAL CALL FOR HOT MEEEALS…"

The scenery got even more beautiful as the ferry approached Port Askaig.

"AAAVE YOUR ATTENTION PLEASE, THE SHOP, CAFETERIA, AND BAARR, WILL CLOSE, INFIVEMINUTES. THAAAT'S THE SHOP, CAFETERIA, AND BAAAR, WILL CLOSE, INFIVEMINUTES."

Finally, I arrived into Port Askaig, a village on the island of Islay which I hadn't visited in nearly seven years. The previous time I was here, just after I had turned sixteen, I had made my way over to Jura and spent a blissful night camping in the north of the island. Alas, I was only going to be in this part of the world for about forty-five minutes this time.

The Hebridean Isles pulled out of the berth to make way for the MV Finlaggan, the ferry I would be getting to Kennacraig. I walked onto the government-monopoly ferry, and found myself looking at the TARDIS centre console on a scaled-down Cunard liner. Overawed by the luxurious presence and attentiveness of the staff, I wandered upstairs to the cafeteria and spent the next two hours eating chips, playing *Call of Duty* and, most importantly, drinking coffee.

The ferry arrived into Kennacraig after sunset, and I had a five-mile night hike to Claonaig on the east side of Kintyre. I put The Fall on and strode out along the B8001 road, arriving into Claonaig just after midnight. This is where my master plan took effect. I knew from previous experiences that the Claonaig ferry terminal – a glorified enclosed bus shelter – didn't have a lock on the door. Or a handle, for that matter. I merely entered the terminal, used my bag to stop the door from blowing open, put down my air bed and sleeping bag on a bench and logged onto the WiFi. It was bliss.

Who needs a tent?

The next morning, I woke up early and packed everything up before anyone could notice that I squatted a ferry terminal the previous night, and breakfasted on beer and anchovies before the ferry to Lochranza showed up. A few hours later, I found myself on board the MV Catriona in the presence of a group of kids from Tarbert Academy, their exchange friends from Austria, and a teacher who was unaware that the buses to and from the north end of Arran ran every three hours. Soon, I found myself at the polling station in Lochranza (did I mention that it was General Election Day?), casting my vote and happily chatting with the SNP canvasser. A neighbour of mine who came to vote gave me a lift home, thus ending my trip to Colonsay.

Many years ago, before my wanderlust took me to the forests of Australia and the mountains of Nepal. I had a lucid dream. In the dream, I was at a party on an island off the west coast of Scotland, but I didn't know which one. A beautiful lassie led me by the arm to the toilet, and before we could make love I awoke.

The dream pretty much came to life over the course of this trip. Several times.

DAY 1

It was the second part of the dream sequence. I walked through the house, shooting zombies by echolocation. Eventually, I found myself in a dungeon-like room – it was probably a dungeon. As I was locked in, a number of trilobites materialised out of the darkness.

"I am General Atana," the commander intoned. "I am here to kill you."

I awoke with a start. General Atana could cut my dick off for all I cared – I was about to set off for Eigg!

An old fart frowned at the presence of the dreadlocked weirdo with the baggage as the bus motored towards Brodick. After the bus got to the ferry terminal, I discovered that the X36 bus from Ardrossan to Glasgow didn't serve Ardrossan Harbour any more. For me, this was a kick in the cock: this meant I would have to spend an extra two-fifty for the train. It was a bit of a shit start to the Eigg trip, but hey, at least I was travelling again.

The train journey from Ardrossan to Glasgow turned out to be vaguely eventful.

"I like your shirt!" the lady who had boarded at Johnstone smiled at me.

This particular shirt had a picture of the Palace of Westminster, with the slogan 'NEVER UNDERESTIMATE THE POWER OF STUPID PEOPLE IN LARGE GROUPS' underneath.

"*Glè mhath!*" I smiled back.

Soon, I had made my way to my friend Hamish's flat, where I would spend the night. We watched a few episodes of *Twin Peaks* and played some music at double speed before I attempted to turn in for the night. Lewis and Katja, his Finnish girlfriend, would show up later in the evening with a kitten named Patrick on a lead, but they were away before midnight. Finally, I could sleep.

DAY 2

I woke early the next morning and made my merry way to Glasgow Queen Street, purchasing a return ticket to Mallaig from the same machine where I shouted at those slow Germans just over a week previous. Boarding the train to Mallaig, I bagged an unreserved table and was joined by Steven, a high school physics teacher from Louisiana who was travelling to Skye. We would spend much of the journey to Mallaig comparing the education systems of Scotland, the United States and Nepal (well, I used to teach there…), as well as discussing the track-side points of interest. As a veteran West Highland Line traveller, I would tell Steven about our current location and he would film part of the journey on his phone, narrating what I had just told him.

Our fellow travellers that day included a large number of other Americans, a few girls wearing Mànran jumpers, and also a large group of scouts who disembarked at Bridge of Orchy. Opposite us was a fat nerd who resembled Bubbles from *Trailer Park Boys*, who was reading a Philip K. Dick novel – I would later bump into him at the party as he was smoking a pipe. The monotony of the most scenic railway line in the world (much of which was hidden in the thick cloud and fog of that particular day) was broken by the toilet door locking from the outside.

A generic picture of Glenfinnan taken by the author, circa 2013

"Ladies and gentlemen, we are about to pass over the famous Glenfinnan Viaduct," the conductress announced over the tannoy system. "As many of you will know, they filmed the *Harry Potter* films here…"

There was a great rush to the left-hand side of the train.

"The Glenfinnan Viaduct was constructed by Robert McAlpine & Sons from 1897 to 1901," the refreshment lady spontaneously announced to our carriage. "The viaduct is built from concrete, and has twenty-one semicircular spans of fifty feet. It is the longest concrete railway bridge in Scotland at four-hundred-and-sixteen yards, and crosses the River Finnan at a height of one hundred feet. Like my friend was just saying, they filmed the *Harriet*, sorry, *Harry Potter* films here…"

"Rule 63…" I chuckled.

"…as well as *Monarch of the Glen* and *Stone of Destiny*. And if you look down there, you can make out the Glenfinnan Monument, which is a monument to Bonnie Prince Charlie raising his standard in 1745.

"And that, ladies and gentlemen, is the information you don't get on the *Jacobite Steam Train!*"

With that, the train pulled into Glenfinnan station. A regal-looking purpose-built train stood at the opposite platform.

"That's the *Royal Scotsman*," the refreshment lady explained to me. "Those people are on a seven-night tour, having paid three thousand pounds per night for a suite."

As the train responsible for briefly raising Glenfinnan's GDP per capita to the highest in Scotland slowly pulled away, I made faces at the dining multi-millionaires and their bratty teenage daughters whilst humming *Ode to Joy*. The Lady Richington and the Emir of Iraqistan looked visibly appalled by the unannounced presence of the Virgin Sex God.

"Sorry folks, I've only got teas and coffees," the refreshment lady was saying. "If you want caviar, get the *Royal Scotsman!*"

Soon, the train reached Mallaig, where I bid goodbye to Steven and procured a return ticket to Eigg. In front of me in the queue for the ferry outside was Pat, a friend of mine from Shotts who, like me, travelled up to Eigg every year. We bantered for a short while before we boarded the *MV Lochnevis* and got separated. I ended up in the passenger lounge and asked to sit down next to two guys (one of whom was also called Steven) and, as per tradition in Scotland, a beer was thrust into my hand before I could sit down. I was later joined by a lady from Fife and her Labrador, the latter of whom just couldn't bear not being stroked.

As I disembarked from the ferry at Eigg an hour later, I re-joined Pat, who had been joined by Claire, his niece, and Stuart, her recently-married husband. We met up with Kevin – another traveller from Shotts who had introduced me to the Eigg Anniversary Cèilidh when I was sixteen – and after I procured a ticket for the cèilidh, we all made our way to the informal campsite on the other side of Galmisdale Bay.

That's when disaster occurred.

I was rushing to put my tent up in the rain before it flooded. It was a cheap festival job, but I still didn't expect the poles to break. With the combined help of Claire, Stuart, Kevin, Pat and a drunk camper from Derbyshire who fortunately had some duct tape handy, we managed to put my tent up for what would be its final time. My initial plan was go camping on Skye after Eigg, but this plan was now scuppered. I returned to the tearoom to act upon my backup plan: book a bed at the Loch Ossian Youth Hostel for Monday night. Sorted, I returned to the campsite to get drunk with my compatriots.

I spent the next few hours getting seriously pissed on cheap cider, describing my adventures in Australia and Nepal to Claire and Stuart.

"…So I went to the Pashupatinath Temple with these people, which is like the holiest Hindu temple in Nepal. Anyway, there were all these wild monkeys there, so I gurned at one and said 'Ee, monkeh! You got any P.G. Tips, lad?'…"

Claire in particular was awed by these tales, but I wouldn't find out how much so until the next day. In the meantime, the cèilidh was just starting, so Stuart and I started meandering towards the source of the music and laughter. A teuchter Transit pulled over as we were walking up the hill.

"Ye needing a lift?" called the driver.

"Sure! Is there enough space for this guy?"

"Fuck aye – this is a van, ya daftie!"

Stuart and I bounced around in the back of the Transit until we reached the community hall, where he ran off to the marquee bar to get even more pissed than he was. I hung around in the hall, watching folks dance to the sounds of the JaMaTha (which, using Gàidhlig phonetics, is pronounced Ya-Ma-Ha) Cèilidh Band. Claire soon joined me.

"Have you seen Stuart?"

"Yeah."

"Well, where is he?"

"I killed him and ate his liver."

"Very funny. Now, where is he?"

"He's outside getting pissed in the marquee."

She looked disappointed.

"The next dance is the Canadian Barn Dance!" announced the MC.

"Wanna dance?" I asked Claire.

She did. We danced the Canadian Barn Dance before Stuart rocked up. Despite the presence of her husband, Claire still wanted to dance with me for the next dance – a waltz. I waved her away.

"No, dance with your husband!" I said, trying to make myself as small as possible.

The rest of the night was, well, weird. Even for the likes of me. A wedding had just taken place on the island, specially dated as it coincided with the twentieth anniversary of the Eigg Community Buyout. These guys and girls must have brought the Spanish Fly with them, because a number of girls were beginning to take a little more than a passing interest in me. A girl who, I think, was on speed attempted to dance with me and fondle my beard as Pictish Trail were playing.

"Get ready for the drop!" she was shouting. "Oh yes, get ready for the drop!"

I managed to get a kiss from a few lassies that night – the second had randomly appeared in front of me on the dancefloor, declared me handsome and covered my mouth with hers before I could protest.

Daimh

After a break where Bob Marley's *Exodus* was put on random, Daimh started their set. I had seen them on Eigg a few years previous, and they had got markedly better since the last gig, but were nowhere near as good as Pictish Trail that night. The guitarist messed around with some primitive electronic gear, causing a number of people in the room to shout 'HAWKWIND!'

Then another lassie named Zoë, who had obviously taken too many eccies, started flirting with me. So, I started flirting back.

"You know, I used to live in Nepal."

"Really? I have an ex who's out there volunteering out there right now!"

"Really! Who's he gone with?"

"Restless Development. He's a Team Leader out in a place called Sindhuli."

"Fuck me, it's a small world!" I exclaimed. "That's the same charity and placement I was on! Except I was just a meagre volunteer…"

We grooved to Daimh for a while, then she touched me on the arm.

"Hey – I'm going to the bathroom!"

"Okay," I said. (Why should I care?)

"No, I'm going to the bathroom…" she grinned, grabbing my arm.

Zoë led me to the bathroom area, where six years previous I had discovered my purpose and the potential of what my own existence could offer. I had flashbacks to the dream I had in 2014, surrendering to the feeling like a zombie. When we got to the disabled shitter, however, we discovered that another couple was shagging in there. As the lassie was loaded up to her eyeballs in eccies, she felt that she had to do something other than wait, so in an anticlimactical manner, she returned to the dancefloor.

Having been close to scoring for the *nth* time, I went to the gents to have a piss, and started having the same feeling that I had when I first came to Eigg when I was sixteen. The toilet started spinning, so I returned to the dancefloor, which was shaking from side-to-side like a ship on the sea. DJ Dolphin Boy's equipment started smiling evilly at me. I realised then I had come full circle – this was probably going to be my last Eigg trip for some years – and had a glimpse of the future (nearly getting laid). I smiled as Daimh rocked on with a cover of 'Pink Elephants on Parade'. As they ended their set, I started shouting 'FIVE MORE TUNES! FIVE MORE TUNES!', to which their response was 'Okay, two more!'

Musically, it wasn't the best Eigg cèilidh – Niteworks had really been on point the previous year – but the soul... oh my!

DAY 3

I woke up just before midday and climbed An Sgurr in an attempt to swim in Lochan Beinn Tighe – the island's water supply. The previous year, Lewis had swum in the loch under the influence of LSD – Hamish, my cousin Lex and I had hidden his clothes, and Lewis somehow came back to the campsite with his clothes on an hour or so later. Today, though, I couldn't find the loch owing to the thick fog. After returning to sea level and having a shower at the tearoom, I returned to the campsite for lunch.

I found out that Claire and Stuart had returned to the mainland when I was looking the other way, and as such, Pat felt it was safe to tell me a few things.

"You know, Claire was really enamoured with you last night!"

"Aye. A lot of girls were – I nearly got laid with this other lassie for fuck's sake..."

"Aye? Well, Claire couldn't stop talking about you, she thinks that you're a really good dancer for a start."

"Pfft. It was just a Canadian Barn Dance. I only know that shit from social dancing in school."

"Aye, but then there were those stories you well telling us last night. You know, like the ones about the wallabies, that time you were on the radio, and that school in Nepal."

"Well, they were all true!"

"Exactly! She found them really interesting because they were sincere!"

"Ah."

"You know, if Claire was up here without Stuart, there would be no doubt that you and her would have ended up shagging last night!"

"How do you reckon that? There's a good reason why people call me the Virgin Sex God!"

"I'm pretty convinced that she was outright fantasising about you last night. Stuart's really fucking jealous of you by the way."

"Why do you think I was encouraging THEM to dance?"

The conversation ended there. I returned to my tent, and ended up watching David Lynch's *Dune* on my phone before sleeping for the rest of the afternoon. That evening was the afterparty at the tearoom. I found myself in the company of Pat and a few other people, including a lassie who had placed a speaker between her breasts and was blasting Neil Young with the volume at eleven. Notably, though, was a fellow traveller named Daniel, a chillum-smoking dude with Asperger's Syndrome who had followed a cosmic path similar to mine, albeit he had a girlfriend and had never left Europe. We discussed life's eccentricities and Rainbow Gatherings for several hours before I went off to the bog for a piss.

As I left, I bumped into yet another lassie who was immediately turned on by my presence. As we made out and hugged, contemplating where this was going, Kevin rocked up with his camera.

"Can I take a picture of you two?" he grinned.

She bolted.

"I think that lassie's into you," he mused.

I glared at him.

"No shit, Sherlock! I almost got laid, ya cunt!"

I staggered back to my tent shortly after, and slept until midday.

DAY 4

I cursed the world as the sky turned blue for the first time during my trip. After ceremoniously burying what was left of my tent in a nearby bin, I made my way back to the ferry. En route, I had an interesting experience after putting a remix of Captain Beefheart's 'Electricity' on – a gent wearing a Beefheart t-shirt materialised and started grooving with me…

On the ferry, after introducing Daniel and his girlfriend to Kevin in a successful attempt to get them a lift back down to Glasgow, I discussed life with a small group of old tourists from Yorkshire, whom I convinced that I was from Huddersfield (well, I was born there).

"I'll tell you summat, lad," one of them was saying, "those Jocks will eat anything, they will. I mean, deep-fried Mars Bars?"

Eventually, the banter turned to the Gàidhlig language.

"*A bheil Gàidhlig agaibh?*" I asked him. (Have you the Gàidhlig?)

"You what, lad?"

"*Chan eil? Chan eil Gàidhlig agaibh?*" (No? No Gàidhlig?)

I laughed as he looked away embarrassed. Once again, I had put the Gàidhlig language to good use.

After we got off the ferry in Mallaig, Pat, Daniel and I meandered along to the chip shop adjoining the railway station, which had just become a little part of Loud America.

"Excuse me chef!" shouted Cody Dempsey II for the third time. "What in hell's a King Rib?"

"It's pork, pal," replied the chef.

"WOW! Ya hear that, Phyllis? Pork!"

I ordered the chicken goujon supper, and bid farewell to Pat and Daniel. I boarded the ScotRail train on the platform bound for Fort William, spending part of the subsequent journey with an old man from Lochailort who had a few tall tales.

"Ye know," he was saying, "there's this wee generator that can fit into the palm of your hand, and it can power an entire hoose!"

"Bollocks," I replied. "Newton's Laws and all that."

"Ach, you're ontae me!"

After a memorable incident where I made faces at a group of kids at the Loch Eil Outward Bound centre who were waving at the train, I reached Fort William and boarded a sleeper train bound for London, travelling as far as Corrour in the presence of yet another American.

Loch Ossian

From Corrour, I walked to the Loch Ossian Youth Hostel in the presence of Dagma, a girl visiting from Berlin. After meeting a relatively-tame stag (which I later learnt was named Honey), I knocked on the warden's door and was greeted by Jan – a beaming lady from the Scoraig scene. She introduced me to Ian and Andy – my bedfellows for the night – and left me to my own devices. After some idle banter, I was more than ready for sleep, so I stuck a dub techno mix on and drifted away into oblivion.

DAY 5

The next morning saw me swimming in Loch Ossian with a lassie named Fiona – Dorothy, her mother, watching on from the bank. After a bracing swim and a much-needed hot shower (available only thanks to a recently-built hydro dam north of Corrour), I walked the mile or so back to the train station.

A train to Mallaig was pulling out of the station having deposited a few middle-aged Scottish hill-walkers, who struck up a conversation with me.

"So where are you going now?" they asked.

"I'm just going over to that bridge to do the *Trainspotting* thing," I replied.

"Now don't you go saying that the Scottish are a shower of wankers!" one of them chuckled.

"Actually, Renton said it was the English that were wankers," I replied.

Silence. One of the hill-walkers smiled and winked.

"You're right there, pal!"

I sat down on the bridge, cracked open a can of John Smiths and stuck some Underworld on. Soon, though, it was time to return to the station to get my train, and just over half an hour later I was back on the West Highland Line and barrelling towards Glasgow. The sound of Hawkwind and Coogan's Bluff filled my ears as the train rapidly descended from the summit of the British railway network back to the sea.

I decided to get off at Dalmuir – the final stop before Glasgow Queen Street – as I knew that there were local trains to Central from here and didn't fancy walking across Glasgow with so much baggage. Correct to my thoughts, a local train for Larkhall via Glasgow Central materialised, as did a hyperactive little shit who shouted "ARE YOU THE CHOO-CHOO DRIVER?" when the driver made his way to the cab, and later declared that it was "BOABY TIME!" just before he got off. I was glad he was away, but not for long – a large group of high school kids boarded the train halfway to Glasgow. They weren't so bad, but there was an occasion where one of the kids was discussing something that happened in his class that day:

"So he was saying to the teacher, 'WHERE'S THE JEW BOOK?' in a loud voice…"

I fought very hard to stop laughing. His friends' laughter was very contagious to say the least…

After spontaneously meeting my old English teacher in Ardrossan, I travelled back to Arran in the presence of a group of Indian tourists who openly laughed at a very morbidly obese CalMac crew member. Soon, though, I had arrived back home after catching the bus from Brodick, but not before I noticed the MV Loch Bhrusda (a ship named after the largest loch on the isle of Berneray) at the pier in Lochranza. I smiled, knowing that this year's Berneray Week was going to be a blast, even if half the people I wanted to see wouldn't be showing up…

Berneray

mats christen prynor anna-marie me liss paul janice

(paul and janice were the ones who introduced me to berneray week in 2010)

For many consecutive years, I have travelled to a little island in the Outer Hebrides for a local festival. It all began when I was sixteen, when I knew my parents needed a court order to stop me from travelling. I attempted to get to the island of Colonsay but failed: after returning home for a few days and picking an island at random, I found myself on the 915 Citylink bus from Glasgow to Portree – the largest village on the island of Skye. After a night camping outside town, where I witnessed a beautiful dawn over Raasay, I made my way to the port of Uig. From here, I caught the CalMac ferry to Lochmaddy, the *de facto* capital of the island of North Uist. Another short bus ride later, and I found myself on the island I had hoped to get to.

Berneray.

The youth hostel there looked pretty decent, so I decided to stay there for a few nights. In the kitchen, I chatted to an English couple named Paul and Janice.
"Are you here for the Berneray Week?" Paul asked.
"What's Berneray Week?" I asked.
And thus began a long love affair with the island of Berneray, or at least the Berneray Week. Over the next eight years, I would associate my time here with many things. A beautiful windswept landscape. The long walk from the hostel to the shop. The call of the corncrake. And best of all, some of the friendliest people I had ever met before my time in Nepal. And it wasn't just the locals – the regular travellers ended up giving me a rare sense of belonging too. Well, apart from the foul Northern Irish git I encountered on my second trip in 2011, who made me feel more unsafe than I ever have been. At least he has a lifetime ban from the hostel now.

Of course, it wasn't just about the island itself. It was also about the satisfaction of completing the long, scenic trip up on the bus from Glasgow to Uig, passing through the best of what the Highlands had to offer. It was about the sounds of the Chemical Brothers, Yes, Yello, Jethro Tull, Klaus Schulze, Gong, Ozric Tentacles, Earthling Society, Sketch, Niteworks and various psytrance mixtapes pulsing through my in-ear buds as I made my way north to the ferry. It was about the surreal thrill of bringing four active mead fermenters on the bus with me to bring to the cèilidhs – not like anyone else wanted any, but still! It was about the smell of cheap *mi goreng* from Glasgow's Chinatown cooking in the hostel kitchen, the taste of powdered milk mixed with aloe vera juice, the relentless taste of baked beans and cheap Lidl sausage.

Much of that changed this year. Even many of the people I know from the area were away this year. Three were away in Africa, one of whom by the name of Daisy maintained an excellent blog during her time volunteering in South Africa. Two were away in the merchant navy. And there were several others whom I just did not see for one reason or another. At least Calum Paterson – the guy who recommended Soft Machine and The Fall to me when I was away in Australia – would be on the island…

Still, I couldn't blame the absentees. For the 2017 Berneray Week was supposed to be my last for some years. As it happened, I would make it to the Berneray Week for the next two years afterwards, but that's spoilers for the next book…

The Journey

Just three days after my twenty-third birthday, I walked to the bus stop in Pirnmill that afternoon laden with more gear than I took to Australia and Nepal. My bags contained – amongst other things – my camping gear, including a green one-man tent that has been with me since I was fifteen, and a significant quantity of alcohol. In contrast to previous years, I only had half a litre of mead in my possession; the rest was made up of absinthe and Whyte and Mackay to make up for the loss. The cèilidhs would be amazing this year…

As I watched one of my neighbours drive his tractor along the beach, forcing a young girl and her grandmother out of the way, the bus arrived.

"Lochranza please, Gary," I smiled to the driver.

"Lochranza? That's a new one!"

"Yep – you caught me sneaking off the island via the back door!"

I paid my fare, and fifteen minutes or so later I arrived in Lochranza, where the MV Catriona was loading. Normally, I would have gone to Brodick, headed for Glasgow and stayed at my friend Hamish's flat, but he was away doing the North Coast 500 with Bòidheach the dog, a hire car and a Dutch model name Rose. Hence my camping gear.

The Catriona – a ferry that ran primarily on electricity – silently departed Lochranza to the cacophony of car alarms, marking the first time I had left the island on a Hebridean trip via Lochranza since 2010. Half an hour later, the ferry had docked in Claonaig, where it was a short wait for the 448 bus to Tarbert, a fair-sized village on Loch Fyne. The driver was talking to a large French family.

"Have you got any apples?"

"Apples? No…"

"Well, Troy over there's expecting one…"

I looked over to a nearby field where Troy, a horse, was eagerly expecting a hand-fed apple. Alas, there were no apples on the bus, so after depositing the French family in the centre of Claonaig, the bus sped towards Tarbert.

I spent a little over an hour in Tarbert, mainly feasting on coronation chicken and cottage cheese from the Co-op. Eventually, the 926 Citylink bus arrived, and with the Celtic-techno fusion of Martyn Bennett's self-titled first album pulsing through my in-ear buds, I relaxed as the bus made its way north to Inveraray. En route, I witnessed the beauty of Loch Fyne, the Crinan Canal and the Slàinte Bar in Inveraray, and a random funfair in Lochgilphead.

Here, a fellow freak boarded the bus. He was an American, who stripped to his underwear, ate his dinner on the bus and, still hungry, phoned the chippy in Inveraray to order a fish supper. Eventually, the bus reached Inveraray, where I was to transfer onto the 976 bus to Oban. With time to spare, I went down the chippy for a delicious king rib supper, and witnessed various police cars (both marked and unmarked) and a fire engine passing through the town at speed. Evidently, something wasn't right. I returned to the bus stop, where the driver of the 926 was waiting for me.

"There's been an accident at the road end for Dunoon," he was saying. "Some loser pulled out onto the main road and got hit by a car doing sixty miles an hour. Don't worry, though, your bus is coming. It will be late, though, really late."

As the American freak boarded the bus with his fish supper in hand, the bus sped off north on the road towards Dalmally, where it would turn right and head south via Crianlarich to get to Glasgow. A few minutes later, I met Martin and Louisa, a Belgian couple who had disembarked from a bus from Dunoon a few hours previous, and were also heading for Oban. I chatted with them for the next several hours, sharing my Tunnock's bars with them and discussing life and *Futurama*. In time, we were considering what to do. A dickhead who worked for West Coast Motors had rocked up with the 486 bus for Dunoon, didn't contemplate radioing the other bus to figure out its whereabouts, and fucked off on the road north to Dalmally in an attempt to get back to Dunoon the long way round.

"You know what we should do?" I asked. "We should give up waiting for this bus."

"Why?"

"Because as soon as we give up, the bus will come. It's like how you usually find what you're looking for when you're on the verge of giving up. Haven't you ever read *The Alchemist?*"

Louisa giggled. As we were about to give up, the 976 bus appeared on the horizon – over two hours behind schedule – and as soon as Martin, Louisa and I had settled at the front of the bus, we were motoring north.

"Anyone for Dalmally?" called the bus driver.

Silence.

"No? Well, we're not going!" she declared defiantly.

The passengers cheered as we passed a number of cars by the side of the road.

"What's going on there?" asked Martin.

"Probably a bunch of people dogging," I replied.

"What's dogging?" Martin asked loudly.

"Sssh, not so loud!" I muttered.

The bus driver supressed her giggles as I quietly explained the concept of dogging to the Belgians. An hour later, we finally arrived into Oban, where Martin, Louisa and I walked the two miles or so to the Kerrera ferry terminal at Gallanach. It was one in the morning when we arrived, but I was skilled enough to put up my tent in the dark in ten minutes. Thank you, Duke of Edinburgh's Award. As I moved into my tent, Martin and Louisa were still figuring out the groundsheet of their tent. I fell asleep that morning surrounded by tent ruffles on one side and magic mushrooms on the rest.

I woke up to a beautiful, peaceful morning and proceeded to take down the tent. I had camped at the Gallanach ferry terminal for a very good reason: I was going to go over to Kerrera that morning. And so, after a chat with a fellow freak from Glastonbury who was sleeping in a nearby van, I found myself on the MV Gylen Lady for the five-minute crossing over to Kerrera.

Half an hour later, I was back on the mainland – I had much to do in Oban before the ferry to Barra. A Kerrera local named Colin, who was on the ferry back with me, offered me a lift into town in the back of his Land Rover Defender 110. A true teuchter wagon, it had seats lifted from an old LDV van welded to the mostly-wood-panelled cargo bay, which I had to sit on due to the presence of a child seat in the front. We chatted idlily about how CalMac taking over the Kerrera ferry was a good thing, and speculated on whether the incoming Carvoria would be a decent ferry or not, before he dropped me off at the Lidl in Oban.

After a bout of shopping, I made my way to the main ferry terminal, where I met Martin and Louisa again. They weren't waiting for the ferry, but for the Citylink bus to Fort William, which was due. I bid them adieu, and sat down in the ferry terminal in the presence of a large number of Americans heading for Iona via Mull. An elderly Irish lady sat down next to me, and we idlily chatted as we watched the mostly-elderly Mull passengers wait up to ten minutes for the lift to the 'departure lounge'.

"You know something?" she was saying. "You look like my grandchildren!"

"Well, are you from the Dingle Peninsula?" I asked.

"No…"

"Well, some of my family emigrated from there many years ago. I went back there in 2014 – it's a nice place."

A few minutes later, she was away to the lift, and I still had a few hours until my ferry to Barra was called. It would be a mostly uneventful, but beautiful, five-hour journey to Barra on the MV Isle of Lewis – I spent my time catching up on some much-needed sleep, reading, eating chips and drinking cider. Eventually, the ferry arrived at Barra, and a vaguely familiar figure in a checked jacket started talking to me just as we were about to disembark.

"You here for the *Fèis?*" he asked in a Celtic/Germanic hybrid accent.

"Nah," I replied. "I'm just passing through. The Berneray Week's on in a few days."

"Oh, really? I'm heading up there too!"

"Really…wait. AXEL? AXEL KOEHLER?"

"Um, yes…"

I knew this guy. He was a legend on Berneray, albeit I hadn't seen him in five years. He was a German, who had spent ten years living in Scotland but had returned to Germany, where lectured in Celtic Studies with emphasis on the Gàidhlig language, although he had recently found a lot of financially-rewarding work teaching German to migrants. We walked through Castlebay – my first time in the village in seven years – and soon we had to go our separate ways. He was heading for a local bunkhouse, and I was heading to a random patch of land about a third of a way up Heaval, where I would pitch the tent once again.

It was a long slog with my camping gear and four bags from Lidl, but I made it up to a good pitching spot. Exhausted from sleep deprivation and the climb, I pitched the tent a few metres away from the road, watched *Sausage Party* on my phone and fell right asleep.

I was rudely awoken early the next morning by a low-flying helicopter slowly buzzing my tent. I had a feeling it would be looking for someone (which it was), but it still wouldn't go away when I was moving around and having my breakfast. You know, sure signs that I was fine and not the person they were looking for. Besides, I was camping next to the main road from Castlebay to the airport – if I was missing, someone would have seen me by then.

An hour and a half later, thousands of pounds of aviation fuel now having burned seemingly needlessly, it finally buzzed off and left me in peace. I would later find out that a diabetic man had indeed gone missing, and had been found dead on a beach on Vatersay. The island had had enough death that year – a few months previous, a fourteen-year-old girl from Vatersay named Eilidh MacLeod had tragically been killed in the Manchester bombing. But that's another story.

I decamped and made my way back into Castlebay: despite waking up early, I had missed my bus to Aird Mhòr – the location of the ferry to Eriskay. Axel was on that bus too, so I was especially annoyed. Well, not really – I made friends with another German teacher, who was heading to Benbecula via the next bus and subsequent ferry.

Eventually, the 1020 bus came – it was a sixteen-seat Transit that served as the stereotypical Outer Hebridean bus. The German and I shared it with a Japanese tourist heading for the airport, who had a penchant for photographing everything including his bus ticket, and a large family from Cape Breton – a part of Canada where there were thousands of Gàidhlig speakers. The German and I had boarded the bus first and sat at the back, and amused ourselves by humming the *Tetris* theme as the eight or so Canadians loaded themselves and their luggage onto the bus. The grandmother sat in front of me, and we chatted idlily.

"*A bheil Gàidhlig agaibh?*" I asked.

"*Chan eil,*" she responded.

"You liar!" I exclaimed.

"What did you say?" asked the German.

"I asked her if she had the Gàidhlig, and she said no!"

"Ah."

Eventually, the bus reached Aird Mhòr, where the German and I realised our folly. We had sat at the back of the bus, and the Canadians (and their luggage…) were going on to the airport, which was after the ferry terminal. Another game of *Tetris* ensured, but soon the German and I were off the bus and on the MV Loch Alainn to Eriskay, where I discovered that one of the metal back supports on my bag had broken. Well, the bag had been with me for seven years and taken a lot of punishment around the world, and this was going to be its final journey after all.

Just over half an hour later, the German and I arrived at Eriskay and boarded the next bus. It was going to Benbecula Airport, but offered through fares to Berneray. I paid up and settled in behind Duncan the D.A Travel bus driver for the first leg of the three-hour journey north. The bus picked up a fair number of people on Eriskay, including a number of local ladies who were about three years old when the SS Politician went down during the Second World War, and an English couple who were also heading for Berneray, but not the Week. The latter quizzed the former on where the Politician went down as the bus crossed the causeway from Eriskay to South Uist, and asked whether or not an island just off the coast was St Kilda (it wasn't…). I watched the desolate landscape go by, listening in to the conversational Gàidhlig flowing between the driver and the locals (which I could understand for some reason – then again, *cupa tì* is a dead giveaway…) as the bus made its way slowly north. In Daliburgh, the drivers switched over, and a lady who knew half my friends on Berneray took us onwards to Benbecula. The German got deposited near his bed-and-breakfast, and I never saw him again.

At Benbecula, there was nearly an hour to kill before the Grenitote bus to Berneray, so I sat in the airport with the English couple, who introduced themselves to me as Alan, who was based on Benbecula during his army days, and Barbara.

"We came from Barra this morning on the bus you were aiming for," Alan was saying, "but we decided to spend a few hours on Eriskay."

"Oh, really?" I asked. "You wouldn't have happened to meet a German guy called Axel by any chance? Strange man, late thirties, checked jacket, spectacles…"

They looked at each other.

"Um, yes we did! He travelled with us to Eriskay, and kept showing us pictures and these short stories he wrote. He's a bit eccentric, isn't he?"

"You could say that. When I first met him five years ago, he was singing Gàidhlig songs to the seals on Berneray…"

"Ah. Well, he told us that he's staying at the Howmore hostel on South Uist tonight, and he'll be on Berneray tomorrow."

"That's good to know."

A Jesus freak handed me a business card reading 'Yeshua HaMashiach is returning very soon…' before Alan, Barbara and I boarded the bus – yet another Transit – to Berneray. For me, it had been an exhausting two-night journey, and I was nearly back on one of many islands which I so loved. Before that, though, the bus picked up a surprising passenger in the middle of nowhere on North Uist.

"Oh, hello Anna-Marie!" I smiled at the newcomer.

Anna-Marie looked surprised. She was a native of the hills of Switzerland, who came to the Berneray Week every two years. After she sat down, we caught up on the past.

"You know, Axel's on his way this year!"

"Really? That's amazing!" she grinned.

"Whoa, whoa, whoa," Barbara chipped in. "Does EVERYONE know this Axel bloke or something?"

"Yes" exclaimed Anna-Marie, the bus driver (who we shall call Catriona) and I simultaneously.

We motored on towards Berneray, stopping briefly in Lochmaddy as per the timetable. Just before the bus reached the causeway, the bus stopped next to a fellow freak to offer him a lift: he was dressed in a kilt, sounded vaguely English (but wasn't), and he was walking the Hebridean Way. So, no bus for him. With that, the bus proceeded across the causeway linking North Uist with Berneray. The bus deposited Alan and Barbara at their bed and breakfast, before taking Anna-Marie and I onwards to the hostel.

After a marathon journey, I was home.

Boreray

There's a lot I could talk about regarding my eighth Berneray trip. For example, I could talk about how the hostel's beds were taken by five o'clock on the day I arrived, owing to the presence of two groups of cyclists. The Berneray hostel can't be booked, you see.

I could talk about Shona and Maya – a teacher from East Kilbride and her daughter, the former audibly in awe of me as I told my friend Eva about how I nearly died on the Insanity Trip.

Ah, yes. Eva. A Danish piano teacher who had been coming to Berneray just about every year for over twenty years; about ten other individuals, including yours truly, show up regularly as well. You can see many of them, including myself, in the music video for Andrew Huggan's 'In the Reek of the Smouldering Peat' (look it up…).

Now, I could talk about traditions that we Berneray regulars hold dear, including the use of our traditional bunks (i.e. the bunks we ALWAYS bag on arrival at the hostel, or move to when the existing occupant leaves…). I could talk about Steve, a mad cyclist from Lancashire who lived on Arran until 2010, and who I passed regularly in the street without recognising him. I could talk about the arrival of Axel the day after me, about how he moved into the bunk below mine in the Penthouse Suite, how he fell asleep listening to traditional Celtic music CDs with the volume at eleven.

I could talk about how the Berneray locals were excited to see me for the *nth* time, including the local canine population.

I could talk about Marie-Hélène, a Québécoise lass who gave me a lift from the hostel to the first Berneray cèilidh, whom I discovered was into Creedence Clearwater Revival, Frank Zappa and ZZ Top.

Ah, yes. I could talk forever about the cèilidhs! I could talk about my consumption of mead, absinthe and whisky. I could talk about the Fifer drinking golden syrup at the cèilidh. I could talk about the Greeks and the Norwegians. I could talk about how I ended up kissing a few lassies! And I could talk about the legendary afterparties – a strange molasse of Orbital, S Club 7, Toploader and good-old hardcore techno music, this year complete with a FaceTime conversation with my friend Daisy who was volunteering in South Africa.

I could, in theory, talk about the meals that Axel and I shared, including his legendary haggis bolognaise. I could tell you about how he wrote a note saying, 'In the name of Cthulhu, please don't touch!' when we discovered that he made too much of it and had to keep it for another day!

Or maybe I should discuss Mats – the Swedish marathon runner/cyclist who frequently visited Berneray in time for his birthday, and the onslaught of cake that we all indulged in. Maybe I should talk about meeting Chris Marks – another regular – and his accompanying family; Kate, who has roots on the island, their children Harvey and Ellie, and Friday and Lilly the labradoodles.

Nah.

Maybe I should talk about how I met the Welsh poet, author, historian and television presenter Dewi Prysor, whom the hostel crowd berated for knocking back copious amounts of Caol Ìla as opposed to savouring it. Maybe I should discuss my lovely experience at the Coralbox shop. Or the relative success of James Bondage – my quiz team, which came second in the Berneray Quiz.

Oh, here's something! Maybe I could talk about my experience timekeeping the orienteering challenge, deducing at the end that the difference between cheating and ingenuity is honesty after a team openly admitted accepting a lift from a local, but by being smart about it?

Nah.

Maybe I should talk about the barbecue, how its allotted time got shifted by a day owing to bad weather. Perhaps I should talk about the idiot in a campervan being a dick to Eva whilst dumping his rubbish in the hostel bins (as opposed to the campervan dump station at the harbour).

Or maybe I should talk more about the rustic, thatched-roof hostel, about Jackie the warden (one of the greatest people on the planet!), about how the hostel now has two stars, but has lost some of its charm in the process.

Maybe?

The answer to the above is a resounding NO. Let's talk, instead, about my visit to Boreray.

When the Berneray Week poster came out in June 2017, my immediate instinct was to book a place on the Boreray trip; it was the first time in many years that they were running boat trips. So, I decided to seize the opportunity, ringing Chrissie to secure a space on the 9am departure.

"You probably know me…" I said.

"What do you mean, 'probably'?", she replied. "You're an institution up here!"

Well, it would be my eighth time on Berneray, after all. I would later find out that virtually all the spaces were booked by the locals, much to the chagrin of some of the regular Berneray travellers.

Fast-forward to the seventeenth of July 2017, and I was prepared to head into the unknown. By that, I mean I was armed with some waterproof trousers and a few Tunnock's bars from a few days earlier. I caught the bus from the hostel to the Berneray ferry terminal, knocking two miles off my walk. I knew that the boat to Boreray was going from the other side of the causeway – Otternish, on North Uist – but I just wanted to use the free WiFi for about an hour or so.

I walked across the causeway, and was greeted by Chrissie and the five or so other travellers who were going over at the same time as me. Soon, a yellow vessel zipped towards the pier; this was the SY59, or Boreas – a small fishing catamaran capable of doing twenty-one knots on the open sea. After donning our lifejackets, the others and I would quickly discover what this experience felt like. I adopted a surfing stance – which I was very well-acquainted with from travelling on the Virgin train from London to Glasgow during the Insanity Trip – and held on for dear life; 'Wipe Out' by The Surfaris stuck in my head for the duration of the crossing.

After just a few minutes, we had arrived on Boreray. Well, almost – we had to be transported to the island on a three-man dingy linked to the shore by a rope, during which time a wave washed over the dingy and flooded the nether regions of my bum. But I finally made it to this, the last Hebridean island I would visit for some time.

Boreray's population had now increased tenfold, and would substantially increase later in the day; the sole permanent occupant being a solitary Australian man. A few Berneray locals – who were over manning a first-aid tent – advised me not to wander onto his croft, and left me to my own devices.

I wandered around the south of the island. My original plan was to climb Mullach Mòr – the island's high point, at just fifty-six metres above sea level, but the idea was quickly shelved after I found out that I only had two short hours to see the island. Instead, I decided to walk anti-clockwise around the south end of the island, passing to the west of Loch Beag and returning via the north side of Loch Mòr.

It was nice to have visited Boreray. The only points of (my) interest, though, were the detritus on the isthmus separating Mol Mòr and Loch Mòr, and the many ruins around the island. Boreray used to have a population of over a hundred, after all. Alas, over-cultivation and the collapse of the kelp trade ensured that there were no people left by 1923.

After two hours on the island, it was time to go back to the hostel. I assisted in roping the dinghy back to the *Boreas*, where I met Alastair – another Berneray regular who only got to visit Boreray after somebody failed to show up for the boat. I took my place in the cabin for the fast trip back to Otternish, much to the envy of the others, and soon we had returned to Otternish. I walked back to Berneray, briefly visiting the shop, and managed to get a lift back to the hostel, where I rested for that night's cèilidh.

Home

It was a sad day for me when I left Berneray. Like I mentioned earlier, it was supposed to be my final Berneray trip for some time, but my experiences in India and Nepal in early 2018 would change all that. But those are stories for the next book.

I packed up my belongings, hugged Jackie the warden and Eva for the last time on this trip (none of the other regulars were around at the time, being out walking), and made my way to the bus stop. Soon, the Grenitote bus came, driven by Charlie – a large man who insisted that everybody on his bus wore a seatbelt. I had known him since 2010, so I knew the drill.

"Sorry Charlie – I've beaten you to it!"

"Ach, you're a good lad!"

As the bus crossed the causeway to North Uist, I had a little spontaneous weep, the sudden realisation that I may not be back for some years washing over me. Soon, though, the bus had reached Lochmaddy, where I went to the ATM before making my way to the ferry terminal.

Now, my original plan was to head north to the isle of Lewis, and come home via the ferry from Stornoway to Ullapool. However, my friend Hamish was on Skye, so I decided to go home the traditional way. At the Lochmaddy terminal, and later on the ferry, I met up with Chris Marks and his family. Chris and Kate had run the Berneray 10k earlier that day – an event which I usually time-keep, but had to forfeit owing to the bus timetable. I chatted with them for a bit before making my way to the outer deck of the MV Hebrides, where I spent the best part of an hour and a half watching the world go by, as well as reading a book on Saudi Arabia I picked up at the book exchange in Lochmaddy.

Soon, the ferry arrived at the port of Uig in the north of Skye, where Hamish was waiting for me, along with his inbred canine. Bòidheach the flat-coated retriever was, once again, delighted to see me. Then again, he was delighted to see everyone, especially if they were male.

"He probably thinks you've come off the ferry from Arran!" Hamish exclaimed.

"Yeah, probably. He knows the ferry at least – remember when I set off for Nepal and you travelled with me from Arran to Glasgow? The Hebrides was doing the Arran run then."

"Ah."

"I remember you going off to the bogs and you left Bòidheach with me – when you were gone, he reared up and started licking the bald patch of the guy sitting in front of us!"

"Ha!"

As we made our way up the pier, the Marks family passed us in their car, where I was thrown into the surreal experience of Friday and Lilly the labradoodles noticing Bòidheach. Soon, though, we made our way to Hamish's hire car, which was driven by Rose. She was a red-headed Dutch model who was taller than me at six-foot-three and, naturally, turned heads wherever she went. Most guys would have looked at Hamish with envy, but not me. I look for personality in girls – everything else is optional. Plus, I knew that Rose and Hamish were just travelling together.

A local border collie appeared just as horny as its owners, though it wasn't lusting after Rose, but after Bòidheach. Now, I mentioned earlier that Bòidheach was gay, but he doesn't receive, just gives. The collie, which we learnt was named Patch after the owner shouted at it through a back door, was a determined bastard though, but not determined enough.

I looked at the collie.

"PATCH!" I shouted.

He looked at me.

"RACH THUSA!"

He cocked his head briefly before returning to Bòidheach.

"What did you say?" asked Rose.

"I just told him to fuck off. Stupid dog – we're in the middle of the Gàidhealtachd and he doesn't understand a word of Gàidhlig!"

By this time, Patch had learnt how to use the pavement as a tool for masturbation, and was crying as he ejaculated, much to our collective amusement. Finally, he ran off, leaving Rose, Hamish and I to plan our next move. Eventually, Rose and Hamish decided to go off and have their dinner, leaving me instructions to find their campsite.

"It's just above the Fairy Glen. Just follow the A87, then follow the sign for 'Shitter'."

"'Shitter?'"

"Aye. Keep following that road until you get to the loch, then climb the hill to the right until you see our great big tent."

Leaving them to their own devices, I followed the main road out of Uig until I saw the sign for Siadair, then turned left and – goodness me, I was in the Pennines and was looking at West Nab! Not really – I was walking up the Fairy

Glen. Ahead of me, facing me, was a car full of Chinese tourists parked in the middle of the single-track road. I decided to have a little fun, and leant into their open window.

"*CHAN EIL THU PÀIRCEADH AN-SEO!*" I shouted. (YOU CAN'T PARK HERE!)

Scared by my presence, they dashed off at a hundred miles an hour or thereabouts. I made my way to the campsite, passing through a surprising number of miniature cairns en route, where I pitched my tent within staggering distance of Hamish's.

The cairns

After an hour or so, Rose, Hamish and Bòidheach finally joined me, where we exchanged banter and alcohol for a few hours. I took the opportunity to put on some music.

"What's this?" Hamish asked.

"'Bug Day,' by The Fall. I was listening to it when I was walking back from Kennacraig to Claonaig last month."

"What's it about?"

"MIDGES!" gurned Mark E. Smith, right on cue.

"What he said! It especially makes sense when he starts saying 'Green is starboard, back Left is port' – maybe he caught a CalMac ferry somewhere back in the day…"

Before long, though, we all retired to bed. Mark E. Smith was right on point with the midges.

The next day was a Sunday – a day of rest traditionally keenly observed by the number of Presbyterians on the island. Being the middle of the summer, though, everybody else in that part of the world just simply did not give a flying fuck. We de-camped and placed our belongings in the car – Rose would be going off to do some kayaking, and Hamish and I would be walking Bòidheach. We meandered back down the road to Uig, imitating the locals.

"Ach, it's the Sabbath, and look at all these godless people on the road! They should all be in the church!"

"Well, it's none of our concern – they'll all be going to Hell. *Obh, obh!*"

We had some time to kill before Rose came back from her water-borne expedition, so we hung around the ferry terminal in Uig, leeching the WiFi. Now, my original plan was to get the bus to Kyle of Lochalsh, get a ScotRail train to either Achnasheen or Achnashellach and camp nearby, going back home via Inverness the next day. Alas, it wasn't to be. The Citylink bus would get into Kyle just after the last train of the day would have departed. Also, a single from Kyle to Glasgow would be about eighty pounds – a bit out of pocket for the likes of me. So, I spontaneously decided to get the bus to the King's House Hotel at the top of Glen Coe.

It was about that point where Hamish decided to duck into the nearby petrol station for some food, during which time he left me looking after Bòidheach. As he was purchasing some tasty comestibles, a coach filled with Chinese tourists wheezed to a halt next to me. Now, like many other tourists in that part of the world, they believed that Skye was a theme park; that everything was planned, sterile and for their exclusive benefit. They liked the look of the big black doggy sitting outside, so they decided to pet him. I mean, Bòidheach was a big dog – if he wasn't as friendly as he was, well…

After some time, Rose joined us, where I took the opportunity to retrieve my luggage from the car. We said our goodbyes, I friended Rose on Facebook, and I was soon left to my own devices. A family who recognised me from Berneray arrived a few minutes later – they were staying at the hostel in Uig that night – and we caught up on the past few days before boarding the bus.

It was a relatively uneventful, but absolutely beautiful, journey down to the Kings House Hotel, punctuated by the sounds of Martyn Bennett, the Earthling Society and Frank Zappa. And when I say relatively uneventful, I mean that a few things caught my eye. In Portree, I noticed there was a pub that sold breakfast until 3pm. In Sligachan, the bus passed the Marks family on the road. They do go straight to Raasay after Berneray Week, after all.

In Dornie, opposite the famous Eilean Donan Castle, a car flying the English flag passed quickly in the opposite direction, much to my displeasure. In Inverinate, I witnessed a troupe of Girl Scouts, all of whom were sporting seventies hair styles!

It was an auspicious day for Scout-spotting. The bus had a meal break in Fort William, where I found myself standing behind a spotty Scout in the queue at Morrisons. He was trying to purchase a 15-rated DVD, but the cashier was having none of it.

"Do you have any ID?"

"No…"

"I can't sell you this DVD, then."

"Come on! Can't you just give me it?"

"No. Sorry."

He sighed.

"FUCK!" the poster child for the Fort William Boy Scout troupe loudly exclaimed.

I praised the cashier for sticking by the law before taking my purchases back to the bus. An hour later, after a short climb through the majestic beauty of Glen Coe, the bus was bearing down on the Kings House Hotel.

"So, you're staying there tonight?" the driver was asking.

"Aye. There's a campsite behind the hotel, with about thirty unpowered sites for tents and a couple for campervans. The hotel owns the place, but the camping's free so to entice people into the bar."

"Jeez-oh! I didn't know that!"

"Aye, you learn something new every day!"

The actual hotel was shut for refurbishment at the time, but they did have a bar operating in a nearby outbuilding. Bombarded by midges, I pitched my tent, and a few short minutes later, I had a cheap cider in my hand. I was surrounded by stereotypical walkers (the hotel is on the West Highland Way, after all…), all of whom appeared to be Germans who favoured socks and sandals as eveningwear. They were a stark contrast to me, a fat bastard dressed for a psytrance festival. After downing the rest of my cider, I retreated to my tent, chewed on some Pringles, and fell asleep very quickly.

The next morning, after dreaming that Chris Marks and I were holidaying at a space-age ski centre, I decamped early and witnessed a beautiful sunrise over Buachaille Etive Mòr. I walked to the road and flagged down a Citylink bus heading to Glasgow, the same driver who took me from Uig to Fort William relatively unsurprised by my presence. I took my seat, and soon I was blasting the Dreamtime album *Strange Pleasures* as the bus crossed Rannoch Moor on a beautiful, clear day. An uneventful journey later, and a music change to an interesting album called *Baron von Tollbooth and the Chrome Nun*, I found myself back in Glasgow. A few more uneventful hours, involving the usual train and ferry rides, and I had returned to Arran, back to life's reality. This, of course, being a pickup truck parked outside my house, the driver unphased that one of the house's occupants had just materialised off a bus.

I sighed, knowing that this reality would soon come to an end. In December, I would be away to INDIA!!!!

POSTSCRIPT

That Sunday, the twenty-third of July 2017, was the last time I met Bòidheach. He developed a very aggressive cancer similar to the one that killed Lemmy from Motörhead, and collapsed as a result of a burst tumour. He died on the twelfth of August 2017, aged about eight years old.

This chapter is dedicated to him in loving memory.

A GLIMPSE OF THE FUTURE

I had been waiting for this moment, as a Nepali might say, 'for some time'.
The laptop screen flickered in front of me.
On said screen was a message:
'EMIRATES FLIGHT GLA-DXB-BOM
PROCEED WITH BOOKING?'
I clicked 'Proceed'.
I smiled, and subsequently sent private messages to a few people.
I made further plans to blow the lid of Epic Voyages I and II.

January 24 2017 – Pirnmill

Ahem.

यो नेपाल मा रहछन कसैको लागि सार्वजनिक सेवा घोषणा छ।[16]

Now that I have grabbed the attention of my target audience and quite possibly alienated them with my terrible usage of the Nepali language, I have an announcement.

Time, whilst seemingly infinite, is frequently perceived to be short, especially in these times of corrupt governments, fake news, and threats of terrorism and nuclear winter; inadvertent or otherwise. It is therefore best to create and live out the good days in life, like what I have done just now.

Every time I watch and/or listen to any media concerning Nepal, and subsequently predict half of what they are going to say ('Hajur?' 'Dhanyabad!', 'Swagarthom!' etc.), I think of the good times that I experienced last year, and make plans to better on them.

Considering the fact that a certain inauguration has recently occurred in a certain land, and I've recently been studying the works of the British-Ghanaian-American philosopher Kwame Anthony Appiah (who advocates that 'Western culture' is merely a myth and we should do away with such an idea), this has further influenced my decision to travel back east once again.

Therefore, on the 20th of December, I will be flying from Glasgow to Mumbai by way of Dubai in order to live out much of my Indian and Nepali-based fantasia. For my Nepali friends, all I can say for certain is that I intend to enter Nepal through the border at Belhiya on the Siddhartha Highway sometime in early 2018 – I cannot give anymore heads up at this time.

Nevertheless, as of this moment, Epic Voyage III officially has the go-ahead.
In other words:

म फिर्ता आउँदैछु।

I'm coming back, guys!

The Future Is Coming

My longest, most epic voyage yet is coming.
Let me tell you what will happen.
There will be craziness.
There will be madness.

---

[16] "This is a public service announcement for anyone residing in Nepal."

There will be happiness.
There will be psytrance.
There will be hallucinogens.
There will be trains.
There will be planes.
There will be great social and personal change.
There will be further avant-garde musings on the state of the world.
Great things will happen.
As for the rest, that's still to be decided.
BUT:
There won't be any shitty sleeper buses!
NEVERTHELESS:
At all times, Misfortune Accompanies Fortune.[17]

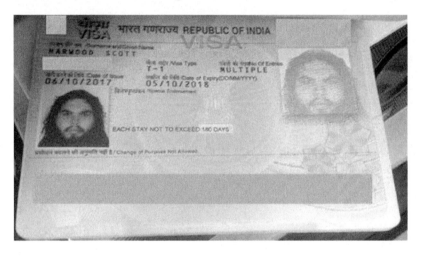

---

[17] A quote from Buddhism for Sheep.

GLOSSARY

AFL   Australian Football League – the pre-eminent professional competition in the sport of Australian rules football.

ArCaS   Arran Cancer Support – a charity on the Isle of Arran that my late grandmother founded.

ashram   a spiritual hermitage or monastery.

autosnelweg   a Dutch motorway.

Beinn Bharrain   a mountain on the Isle of Arran.

Bogan   an Australian term used to describe a person whose speech, clothing, attitude and behaviour exemplify values and behaviour considered unrefined or unsophisticated.

CalMac   Caledonian MacBrayne, the Scottish government-monopoly ferry service.

charas   more commonly known as hashish.

chiya   tea

Citylink   a Scottish long-distance bus company.

CSG   coal-seam gas – obtained by hydraulic fracturing, or fracking.

daal bhaat   the national dish of Nepal – consists of lentils and rice. Often served with *takaari* – mixed vegetables.

dim sim   a Chinese-inspired meat and vegetable dumpling-style snack food popular in Australia.

frituur   a Dutch chip shop

Gàidhlig   a Celtic language spoken in Scotland, pronounced 'Ga-lig'.

ghat   a series of steps leading down to a body of (often holy) water.

gulab jamun   a ball-shaped sweet made from *khoa* (milk solids) and saffron and coated in enough syrup to drown a Malaysian rat. Also known in Nepal as *lal mohan*.

Hungry Jack's   also known as Burger King.

khola   Nepali river

Koori   indigenous inhabitant of New South Wales and Victoria.

Losar   the Tibetan New Year. Not exactly celebrated in the lowlands of Nepal, but since Nepal gained a new constitution in 2015 which granted equal rights to all Nepalis, no matter what their background, all major ethnic holidays were made public holidays.

Madainn mhath   "Good morning" in Gàidhlig.

Madhesi   a demonym given to the people residing in the Terai plains of southern Nepal.

mi goreng   fried noodles with spices native to Indonesia, Malaysia and Singapore; can be picked up for as little as twenty cents per packet in Australia.

middy   a 285ml beer glass.

momo   a very, very delicious fried or steamed dumpling popular in Tibet, Nepal and Bhutan, as well as parts of India. Typically filled with buffalo, lamb, goat, chicken or mixed vegetables, less so with chillies (these are known as *c-momos* – spicy as fuck but worth it for the taste!) and cheese. If there is a Nepali eatery in your vicinity, stop reading this book, put it down immediately and order some momos. So sayeth the author!

nasi lemak   the national dish of Malaysia – traditionally consists of coconut rice, chili sambal, *ikan bilis* (fried anchovies), peanuts and a boiled egg. Typically eaten for breakfast.

Newari   a traditional inhabitant of the Kathmandu Valley, typically practicing both Hinduism and Buddhism simultaneously and speaking the Newar language (a Sino-Tibetan tongue) as their native language.

Opal card   a contactless smart card system used for all public transport in the Sydney area, plus a surrounding chunk of New South Wales covering an area roughly the same size and population as Scotland.

OV-Chipkaart   a contactless smart card system used for all public transport in the Netherlands.

Pastafarianism   a social movement that promotes a light-hearted view of religion and opposes the teaching of intelligent design and creationism in public schools. More commonly known as the Church of the Flying Spaghetti Monster.

purdah   gender-segregation – also a term for a type of curtain.

rangichangi   a Nepali word that means either 'multicoloured' or 'drunk' depending on the context. An especially auspicious word to use during Holi considering the potent charas floating around…

Red Stripe   a lager brewed in Jamaica.

Rule 34   'If it exists, there is porn of it – no exceptions'.

Rule 63   'For any given male character, there is a female version of that character.'

sannyasi   a Hindu holy man.

Sassenich   English people (in the plural, the singular is 'Sassenach')

Selfie Hanulah   'Take a Selfie' – the most popular song on the radio when I was volunteering out in Nepal.

servo   an Australian service station.

String Road   a road connecting the villages of Brodick and Blackwaterfoot on Arran.

sumo   a ten-seater jeep used as a shared taxi in Nepal. Named after the Tata Sumo.

TEFL   'Teaching English as a Foreign Language'.

tempo   A Nepali auto-rickshaw, or tuk-tuk.

teuchter   Slang term for a Highlander or something from the Highlands. A few non-Highlanders also use it as a derogatory term.

thobe and ghutra   the traditional man-dress of the Arabian Peninsula.

topi   a small hat, shorter at the front and back, which gives the wearer the demeanour of a corrupt politician. As if there is any other kind in so many cases…

Tristan da Cunha   the most remote inhabited archipelago in the world, lying two thousand kilometres from the nearest inhabited landmass – the island of Saint Helena.

ute   the Australian term for a pickup truck.

VCS3   'Voltage Controlled Studio, version #3', a portable analogue synthesizer.

Whyte & Mackay   a strong, blended Scotch whisky.

Yang di-Pertuan Agong   literally "He Who Was Made Lord", the King of Malaysia.

Printed in Great Britain
by Amazon

24543238R00116